# The Greening of
# U.S. Foreign Policy

The Hoover Institution and the
Political Economy Research Center
gratefully acknowledge

EARHART FOUNDATION
EXXON CORPORATION
SARAH SCAIFE FOUNDATION

for their generous support of the conference
and this publication.

# The Greening of U.S. Foreign Policy

*Edited by*
*Terry L. Anderson*
*and*
*Henry I. Miller*

HOOVER INSTITUTION PRESS
STANFORD UNIVERSITY   STANFORD, CALIFORNIA

POLITICAL ECONOMY RESEARCH CENTER
BOZEMAN, MONTANA

www-hoover.org

Hoover Institution Press Publication No. 478

First printing, 2000

Manufactured in the United States of America

06 05 04 03 02 01 00                9 8 7 6 5 4 3 2 1

The paper used in this publication meets the minimum requirements of American National Standard for Information Sciences—Permanence of Paper for Printed Library Materials, ANSI Z39.48-1984. ⊗

Library of Congress Cataloging-in-Publication Data

The greening of U.S. foreign policy / edited by Terry L. Anderson
    [and] Henry I. Miller.
        p. cm.
    Includes bibliographical references and index.
    ISBN 0-8179-9862-4 (alk. paper)
    1. United States—Foreign relations—1989– 2. Environmental policy—United States.    3. Green movement.    4. Global environmental change—Politics.    5. Environmental policy—International cooperation.    I. Anderson, Terry Lee, 1946– II. Miller, Henry I.

E840.G72 2000
327.73—dc21                                         00-029588

# Contents

*Acknowledgments*                                                         vii

*Introduction: The Green Hand of Foreign Policy*                           ix
   Terry L. Anderson

CHAPTER 1
*The Value of Sovereignty and the Costs*                                     1
*of Global Environmentalism*
   Jeremy Rabkin

CHAPTER 2
*Environmentalism, the Transformation of International Law,*                31
*and the Pursuit of Political Objectives*
   Fernand Keuleneer

CHAPTER 3
*Green Creep: The Increasing Influence of Environmentalism*                41
*in U.S. Foreign Policy*
   Brett D. Schaefer

CHAPTER 4
*U.S. International Efforts, Sustainable Development,*                     115
*and the Precautionary Principle*
   John J. Cohrssen

CHAPTER 5
*Sustainable Development: The Green Road to Serfdom?*                      143
   James M. Sheehan

CHAPTER 6
*The War Against Warming: Climate Change, Kyoto, and*                      167
*American National Security*
   Jeffrey Salmon

CHAPTER 7

*Bootleggers, Baptists, and Global Warming*                          195
   Bruce Yandle

CHAPTER 8

*Biotechnology Regulation and Foreign Policy: Eccentric*             221
*Environmentalism Instead of Sound Science*
   Henry I. Miller

CHAPTER 9

*Bucking the Tide of Globalism: Developing Property Rights*          249
*from the Ground Up*
   Terry L. Anderson

CHAPTER 10

*International Environmental Agreements:*                            267
*Developing Another Path*
   Julian Morris

*Contributors*                                                       303
*Conference Agenda*                                                  305
*Index*                                                              307

# Acknowledgments

This book is the result of much more than our efforts as editors. Of course, we owe a debt of gratitude to the authors who have given us their innovative thoughts, stuck with us through the editing process, and responded to our requests for changes. This book is their book too.

Investing in intellectual exercises such as this one requires a commitment to the long term, and for this commitment, we thank the Exxon Corporation (now ExxonMobil Corporation), the Sarah Scaife Foundation, and the Earhart Foundation. We especially thank Bill Hale from Exxon and Dick Larry from Scaife for their support of the research, conference, and volume.

Finally, we must thank people at the Hoover Institution and at the Political Economy Research Center (PERC) for helping make this project possible. John Raisian is always the intellectual entrepreneur, seeking innovative projects and finding resources to make them happen. The staff at PERC helped organize the conference and coordinate production of the manuscript, and the staff at the Hoover Institution Press made the volume come to life. Thanks Michelle, Colleen, Monica, Sheila, Pat, and Ann. You all certainly made our task easier and deserve much credit for this final product.

# Introduction:
# The Green Hand of Foreign Policy

*Terry L. Anderson*

In the past few years, globalization has become a buzzword that permeates both economics and ecology. Under the globalization banner, economists study the interconnections between diverse economies, and environmentalists worry about local actions having global consequences. Environmentalists allege that better science makes us more aware of global interconnections and that new technologies make environmental effects broader-reaching. So the Gaia principle suggests that a butterfly flapping its wings in Japan might cause hurricanes in the Caribbean. Allegations of global warming, ozone depletion, and species extinctions—all are blamed on market and ecological processes that span the globe.

Not surprisingly, armed with these allegations, the environmental movement has moved the policy agenda beyond local and even national boundaries into the foreign policy debate. By arguing that actions in one country have adverse environmental effects in another, environmentalists call for international agreements that abrogate national sovereignty and delegate foreign policy to nondemocratic international agencies. The Kyoto accord aimed at curbing the emission of greenhouse gases is perhaps the best known of these efforts in recent years, but the list of international regulations rationalized by environmental concerns is long and growing. Biodiversity, biotechnology, chlorofluorocarbons, endangered species, hazardous wastes, and nuclear wastes are but a few of the driving forces for international regulation. Even military operations cannot escape the green hand of regulation. In the midst of the Kosovo conflict, environmentalists raised concerns about the environmental effects of bombing oil refineries, power plants, and ammunition dumps. One wonders if the filing of environmental impact statements will become prerequisite for all military operations.

Believing that the greening of foreign policy has continued too far without analytical scrutiny, the Hoover Institution and the Political Economy Research Center (PERC) brought together a group of scholars to focus on the law, economics, and politics of extending the green hand of regulation beyond national borders. The critical analyses undertaken by these scholars focus on three main questions:

1.   What are the implications for national sovereignty if international green regulations are imposed?

2.   What politics drive the greening of U.S. foreign policy, and is that policy likely to have any positive effect on environmental quality?

3.   If global concerns are real, are there alternative approaches based on markets and property rights that can do a better job?

The first few chapters in this volume help us understand the nature of sovereignty and the threat to it posed by global environmentalism. Political scientist Jeremy Rabkin begins with an essay that summarizes exactly what the trade-offs are between sovereignty and environmental regulations at the international level. He puts forth three possible implications of increased international environmental regulations: (1) greater international environmental regulations implies a new understanding of international affairs where national sovereignty is weakened and international institutions find increased authority; (2) the checks and balances of our federal system will be eroded by global environmentalism; and (3) the greening of foreign policy increases the risk of international tension, reduces free trade, and undermines the confidence and trust of U.S. citizens in their government.

Fernand Keuleneer follows this lead by discussing how international law is changing with pressure from global environmentalism. He argues that the new environmentalism is not as concerned with the environment as it is in "a radically new allocation of power in a globalized international system." The new environmentalism has become an important justification for the United Nations' attempt to define a new global consensus in which the global society can form a new global order based on three principles: people's centeredness, sustainable development, and holism.

If there are any doubts that "green creep" is infiltrating U.S. foreign policy, Brett D. Schaefer dispels them. He documents how environmental issues are influencing domestic as well as international agencies to move away from their original goals toward "greener" missions. Schaefer presents a domestic history of environmental groups and catalogs examples of how these groups have influenced U.S. foreign policy, especially in the departments of state and defense.

John J. Cohrssen gives a view of the world through emerald-colored glasses. He documents how the executive branch under the Clinton administration has used green foreign policy to justify foreign aid programs and climate change proposals. Cohrssen shows how sustainable development and the precautionary principle, both commonly accepted but ill-defined policy guides, have infiltrated the rhetoric of foreign policy.

On the one-hundredth anniversary of British economist Friedrich Hayek's birth, James M. Sheehan explains how the road to serfdom may be paved with green bricks. He shows that sustainable development has become enshrined in a growing number of environmental treaties and international agreements. On its face, sustainable development sounds innocuous, but it is based on the premise that current consumption levels are not ecologically sustainable. Sustainable development, therefore, calls for international regulation of both consumption and production.

From the general chapters focusing on the interface between foreign policy and environmentalism, the volume moves to specific applications. The issue of global warming dominates this interface as explained by Jeffrey Salmon. He illustrates how the

Kyoto treaty could affect the ability of the United States to carry out military missions and cautions that the price of signing the Kyoto agreement is too high.

Building on his well-known "Bootleggers and Baptist" theory, Bruce Yandle explains that the Kyoto protocol has less to do with reducing greenhouse emissions and more to do with private efforts to use foreign policy to restrict competitors. Yandle explains how energy companies and environmentalists who might seem to be strange bedfellows come together in coalitions that thwart competition and restrict sovereignty without much positive impact on the environment.

Before the hype about global warming, the 1992 "eco-summit" in Rio de Janeiro, with its Convention on Biological Diversity, set the stage for the greening of U.S. foreign policy. Henry I. Miller examines the effect of this convention as it relates to biotechnology. He explains how we have moved from scientific-based regulation of biotechnology to a political-based regulation that plays off "eccentric environmentalism." His biotechnology example illustrates just how expensive the greening of foreign policy has become.

The volume closes with two chapters offering alternative approaches to the green hand of international environmental regulation. Terry L. Anderson offers an alternative to government intervention based on free market environmentalism. He argues that the traditional focus of foreign policy on supporting democratic countries based on a rule of law can do more to improve environmental quality than international regulations can.

Finally, Julian Morris explains how international environmental agreements might be restructured. He concludes with a list of four criteria that might be used in restructuring these agreements: (1) The agreements should flow logically from a body of evolved private law and should protect property rights; (2) they should rely on national and local regulation where spillover effects do exist; (3) they should be restricted to those nations with direct interest in the issue; and (4) they should require the same scientific balancing procedures required by civil law.

The green hand of foreign policy is a threat to national sovereignty without the offsetting benefit of improved environmental quality. This volume provides a theoretical basis for understanding how global environmentalism has come to the forefront of foreign policy. The growing list of issues that now drive international treaties and agreements have high costs with low benefits. If the threats of environmentalism are as real as we are led to believe, they can be better handled by returning to the traditional principles of the free society based on a rule of law. This volume is dedicated to returning us to that path.

# CHAPTER 1

# The Value of Sovereignty and the Costs of Global Environmentalism

## Jeremy Rabkin

War still raged in Southeast Asia in 1972. America was still convulsed by internal dissension over U.S. military actions. U.S.-Soviet relations still teetered between Cold War and détente. Only two years after the first Earth Day, environmentalism was still a relatively new force in American domestic politics. Yet in that year a United Nations conference in Stockholm, Sweden, had already sought to place environmental protection on the international agenda. The conference resulted in the founding of a new international agency, the United Nations Environment Program (UNEP).

In more than a quarter century since then, hopes for international cooperation have gone through cycles of hope and despair in many other fields. International environmental regulation, however, seems to have followed a path of ever-increasing hope and ambition. A survey of international environmental agreements in the early 1990s found that more than half of the 140 multilateral agreements concluded in this field over the preceding seventy years had actually been negotiated in the two decades since the founding of UNEP (Haas, Keohane, and Levy 1993, 6). In what follows, I view this trajectory in political or constitutional terms, making three main points.

First, international environmental regulation implies—as its most fervid advocates freely acknowledge—a new understanding of international affairs. To see the point more clearly, one must recognize how much the new environmental agenda departs from the classical conceptions of international law, which placed central importance on the internal autonomy of sovereign states. The outlook of international environmentalism, by contrast, implies a considerable reduction in national sovereignty, a considerable increase in the authority of international institutions, and a large new role for nongovernmental advocacy groups.

Second, ambitious approaches to international environmental protection imply, by the same token, a change in the traditional constitutional scheme within the United States. The traditional scheme sought to limit government through a system of checks and balances, most notably in a division of powers between the federal government and the states and at the federal level by a complex legislative process. New schemes of international environmental regulation will erode these already enfeebled checks, as policy initiative shifts from American constitutional organs to international policy-making forums.

Third, the developments sketched above carry sizable new risks in themselves, quite apart from their most obvious tendency to deliver more regulation of economy and society than we might otherwise choose for ourselves. Ambitious new programs threaten to exacerbate existing conflicts in international affairs and to put dangerous strains on international trade agreements. At the same time, such programs may undermine confidence and trust in both law and government at home. All of these costs are worth careful reflection, even if they cannot be readily quantified or fully understood in the early stages of new commitments.

## THE PREMISES OF INTERNATIONAL LAW: LIBERAL ORIGINS AND COMPETING NEW VISIONS

### LIBERAL ROOTS

The Charter of the United Nations, already looking to new international arrangements in some ways, still acknowledges the traditional principle of international law. Near the outset, the Charter stipulates that none of its provisions can "authorize the United

Nations to intervene in matters which are essentially within the domestic jurisdiction of any State" (Art. 2.vii). Precisely what this meant in 1945 is a subject of ongoing scholarly debate. But the clause was certainly not voicing a new principle. It invoked a long-established tradition, perhaps the central tradition in international law: A sovereign state is not answerable to others for what it does on its own territory, unless it injures the citizens or established rights of some other state.

As sovereignty has come to be viewed with distrust in recent decades, it is worth pausing at the outset for some clarification. Sovereignty is not a concept that was entrenched in statecraft by medieval warlords. On the contrary, it is a concept that entered Western political thought during the Renaissance and flowered during the Enlightenment. Though it certainly has been invoked by tyrannies of many descriptions, sovereignty owes its main philosophic development to that stream of thought called *liberalism*.

Thus Grotius, the seventeenth-century Dutch jurist often regarded as the father of international law, made sovereignty a major theme of his work. But he was also the first writer to use the term *right* (*ius* or *jus*) in the sense of subjective rights—as in "my rights" rather than "what is right by law" (Tuck 1979, 66–69). An advocate for the Dutch East India Company, Grotius defended the proposition that no nation can rightfully lay territorial claim to the high seas and exclude ships of other nations from making use of the seas. Yet this famous argument for freedom of the seas rests, in its turn, on a strong notion of territorial sovereignty on land. Grotius treated sovereignty as a form of ownership, developing most of his doctrines on explicit analogy with Roman property law.

Although most of Grotius's great treatise, *De Jure Belli ac Pacis* (The Law of War and Peace) deals, as one might expect, with laws of war, the expressed aim of the work is to establish principles of peaceful coexistence among states for their mutual benefit. And the Grotian premise is that peace—and the mutually beneficial trade it allows—will be most secure when ownership rights entailed in the term *sovereignty* are most clear. It is only a slight oversimplification to see Robert Frost's poetic dictum—"good fences make good neighbors"—as the central theme of Grotius's work.

By the eve of the American Revolution, the philosophic development of international law was even more congenial to liberal thinking about rights, while remaining quite emphatic about the importance of sovereignty. *Le Droit des Gens* (The Law of Nations), published by the Swiss diplomat Emmerich de Vattel in 1758, quickly established itself as the leading authority on the subject, a distinction it held until well into the nineteenth century. Not only Vattel's specific doctrines but also his mode of argument appealed greatly to the American Founders. "Since Nations are free and independent of one another as men are by nature," Vattel holds, ". . . each nation should be left to the peaceable enjoyment of that liberty which belongs to it by nature. The natural society of nations can not continue unless the rights which belong to each by nature are respected" (Intro., §15). "Of all the rights possessed by a nation, that of sovereignty is doubtless the most important" (II, iv, §54). Accordingly, "No foreign state may inquire into the manner in which a sovereign [government] rules . . . it is for the nation [which it governs] to take action"(II, iv, §55).

Thomas Jefferson, who would later make Vattel required reading at the University of Virginia, seems to have paraphrased Vattel, as much as he paraphrased John Locke, in the Declaration of Independence. The Declaration actually invokes God and Nature in its opening sentence, not on behalf of individual rights but to defend the claims of sovereignty: "When in the course of human events, it becomes necessary for one people to . . . assume among the powers of the earth, the separate and equal station to which the Laws of Nature and of Nature's God entitle them. . . ." The ensuing paragraph of the Declaration is a reminder of the strong link that Enlightenment thinkers saw between the rights of individuals and the rights of sovereign states. Why are sovereign states "entitled" to "separate and equal station" in relation to other states? Because, as the rest of the Declaration implies, sovereign states derive their authority from the consent of free and equal men. And the governments of independent states remain free and equal because, like individuals in a state of nature, they have no common superior.

Or rather, there is no *human* authority above the authority of independent states.

The wording of the Declaration implies that it would be blasphemous—and certainly tyrannical—to establish a human authority with the power to dictate to independent nations. A universal power of this kind, which cuts off all possibility of escape, would seem to undermine the possibility of meaningful consent. For in most instances (as Locke and Vattel both argued), an individual's consent to a government is inferred from the fact that he does not leave the territory in which that government rules.

The point of territorial sovereignty, then, was not to confine people within the boundaries of their own states. Rather, more reliable exchange was always a central purpose of international law. Vattel depicted the fostering of trade and commerce as a duty of nations. And a multiplicity of sovereigns was assumed to have benefits reaching across borders. Only a decade before Vattel published his treatise, the Scottish philosopher David Hume, friend and mentor to Adam Smith, emphasized that the "progress of the arts and sciences" owed much in modern Europe to the existence of "a number of neighbouring and independent states, connected together by commerce and policy." Hume laid particular stress on intellectual exchange: "The emulation, which naturally arises among those neighboring states, is an obvious source of improvement: But what I would chiefly insist on is the stop which such limited territories give both to *power* and to *authority*" (Hume 1985, 119–120).

In the nineteenth century, the development of international law was very centrally concerned with protecting trade, as nations sought to ensure fair treatment of their own nationals traveling abroad (usually for business reasons, but also for study and professional or scientific exchange). Even in the first decades of the nineteenth century, James Kent's *Commentaries on American Law* (1826), the first American treatise to provide sustained treatment of the law of nations, devoted almost half of its exposition to legal protections for private property and private commerce in time of war.

The nations most active in international trade, notably Britain and the United States, were avid in their support for new methods of international arbitration for the peaceful settlement of international disputes. Some of the most important precedents for this practice were indeed established by special panels of jurists convened to settle disputes between the United States and Britain. The classical scheme of international law, which built on precedents established in such arbitrations (and in rulings of national courts on disputes involving foreigners), continued to work by analogy with property rights in municipal law.

Experience in the first decades of the twentieth century demonstrated that even environmental disputes could be handled within the classical scheme of international law, for all its emphasis on national sovereignty. Environmental concerns did not intrude into international law until the twentieth century, since earlier generations gave little attention to industrial pollution, even at home. But in 1935, the United States complained about sulfur dioxide emissions drifting over the border from a smelter in Trail, British Columbia. The United States and Canada agreed to establish a special tribunal to assess whether Canada should pay damages to the state of Washington for resulting property damage. The tribunal, reasoning by analogy with rules applied in interstate disputes within the United States, found Canada liable for $78,000 in damages, which was duly paid. Decades later, Canada invoked the precedent of the *Trail Smelter* ruling in a successful claim for damages from the U.S. government after an oil spill in the United States, which contaminated beaches in neighboring British Columbia.

It would be an exaggeration to claim that transborder pollution damage is now subject to clear and well-established rules in international law. A UN international law commission struggled in vain throughout the 1980s to formulate a set of liability rules that would have broad international support. What *is* clear, however, is that neighboring countries can address such concerns in direct negotiations, and, where there is a will to settle differences, mechanisms can be put in place to resolve such differences. So the United States signed a special agreement with Canada in 1979 to reduce sources of acid rain in the Great Lakes region and subsequently negotiated a similar agreement with Mexico regarding air pollution from copper smelters on each side of the border. A broader series of conventions on oil spills from ocean tankers have worked reasonably well by focusing liability (to injured states) on the firms operating the tankers (Pritchard 1987). In Europe, multilateral agreements for reducing water pollution in the Baltic and Mediterranean Seas also seem to have worked reasonably well, as more environmentally conscious states have prodded neighbors to adopt parallel precautionary measures (Haas et al. 1993, 133–182).

In essence, environmental agreements of this sort are contractual. A country that cares more about the problem may urge greater effort from its neighbors and offer various inducements for such action. But whatever asymmetries of wealth or concern may complicate the negotiations, the bargaining centers on the application of a very old principle: One country should not interfere in the internal affairs of another, unless the other invades the territorial rights of the former, as drifting pollution might be seen to do.

## NEW VISIONS

Such localized agreements have not satisfied environmental advocates. The past two decades have seen the emergence of far more ambitious ventures in international environmental regulation. The new agreements are not simply bilateral, contractual agreements between directly affected states. Rather they are ventures in international cooperation that aim at securing near-universal participation. These ventures seek to deal with problems seen as global threats—potentially threatening to everyone and hence to no country in particular.

Among the landmarks in this new trend are the Basel Convention on Transboundary Movement of Hazardous Waste (1989), which limits exports of materials judged hazardous by subsequent decisions of the member states, even when other countries would agree to receive the materials; the Vienna Convention on Protection of the Ozone Layer (1986, with follow-on protocols, notably the 1990 Montreal Protocol), which seeks to phase out use of chemicals thought to threaten the atmosphere's ozone layer; the Convention on Climate Change (1992, with follow-on Kyoto Protocol, 1997), which seeks to reduce emission of carbon dioxide (from burning of fossil fuels) and other gases thought to threaten a long-term warming of the earth's atmosphere; and the Biodiversity Convention (1992, with a follow-on protocol on biosafety, now in preparation), which preserves diverse animal and plant species and ensures their safe and fair use in biotechnology.

Older ventures in bilateral dispute resolution might be seen as the international counterpart to a common-law action, where a neighboring landowner seeks damages and abatement for injuries inflicted by industrial smoke from a particular factory. The new schemes of international control are more like setting up an administrative agency to enforce a general reduction of smog in the Los Angeles basin, where no one automobile and no one factory can be held liable for the harm done to any particular homeowner. For example, once the issue is chlorofluorocarbons (CFCs), thought to be thinning the atmosphere's ozone layer, it is impossible to trace particular harms experienced by one country to the particular aerosol sprays in use in another country (even though the buildup of CFCs in the atmosphere was linked to ozone depletion and CFCs were a known ingredient in many aerosol sprays). A common response seems to be required if anything substantial is to be achieved.

But the change in focus brings a number of other changes in its wake. First, as the focus shifts from specific transborder pollution to concerns about the global commons, it is easy to conclude that borders are no longer relevant. The Kyoto agreement is, of course, the most extreme example, with its effort to impose limitations on carbon dioxide emissions (and so, in effect, on energy consumption) on industrialized nations around the world. What is done by the driver of an automobile in Kansas City or the homeowner who pushes up his thermostat in Minneapolis has now become the concern of people in Belgium and in Australia, though there is no way of weighing, let alone tracing, the effect on other continents of what these people do in the American Midwest. The same can be said of the Convention on Biodiversity, which seeks to preserve vast numbers of uncounted and unknown plant and animal species in special habitats around the world, on the theory that the world as a whole—though no one can say which country in particular— would be impoverished by the loss of such species.

The more ambitious the agenda, the more it requires not just an initial agreement, but an ongoing authority to implement and direct its details. In a traditional bilateral dispute, the issue is pursued by the immediate parties; if it is not so pursued, there is no issue. A truly international program is, almost by definition, something that cannot simply depend on the initiative of particular aggrieved states. It aims at achieving a global result, not just at satisfying individualized grievances. In domestic affairs, this sort of ambition has encouraged the establishment of administrative agencies that have a more result-oriented and more continuous involvement than courts and more flexibility than legislatures. Something similar happens in the most ambitious schemes of international regulation. The Kyoto scheme proposes separate authorities and agencies for tracking, monitoring, and assessing a whole series of phases in its overall program.

Another result seems to follow from the blurring of boundaries (between domestic and international) and the rise of specialized bodies and forums—that is, an expanded role for nongovernmental organizations (NGOs). Because the harm is no longer localized and is no longer readily conceptualized as an injury to any particular state, it becomes easier to think of the aggrieved party as humanity or the earth—for whom environmental advocacy groups might seem to speak as well as governments do. Or perhaps, more to the point, private advocacy groups come to play a larger role as more doubt and ambiguity arise about the stakes for any particular government.

Something similar has happened in domestic regulation. Regulatory schemes generally involve a reduction in the property rights of regulated firms. At the same time, however, they frequently entail an extension of new rights—or more ambiguous legal claims—to third parties. When the Interstate Commerce Commission began to regulate railroad rates and terms of service, it acted not simply on behalf of the general public (whose claims or expectations were, in any case, very hard to determine) but most often in response to formal protests from particular shippers or competing railroads. The Federal Communications Commission would rarely hold formal proceedings for a license renewal except at the initiative of a competitor (or would-be competitor) of the broadcaster seeking renewal. Environmental statutes in the 1970s extended the pattern by allowing environmental advocacy groups to sue federal agencies to ensure proper regulatory action for the public. When the aims of programs are too vague to chart their implementation, it seems to be a natural progression to fall back on interested constituencies to help give such direction and mobilize political support for it.

In the past decade, this pattern has become evident in international environmental regulation. It is not simply a matter of informal practice to have NGOs huddling on the margins of international conferences; it is now a matter of official policy to incorporate them. The Basel Convention, the Montreal Protocol, the Climate Change Convention, and the Biodiversity Convention all make explicit provision for attendance and participation of qualified private organizations. In turn, environmental advocacy organizations have invested much effort in trying to influence both official conference negotiations and the postures of governments in between. (Raustiala [1997] compares the process to the changes in U.S. administrative law in the 1970s that enhanced the legal leverage of environmental advocacy groups.)

The UN's Commission on Global Governance, which urges major changes in the way the United Nations operates, noted this trend toward involving NGOs as a particularly promising development in the environmental field:

> In the interlinked global conferences that have followed the Rio meeting, NGOs continued to have a strong impact on both the preparatory processes and the conferences. . . . More and more, NGOs are helping to set public policy agendas—identifying and defining critical issues, and providing policy makers with advice and assistance. It is this movement beyond advocacy and the provision of services towards broader participation in the public policy realm that has such significance for governance. (UN Commission on Global Governance 1995, 255)

All of these changes are, in some sense, a matter of degree. Specialized international unions for postal and telegraph coordination go back to the nineteenth century. Efforts to deal with tanker spills at sea and other sources of ocean pollution have been helped by the International Maritime Organization, in which petroleum companies have played a major role. But for governments, the costs of cooperation in such ventures have been relatively small and the benefits clear and immediate. For projects as ambitious as the Kyoto Protocol, however, nobody knows what benefits may be secured, but its costs may be very great indeed.

As the costs increase, redistributive agendas begin to surface, along with maneuverings for commercial advantage among the participating countries. The Montreal Protocol sought to win support from less-developed countries by offering technological and financial assistance from the more developed countries. This assistance was to help poor countries find substitutes for refrigerants with CFC (substitutes that, as it happens, were principally produced by U.S. companies, which strongly supported the Montreal Protocol). The parties to the Basel Convention, which include some countries (notably Germany) that have already invested heavily in recycling facilities for toxic wastes, decided to limit exports to a small list of developed countries and in March of 1998 refused the request of Israel and Monaco to be added to the list of eligible recipients, thus preserving a cozy cartel arrangement. The Biodiversity Convention seeks to enlist support from less-developed countries by promising rebates from private commercial success with any products developed from biological specimens in these countries. In short, these conventions have moved quickly from technical cooperation to the international equivalent of legislative horse-trading.

The ambitious scale of new ventures is not the only thing that reinforces the sense that these ventures are something quite different. The old schemes sought to coordinate existing policies—international mail delivery makes no sense unless there is already domestic mail delivery. By contrast, the issue for some new conventions is not so much coordinating as sponsoring, not so much protecting against externalities as generating new preferences. And hovering in the background is a new ideology that is, in its own logical way, hostile to markets, hence to property and to boundaries. "The ecological truism that everything is connected to everything else may be the most profound challenge ever presented to established notions of property," as one environmental theorist put it (Sax 1992, 32). So, by similar reasoning, environmentalists call for a reevaluation of the principle of territorial sovereignty: "Our accepted definition of the limits of national sovereignty as coinciding with national borders is obsolete" (Mathews 1989, 174).

Of course, few national governments are prepared to follow this vision to its full logic. But even partial attempts—along the lines of regulatory conventions launched in the past decade—would imply a major change in the way the United States has been governed. Our Constitution, framed in the era when "Nature" was thought to dictate a "separate station" for a sovereign state, is not easily adapted to a world where nature is understood to mean that "everything is connected to everything else."

## A NEW CONSTITUTION?

International environmentalism implies a change in the U.S. Constitution. One can say this with some confidence because we have already witnessed similar trends within the United States. Disdain for boundaries has produced a swelling in federal authority, at the expense of state and local governments within the United States. At the international level, such attitudes invite a similar expansion of international authority at the expense of the U.S. government. In much the same way, the expansion of regulatory programs within the United States has led to a shift of decision-making authority from the legislative process in Congress to the more obscure deliberations of administrative agencies. International environmental programs would reinforce this shift of power—and accountability—this time from Congress to specialized, even more obscure and less accountable international agencies or policy forums.

### DEFEATING THE RECOVERY OF FEDERALISM

One of the few postulates of political science that still commands broad assent is that institutional arrangements matter. How decisions are made affects what decisions are made. The U.S. Constitution, as a system for regulating decision making, has two architectural features designed to discourage or inhibit governmental overreaching. One is the separation of powers (discussed in the next section). The other is the division of power between the federal government and the states—federalism.

Because the Constitution stipulates that states cannot restrict the movement of products or persons across state lines, state governments are, to some extent, restrained from imposing overly severe burdens in their own territory, lest they drive business firms, along with individual taxpayers and consumers, to other states where burdens are lighter. The federal government can, to some extent, escape this problem because its authority extends to people and firms in all states. So the federal government can impose tax burdens far beyond what any individual state would dare to attempt. If one thinks of the states as competing in a market for government services (where those that provide better or cheaper service will prosper and those with less-reliable service or higher costs will lose out), then the federal government might be seen as holding the power to impose a cartel arrangement, shutting down competition among states by imposing a single standard throughout the country.

The constitutional scheme, as traditionally conceived, put a brake on this sort of federal control in two ways. The Constitution provides a complex system of checks and balances on the internal operations of the federal government, which we will consider in the next section. But the Constitution also seeks to restrain federal power, at the outset, by limiting the reach of federal legislation to a limited set of enumerated powers. Most notably, it limited federal regulatory power to international and interstate commerce, implicitly denying the federal government power to regulate commercial activity that does not cross state lines. Until the late 1930s, the Supreme Court sought to enforce this limitation. The demise of traditional doctrines in this area, following the Court's confrontation with the New Deal, allowed for a vast expansion of federal regulatory activity in the ensuing decades. Until recently, therefore, brakes on government implicit in the federal system seemed to be a constitutional dead letter.

But during the 1990s, the Supreme Court has revived this jurisprudence, striking down a series of federal regulatory measures for improperly preempting matters reserved to the states. How far this revival will go is certainly open to question. But the mere existence of a few prominent precedents may help to alter the political atmosphere. A few decisions of the Supreme Court can give plausibility to constitutional objections voiced in Congress against new measures. Indeed, if constituencies favoring limitations on federal power rally support for the Court's new direction, this support may embolden the Court to insist more confidently on the contours of a system that does indeed divide power between federal and state governments and does not simply leave states—and the market for government between states—to the whim or grace of federal decision makers.

International conventions are a serious threat to such trends, however. Even before the New Deal, the Supreme Court had held that Congress had a power to implement treaty commitments, separate from and broader than any of its particular enumerated powers. In *Missouri v. Holland* (252 U.S. 416, 1920), the Court held that Congress could enact measures to protect migrating birds pursuant to a treaty with Canada, although such legislation, standing alone, had previously been held to be improper under the enumerated powers of Congress. This decision was not unanimous, and it ignored contrary constitutional dicta from eminent authorities (and some Supreme Court justices) in the past. Some legal scholars have recently raised new questions about whether it is still good law (Bradley 1998). But this ruling seems to have become generally accepted, and it does, after all, have a strong intuitive appeal: It is strange to think that the Constitution gives the federal government power to make treaty commitments while denying it the power to make good on them in subsequent implementing legislation.

Historically, however, this dilemma could be left to the margins of scholarly journals. Whether Congress had full power to implement treaties was not a burning question in most of American history because few treaties committed the U.S. government to undertakings that actually threatened the power of the states. And that was so, in turn, because the treaty power was assumed to have definite limits. Not just anything could be a treaty. James Madison—surely one of the leading authorities on the meaning of the Constitution—put it this way: "The exercise of the [treaty] power must be consistent with the objects of the delegation [of that power to the federal government]. . . . The object of treaties is the regulation of intercourse with foreign nations and is external" (Elliott 1888, III, 513). Proponents of the Constitution identified the power with "war, peace and commerce" and therefore insisted that the treaty power would rarely affect the rights of Americans in domestic law.

The traditional view was still affirmed by Chief Justice Hughes in 1929 (after his service on the Permanent Court of International Justice): "[T]he treaty-making power is intended for the purpose of having treaties made relating to foreign affairs and not to make laws for the people of the United States in their internal concerns" (Hughes 1929, 194). The Second *Restatement of Foreign Relations Law* explicitly reaffirmed this doctrine in the mid-1960s (§117, Cmt. b). Although only a privately sponsored treatise, the Restatements (published by the American Law Institute) purport to summarize existing law and carry a good deal of influence. By the mid-1980s, when the Third *Restatement of Foreign Relations Law* appeared, this doctrine had been expressly repudiated, however, on the grounds that no limits on the treaty power could be discerned or insisted upon, given modern circumstances (§302, Cmt. c).

Human rights conventions seem to have been a central consideration in the shift. These conventions deal with entirely internal concerns (how a government treats its own citizens within its own territories) and have only the most notional or metaphysical sense of international exchange (the United States would not turn to torturing its own citizens merely because another signatory to a human rights convention had resumed such practices on its own territory toward its own citizens). In fact, the United States had long refused to commit itself to UN human rights conventions precisely because of constitutional objections in the Senate to internationalizing matters traditionally conceived as internal—and in many respects, reserved to the states. When the Senate did ratify a number of human rights conventions in the Bush administration, it did so with reservations stipulating that they would not have domestic effect and would not commit the United States to change any domestic law that might seem in conflict with the conventions. In other words, the Senate was persuaded to ratify such conventions only on the understanding that ratification was essentially a symbolic gesture rather than a serious legal commitment. So even now, the view that anything at all can be a proper exercise of the treaty power is not well accepted, at least not in the Senate.

But international environmental treaties do seem to open a vast range of internal concerns to international negotiation. The Senate has, in fact, balked at ratifying the Basel Convention and the Biodiversity Convention, despite support from the Clinton administration. The Senate has also expressed strong misgivings about the Kyoto Protocol. None of these international conventions has been ratified by the Senate, but they have not been formally rejected, either. Should the Senate come to ratify them, it might be seen as endorsing the theory that anything can be the proper subject of a treaty. And if more and more treaties of this kind enter into the stream of federal policy, any serious hopes for a further revival of federalism may be strangled. For if treaties do gain more support, international conventions would be a ready pretext for federal action on anything that might otherwise seem denied to the jurisdiction of the federal government. It has happened elsewhere in just this way. In Australia, to cite the most notable case, federal powers have been more restricted than in the United States, but in recent decades Australia's High Court has approved the extension of federal authority in labor relations, environmental protection, nondiscrimination measures, and a host of other new areas—in deference to international treaties involving such subjects (Alston and Chiam 1995).

## Streamlining the Legislative Process

This brings us to the second and perhaps more important constitutional issue—how federal power is exercised (rather than where or on what it is exercised). The traditional constitutional scheme did not simply divide power between the federal government and the states. It also divided power within the federal government. More to the point, it imposed a rather difficult legislative process for making new federal laws. Normally, a law must pass muster in the House and the Senate and then receive support from the President. The treaty power is different, but still onerous: After negotiation and submission by the President, treaties require two-thirds approval by the Senate, which is a difficult burden.

In the course of the twentieth century, however, advocates of regulation have found ways to streamline the legislative process in domestic affairs. Because it is difficult to secure the agreement of concurrent majorities in the House and Senate (with concurrent approval from the White House), the path to regulation has been smoothed by formulating a statute in the most general terms and then leaving it to an administrative agency to fill in the details. If the details are of a minor, technical nature, such administrative decision making may be an inevitable and entirely acceptable aspect of large governmental undertakings. But constitutional doctrine was once understood as prohibiting wholesale delegation of legislative authority to administrative agencies. Here, too, the Supreme Court was forced to relax traditional doctrine during the 1930s to accommodate the ambitions of New Deal regulation. Many scholars have warned that allowing such end runs around the constitutional scheme of checks and balances has been an invitation to the domination of policy by special interests, once policy has been relegated to specialized agencies in specialized political arenas (Schoenbrod 1993; Lowi 1979).

The same problem arises in international regulatory ventures. Just as modern environmental legislation delegates broad rule-making discretion to administrative agencies (like the Environmental Protection Agency [EPA]), so ambitious environmental treaties characteristically set out a broad framework, which is then given more definite content through subsequent elaborations. Often the subsequent development is by a new international conference at which the parties to the original framework treaty commit themselves to new details in a new treaty—or, as favored usage now tends to style such subsequent agreements, to "protocols" (a term that emphasizes the subsidiary character of the new agreement and suggests that it ought to be seen as a more or less expected follow-up of the original treaty). In some cases, the U.S. government may decide to treat such a follow-up protocol as a new treaty, requiring a new ratification vote in the Senate. That approach has been promised for the Kyoto Protocol, which is designed to implement the earlier Framework Convention on Climate Change.

There is already an evident tendency to short-circuit this process, however, by allowing the executive to commit the United States to new international agreements by the simple expedient of a unilateral executive agreement or declaration. For example, in the Clean Air Act Amendments of 1990, Congress delegated to the EPA the authority to implement any new restrictions on CFC use that were then being negotiated, as refinements to the earlier Vienna Convention on Ozone Depletion. The United States adhered to subsequent protocols on this subject by executive action of the President, without any ratifying vote in the Senate (and without the need to muster a two-thirds majority in the Senate). More ambitious and speedier phaseout of CFCs was put into American law without any need for a direct vote by Congress.

Executive agreements have been endorsed by the Supreme Court as a legitimate way of making international commitments. But the traditional understanding is that these agreements would deal with specialized military or diplomatic matters and would be auxiliary to treaties. Thus, during the first century of American diplomacy (under the Constitution), the United States adhered to 265 treaties (with Senate ratification) and presidents made 265 executive agreements on their own. Over the next century, the number of formal treaties (with Senate ratification) had tripled, but the number of executive agreements increased 25-fold. Between 1980 and 1992 alone, the United States ratified 218 treaties and 4510 executive agreements (Steiner, Vagts, and Koh 1994, 561). Few of these agreements affect the rights of American citizens in any direct or substantial way. But if the United States begins to participate in ambitious international regulatory ventures, more and more basic policy matters may escape the checks and balances of Senate ratification.

The threat to normal constitutional decision making, however, goes beyond a simple shift of decision-making authority from Congress to the executive. Some treaties envision an elaboration not simply by subsequent agreements but by majority vote of the participating countries (so that even those voting against the new rule would be bound by it) or even by freestanding international administrative authorities. The former arrangement (majority voting to bind even dissenting states) is provided for the development of regulations on deep-sea mining under the UN's Law of the Sea Treaty and was one of the reasons that President Reagan cited for refusing to submit the treaty to the Senate. The latter arrangement—delegating to a freestanding international agency—appears at several places in the Kyoto Protocol, where international agencies are supposed to develop their own rules for measuring greenhouse gas emissions and for calculating the trade-off value of efforts to reduce the atmospheric concentration of such gases in other ways. Billions of dollars in cost for the U.S. economy may be in the balance, depending on whether the international agency concerned adopts one rule or another. The Protocol seems to say that the United States would be bound to follow the rule adopted by the international authority set up to make such determinations.

Such arrangements may cause much more trouble than delegations to our own EPA. Even with a relaxed view of the traditional doctrine against delegations of legislative power, federal administrative agencies are subject to a whole series of checks under the Constitution. Thus, top officials of domestic agencies are subject to Senate confirmation, and the confirmation process is often used to air concerns about the agency and sometimes even to extract promises or understandings from nominees about their future policy course. Such promises may not be legally binding, but the top officials of domestic agencies do need to retain congressional favor. Congress provides the funding for domestic agencies and can expand or reduce that funding from year to year. Congress can initiate legislative restrictions on the agency's authority or agree to expand its authority. None of this applies to international agencies (or international negotiating conferences), where Congress has little direct leverage on what is done.

Because the delegation of broad powers to domestic agencies has raised great concerns about abuse of power, the United States has imposed a whole series of general, statutory checks on administrative authority. The Administrative Procedure Act requires agencies to provide advance public notice of new rules and to consider subsequent comments from the public. Some statutes impose even more severely constraining rule-making procedures. The Freedom of Information Act allows anyone to force an agency to release relevant policy documents, and the Federal Advisory Committee Act requires policy discussions between agency officials and private parties to be accessible to the public. Both the procedural requirements for rule-making and the substantive limits on the resulting rules (that they accord with statutory authority and not violate other relevant limits in statute law or the Constitution) can be enforced by litigation in U.S. courts. None of this, however, applies to international regulation. Executive officials of the U.S. government may participate in the formulation of new international standards, but if the resulting rule or standard is not formulated as a treaty requiring Senate confirmation, the whole matter seems to be left up to the President. The rule or standard would be binding on the United States if the President decided that it should be—or if the prior treaty committed the United States to accept the result.

Earlier generations would have seen this as a disturbing challenge to constitutional norms. Alexander Hamilton, who was perhaps the warmest defender of executive power among the Founders, acknowledged that treaties could "not change the Constitution. . . . A treaty, for example, cannot transfer the legislative power to the executive" (Hamilton 1885, V, 30). Hamilton would certainly have been aghast at the thought that a treaty could transfer the legislative power not simply to the U.S. executive but also to some international executive, not directly accountable to American voters or the U.S. Congress. In the 1920s, the leading treatise on foreign relations law, while eager to defend U.S. participation in the League of Nations, remained emphatic about the constitutional limits on such participation: "The treaty making power [of the United States] exercises legislative power which cannot be delegated. . . . A delegation of political power, that is legislative or treaty-making power, to such a body [an international commission] would be unconstitutional" (Wright 1922, 104, 125).

Today, by contrast, Professor Louis Henkin, chief reporter for the Third *Restatement of Foreign Relations Law* and one of the leading scholars in the field, takes a very different view: Where "legislative" or "regulatory" powers are given to international agencies, those powers may be "properly seen as implementations of the original treaty establishing the organization and giving it 'regulatory powers' and, in consenting to that agreement, the Senate may be said to have consented in advance to any regulations authorized by that agreement" (Henkin 1996, 263). In other words, the notion that there are constitutional limitations on the delegation of policy-making authority to international bodies has disappeared.

None of this implies that the United States will be coerced against its will to undertake policies to which it is vehemently opposed. In the United States, it is well settled that treaties have no more authority than ordinary statutes and so can always be overridden by new statutes. Congress can certainly put a stop to any international policy it does not like—or at least, it can put a stop to the implementation of the policy so far as it requires American cooperation. But this ability of Congress is not, by traditional understandings, a sufficient reassurance. It is equally true that any agency regulations that cause sufficient protest can, in the last analysis, be overridden by a new statutory enactment. But almost no one thinks it is adequate to let administrative agencies do whatever they please, subject only to this one ultimate check. The whole point of constitutional procedures—and the new levels of administrative procedures that Congress and the courts have imposed on agencies in recent decades—is to promote better decision making at the outset.

There is a further point to consider in this context. When Congress contemplates changes in its own statutory directives to a domestic agency, it may face disapproval from private interests favoring the original statute and that may often make it difficult to reconsider the policy. A treaty, however, is literally a contract with foreign states. For the United States to back out of a treaty is to break its word. Although it is certainly possible to do that (as a matter of U.S. law), backing out remains costly (or potentially costly), because it undermines the worth of future American promises or the sense of obligation that foreign states feel in their promises to the United States. A statute is not, in the same way, a bargain between Congress and the particular constituencies that may support the provisions of that statute. At the least, no one supposes that a change in political administrations lessens the obligation of U.S. commitments to other countries. But everyone supposes that a Congress with a new partisan majority—or a new mood, owing to shifting political opinion in the electorate—will feel entitled to reconsider the policy decisions made by a previous Congress.

What all of this means is that international commitments, while they have fewer institutional safeguards in their development, have stronger protections against reconsideration. All of this is perhaps in the nature of international commitments. But this means that the more we allow our internal policies to be formulated in international forums, the more we end up with a different scheme of government than we thought we had. If we cannot insist on limiting the delegation of policy-making power by treaty, we invite a gradual erosion of our sovereignty.

The whole point of sovereignty, after all, is to localize responsibility for policy making. Property rights internalize the costs and benefits of decisions about the use of the property—so the owner will gain or suffer depending on the choices that are made. In much the same way, territorial sovereignty localizes or focuses responsibility for government policy on those most directly affected. Every sovereign state has its own constitutional scheme for regulating the way that decisions are made by the governing power in that state. It was always one of the central tenets of international law that how a nation chooses to arrange its domestic constitution is no business of other nations. It is not a mere slogan to say that we lose some of our sovereignty if we have to alter our domestic decision-making patterns to accommodate international obligations.

Certainly, it does not answer the objection to say that the Constitution itself authorizes the United States to commit itself to international obligations. The traditional view was that treaties would be exceptions to the normal pattern of policy making, that they would not affect internal matters and would not involve ongoing delegation of policy-making authority to extraconstitutional bodies. All of these doctrines were, in effect, safeguards of American sovereignty.

To see the point, one has only to imagine the treaty power stretched a bit further than is now contemplated in existing agreements. Suppose that the United States entered into a treaty, ratified by the Senate, to give more force to the North American Free Trade Agreement (NAFTA). Suppose the United States authorized a NAFTA Executive Commission to make detailed rules for health, safety, environment, labor, and a score of other matters and then gave enforcement authority to a NAFTA High Court, whose rulings would enter directly into U.S. law. This is precisely what European nations have done in gradually building the European Union (EU) from the sort of customs union that NAFTA now is. Not even defenders of the EU claim that it leaves the sovereignty of the member states unimpaired. Instead, it is said that their sovereignty has been pooled—meaning that no member state now has the sovereignty it started with.

The United States is a long way from such arrangements. Even today, most constitutional scholars probably would acknowledge that such arrangements would cross some line beyond which the treaty power would no longer be a valid exercise of constitutional authority, but rather it would be an improper vehicle for imposing an entirely new constitutional scheme. The question about international regulation is whether it is, by degrees, taking us into a constitutional limbo where traditional constitutional norms no longer apply. It is not engaging in rhetoric to think of this as a threat to sovereignty.

## POLICY RISKS: OUTSIDE AND AT HOME

The Constitution, as Chief Justice Marshall famously put it, must be "adapted to the various crises of human affairs" (*McCulloch v. Maryland*, 4 *Wheat* 316 [1819]). In past crises, the United States has certainly done things that nobody now challenges, but that probably nobody would want to repeat. The constitutional history of the Civil War and the world wars of this century provide many examples. Extreme circumstances may justify powers that we would not want to see as part of the normal scheme.

On some such theory, it would be easy to say that the implementation of the ozone protocols was an exceptional matter. Extraordinary measures might even be justified to deal with the threat of global warming, if those measures had reasonable prospects of averting otherwise inevitable catastrophe. But we should be careful to ensure that extraordinary measures are understood to be extraordinary—that is, exceptions to normal practice.

Unfortunately, advocates of international environmental regulation do not present individual treaties as exceptions. On the contrary, the ozone protocols were presented as merely a first step toward other necessary measures. The Rio Earth Summit in 1992, which produced the Framework Convention on Climate Change, also produced a convention on biodiversity on the premise that threats to biodiversity would also, like global warming, entail catastrophic loss. Indeed, the same summit also produced a Declaration on Environment and Development, which moved right along to the "indispensable requirement . . . to decrease the disparities in standards of living" (Principle 5) and to recognize that "women have a vital role in environmental management" (Principle 20). At the same time, the Declaration urged that the "creativity, ideals and courage of the youth of the world should be mobilized to forge a global partnership" (Principle 21), but admonished that, amidst all this youthful enthusiasm, governments must not neglect the "vital role in environmental management" of "indigenous people and their communities" whom states should "duly support [in] their identity, culture and interests and enable their effective participation." In other words, the focus is not on extreme, overriding challenges but on fostering a "global perspective," which invites an ongoing grab bag of special concerns, piled onto the international environmental agenda like baggage on an airport carousel.

Thus, the first risk in international environmental regulation is that it smooths the way for more and more international regulatory ventures. There is a clear and evident reason for this tendency: To gain support for new programs, it is necessary to offer more carrots to recalcitrant states. To do that, it is necessary to have more bargaining chips. In other words, to ensure the viability of one measure, it is necessary to have other measures to buy support for the first measure. In Congress, this is called logrolling and has encouraged a continuing expansion of federal programs. International forums with great ambitions will want to duplicate the experience. That has been part of the explanation for the remarkable growth of the European Union in recent decades. Each new expansion in the authority or resources of the EU helps solidify or entrench previous ventures, so that politicians of very different aims can cooperate if there is enough in the pie to serve all their diverse constituencies. We have already seen the pattern in international environmental programs—as in the Biodiversity Convention, which links support for conservation programs in less-developed countries to promises of special taxes on foreign corporations to reward such countries for their efforts. The Rio Earth Summit eagerly advertised its dual—or multiple—agendas by calling itself the Conference on Environment and Development, with each part of its name seemingly aimed at a different global constituency.

The international arena is not, however, like that of a sovereign state or even of the EU. What makes the United States one country—as the authors of *The Federalist* argued so insistently— is that the federal government can reach directly into any part of the country and enforce compliance with its own laws by its own executive, supported in the last analysis by its own army. The EU has not been nearly so ambitious, but it still has its own court system which has successfully asserted the power to overrule courts of member states and to overturn parliamentary enactments of the member states. International authorities have nothing like this sort of power. And they are not likely to acquire it anytime soon, because few nations are prepared to cede such authority to a global entity.

Several risks follow from this fact. The first is that ambitious international regulatory schemes are bound to give rise to disputes about compliance. The more demanding the obligations, the more there is likely to be cheating or resistance. This, in itself, is bound to increase international tensions, as the countries that make more sacrifice protest the free riding of others. But efforts to enforce compliance will almost necessarily divert attention from other, perhaps more urgent priorities.

To see this first point, one should focus on the likeliest tensions. They are not between countries like the United States and Canada. Rather, a recurring theme in almost every great international conference on environmental issues is the resentment of less-developed countries, which feel that they cannot afford to make sacrifices for the environmental ambitions of more-developed countries. While more-advanced countries are focusing on the threat of skin cancer (to light-skinned peoples and to people in the later years of life), less-developed countries try to cope with mass death of children from diarrhea epidemics. So the less-developed countries insist that the wealthier, developed countries should buy their cooperation. Their insistence is not unreasonable, but it is never likely that western taxpayers will pony up money on a scale that would ease resentments. So continued friction should be expected. Also, because environmental protection is mostly the enthusiasm of rich western nations, one should expect China and other leaders of the less-developed world to keep harping on the selfishness and inequity of the rich nations. At the Kyoto Conference, in fact, China led other, less-developed countries in the refusal to make any commitments at all to reducing increases in energy use or making any other contributions to the climate control project.

Suppose that China does agree to make some contribution but then does not keep its pledge. Somewhere down the road, western countries will have to decide whether they care more about China's compliance with efforts to combat global warming or about its sale of ballistic missiles to renegade regimes or its saber-rattling (or worse) against Taiwan or some other, more immediate, security risk. Although piling on more and more international responsibilities may help to win support for particular new programs, it also makes it harder to maintain international focus on genuine priorities. That may hold serious risks, too.

But the most immediate and perhaps most pervasive risks may be to the international trade system. Since 1947, successive rounds of negotiation under the General Agreement on Tariffs and Trade (GATT) have brought about dramatic, worldwide reductions in barriers to international trade. Although mutual tariff reductions and other mutual accommodations have been negotiated in large multilateral forums, the system has the admirable characteristic of seeking to localize rather than globalize disputes. Even with the advent of more formal machinery under the World Trade Organization (WTO), disputes about trade policy are still essentially complaints of a particular exporting country against the particular import barriers of another country. The point of the WTO is to help arbitrate such disputes, but when (as usually happens) the two countries involved work out an agreement between themselves, the concern of the WTO or the international community is ended. In this way, the trade system conforms to the traditional contractual arrangements of international treaties in the past. As with other contractual undertakings, however, a country may submit to unfavorable rulings (or obligations that prove more burdensome than expected) in the expectation that the other party will respect its own obligations in future disputes.

At present, the WTO has been deadlocked on how to mesh environmental agreements with GATT rules, which do not allow trade barriers to be used as an enforcement sanction—even though some environmental agreements expressly invite such sanctions and others seem to assume that economic sanctions will be available. The more ambitious the scope of international environmental agreements, the more they invite such retaliation in disregard of existing trade commitments. At some point, there is a risk that the expectation of reliable compliance by others becomes less secure. Trade disputes may then be harder to settle amicably or quickly, as the rules and the dispute resolution system lose their moral authority.

Down the road, ambitious environmental regulation poses an even more fundamental challenge. If the system does accommodate trade sanctions to punish environmental dereliction, why not also use sanctions to protect environmental commitments? Environmental advocates have demanded this latter use of sanctions, because they fear a race to the bottom if some countries gain competitive advantage by lowering environmental burdens on their own industry. In May 1998, President Clinton expressed the urgency of such protections in his speech to the WTO (Clinton 1998). But if sanctions can be used for environmental regulation, why not for other worthy causes—such as labor standards and safety and consumer standards or human rights? In fact, this is exactly what other advocates have demanded and what President Clinton has endorsed. So, instead of a system for freeing trade on essentially the same terms for everybody, we may back into a system that allows participants to reward, punish, and protect according to their own differing estimates of who deserves credit and who deserves censure. It is not, to say the least, a recipe for stable and reliable trade rules.

If trading norms become more uncertain, there will be great temptation for developed countries to reach common standards, whether less-developed countries accept them or not. It is easy to imagine, in this context, that the United States will feel some pressure to follow common policies with the European Union. This has been the pattern within the EU, where Germany and other northern countries have forced less affluent or less green member states to adopt more ambitious labor and environmental standards as the price for freer trade within Europe (Rhodes 1995, 120; Vogel 1996, 96–97). Even so, it may still be, in purely economic terms, a good deal for Portugal or Greece. Indeed, the EU rules have helped liberalize markets even within member states. Also, some part of the EU's support in many member states seems to reflect popular distrust toward their own governments.

Still, the United States has not thought to improve itself in the past by allowing its government to bind itself to the decisions of other governments. Self-government has perhaps more prestige in the United States than in other countries, because it has been maintained here over a longer period and has been more continuously associated with stability and prosperity. Perhaps the ultimate cost of entering unreservedly into the brave new world of international environmental regulation is that it puts at risk the large element of trust and respect that Americans still have for their own government. There are, after all, still many conflicts and tensions in American society. If we can no longer say that laws must be obeyed because they are our laws, made by our representatives, what do we say?

If that point seems overly abstract or remote, one might recall the immense political bitterness generated in the 1970s by activist court rulings on such contentious issues as busing for school integration or access to abortion. Citizens on the losing sides in these disputes were not simply opposed to the eventual policy, they were particularly enraged at having the matter taken out of the hands of local legislatures. On the whole, courts seem to have backed away from activist agendas in more recent decades, partly from fear that public resistance to controversial rulings would undermine public respect for law in general. If international policies come to impose serious costs or controversial measures, there is no reason to think Americans will be more accepting of such intrusions from outside than they were of policies developed by U.S. courts, from the U.S. Constitution. But just as there were loud and insistent constituencies for particular decisions of activist courts in the 1970s, there will be those who insist that international policies must be applied and respected— particularly when those people favor the particular policies involved. Once we move away from the notion that our own legislatures are the dominant policy makers, we will have more difficulty resolving these sorts of disputes. And the disputes may become quite bitter.

The underlying point can be put quite simply: Before we commit to visionary schemes of global governance, we should be sure we have given adequate protection to our own constitutional system at home, which has served us so well for so long.

## REFERENCES

Alston, Philip, and Madelaine Chiam, eds. 1995. *Treaty-Making and Australia, Globalization Versus Sovereignty?* Sydney: Federation Press.

Bradley, Curtis. 1998. The Treaty Power and American Federalism. *Michigan Law Review* 97 (November): 390.

Clinton, William J. 1998. Statement at the Conclusion of the World Trade Organization Meeting. *Weekly Compilation of Presidential Documents* 34 (10 May): 934.

Elliott, Jonathan, ed. 1888. *Debates on the Adoption of the Federal Constitution,* 2nd ed. Philadelphia: J. B. Lippincott.

Haas, Peter, Robert Keohane, and Marc Levy. 1993. *Institutions for the Earth.* Cambridge: MIT Press.

Hamilton, Alexander. 1885. Camillus. In *Works,* edited by Henry Cabot Lodge. New York: G. P. Putnam's Sons.

Henkin, Louis. 1996. *Foreign Affairs and the Constitution,* 2nd ed. New York: Oxford University Press.

Hughes, Charles Evans. 1929. Remarks to the American Society of International Law. *Proceedings of the American Society for International Law* 23: 194.

Hume, David. [1742] 1985. Of the Rise and Progress of the Arts and Sciences. In *Essays, Moral, Political and Literary*. Eugene Miller, ed. Indianapolis, Ind.: Liberty Classics.

Lowi, Theodore. 1979. *The End of Liberalism*. 2nd ed. New York: Norton.

Mathews, Jessica Tuchman. 1989. Redefining Security. *Foreign Affairs* (Spring).

Pritchard, Sonia Zaide. 1987. *Oil Pollution Control*. London: Crom Helm.

Raustiala, Kal. 1997. The "Participatory Revolution" in International Environmental Law. *Harvard Environmental Law Review* 21: 537.

Rhodes, Martin. 1995. A Regulatory Conundrum, Industrial Relations and the Social Dimension. In *European Social Policy: Between Fragmentation and Integration,* Stephen Leibried and Paul Pierson, eds. Washington, D.C.: Brookings.

Sax, Joseph. 1992. The Constitutional Dimensions of Property. *Loyola Los Angeles Law Review* 26 (23): 32.

Schoenbrod, David. 1993. *Power Without Responsibility: How Congress Abuses the People Through Delegation*. New Haven, Conn.: Yale University Press.

Steiner, Henry, Detlev F. Vagts, and Harold Hongju Koh. 1994. *Transnational Legal Problems,* 4th ed. Eagan, Minn.: Foundation Press.

Tuck, Richard. 1979. *Natural Rights Theories: Their Origins and Development*. Cambridge: Cambridge University Press.

United Nations. Commission on Global Governance. 1995. *Our Global Neighborhood*. New York: Oxford Press.

Vogel, David. 1996. *Trading Up: Consumer and Environmental Regulation in a Global Economy*. Cambridge: Harvard University Press.

Wright, Quincy. 1922. *The Control of American Foreign Relations*. New York: Macmillan.

# CHAPTER 2

# Environmentalism, the Transformation of International Law, and the Pursuit of Political Objectives

## *Fernand Keuleneer*[1]

## THE MULTIPLE MEANINGS OF ENVIRONMENTALISM

As an undefined term, *environmentalism* can have multiple meanings. It may indicate a sensitivity for real problems having to do with the hazardous effects of various types and forms of pollution, or it may refer to proenvironmental political action. There is also, however, a type of environmentalism that is not so much interested in the environment, but rather more in a radically new allocation of power in a globalized international system. Such an environmentalism is of particular interest to us today. It is one of the centerpieces of the "new global consensus," as generated and defined by the United Nations and its agencies.[2] This new global consensus is meant to provide a new framework in which the "global society" must evolve. The consensus ties together the different facets of the "new paradigm," a term coined by UN officials to describe the set "constituting principles of the global order" as they have been developed in various UN bodies. Key elements of these constituting principles are people-centeredness, sustainable development, and holism or integration of all components.

### THOSE KEY ELEMENTS COMPLEMENT EACH OTHER

People-centeredness stands for a law-driven, rights-based strategy, identifying new needs and creating new individual rights and entitlements. Sustainability is the proposed litmus test for each and every policy, wherever in the world, and includes a strong environmental component. It necessarily implies the knowledge of the criteria that make a particular policy sustainable and that allow saying that one policy is less sustainable than the other. Holism integrates all components of the new consensus. Human rights, the environment, population control, and development are interconnected and come, so to speak, in one package.[3] This description may sound like phraseology, but it would be a momentous mistake to overlook the far-reaching effect these terms may have on the way societies function.

## WE WITNESS THE RISE OF A NEW GLOBAL ORDER

This new global order seeks its legitimacy in "civil society"; direct links are established between this new level and nongovernmental organizations (NGOs), deemed to represent various kinds of formal and informal groups and interests in society. States and governments are put on the same level as the NGOs or are bypassed altogether.

Environmentalism thus emerges in a new context, as a prominent component of the constituting principles of a new international order, the newness of which is also reflected in its legal aspects. In connection with the other components, including the (random) creation of new individual rights, environmentalism must be recognized for what it really is today: a powerful tool for realizing and justifying a global power shift where law is increasingly replaced by rights, States by networks, and elected officials by judges and appointed NGO experts, often operating in a system of auto-reference. This new role of environmentalism on the global scene squarely confronts us with the changing substance and role of international law.

## EFFECTS ON INTERNATIONAL LAW

Talking about rights is talking about law, a system of directly or indirectly enforceable rights and obligations. The new global consensus is increasingly also reflected in a new international law, the international system of enforceable rights and obligations.

To appreciate fully the implications of this new international law, we should try to grasp it in the substance and role of international law, which has primarily happened as a result of the predominant place that an expanded notion of "human rights" has gained in the international legal system.

Classical international law governed the legal aspect of relations among entities legally recognized on the international level, that is, States. Traditionally, the individual, or nongovernmental entities, were not considered as subjects of international law. The international system did not have any direct authority vis-à-vis the individual, who was considered a citizen of a State, and who depended on the State and its political and legal system for the protection of individual rights.

Only after the creation of the United Nations did the individual become a subject of international law, following the 1948 Universal Declaration of Human Rights. At that time, international law became a direct source of individual rights and obligations. Today, the once crucial role of the State in shaping, receiving, and implementing international law becomes less and less the general rule. The balance between international and national (domestic) law is being modified profoundly to the detriment of the latter. As a result, the role of the State itself in law and politics is at stake.

Until recently, the absence on the international level of a legislator acting in the framework of a constitution (or a set of constituting principles) remained one of the major differences between the creation of rules and norms of international law, as opposed to rules and norms of national law. The principal sources of classical international law are treaties and customs rather than legislative acts. Whereas a treaty only binds the parties that entered into it, all subjects of international law must respect customary law. To be recognized as custom, a norm or rule should express a universal consensus and must be perceived as a norm or rule of a legal rather than a political or moral nature. Consensus must not be confounded with unanimity; the presence of a consensus is recorded not only by the institutions in charge of the application of international law, such as the International Court of Justice, but also by domestic courts as they apply rules of international law. These days, the conclusions of specialized UN agencies are presented as the expression of a new consensus in the international community. Consequently, these conclusions are meant to be part of the set of international law norms, which only require acceptance as such by the competent courts, even if the institutions that convoke those UN conferences and set their agendas do not exercise any formal legislative power.

## THE NEW ROLE OF HUMAN RIGHTS

By referring to human rights, a program of political action can fairly easily be translated into legal norms and, by doing so, promote its acceptance and application in international law. Indeed, it can no longer be doubted that human rights have obtained the status of an international legal norm. An international consensus referring to the concept of human rights suffices to enter this consensus into international customary law, thereby assuring its application as a norm of international law. There exists no mechanism that would prevent the concept of human rights to be interpreted, updated, or expanded, as is the case today in different UN institutions, agencies, and conferences. This may be accurately described as a system of auto-reference.

Two features make the use of the concept of human rights very powerful and efficient in terms of its political and ideological objectives: (1) human rights are addressed to individuals, and (2) human rights fall within the category of fundamental rights.

Even if, formally, international law is still addressed in the first place to States, the role of States is often reduced to the implementation and application of fairly detailed and specific rules and prescriptions established under international law. A "negligent" State would be exposed to legal action.

Human rights considered as fundamental rights have the following characteristics:

• Human rights must be upheld by everyone, including the international community and civil society, against each violation by a State, by any center of political power, or by any other group in society.

• The introduction of the human rights concept transforms political issues, which are normally decided upon after a political debate, into legal issues, ruled upon by judges.

• In the hierarchy of legal norms, human rights are at the highest level.

## HUMAN RIGHTS AND THE PREVALENCE OF INTERNATIONAL LAW

Many States already accept the priority of international law, meaning that in the event of a conflict between a norm of national law and a norm of international law, the latter will prevail. The monistic position, similarly accepted by a large number of States, holds that the superposition of international law does not even require any prior intervention on the part of the receiving State. No legislative act or even constitutional provision can prevent the application of whichever international legal norm. The new role of human rights will accelerate this development.

In practice, it will become sufficient for a court or tribunal, domestic or international, to invoke a fundamental international right (human right) to render obsolete any provision of national law, even a posterior legislative act. The scope and the undefined and vague nature of many new human rights lead to a loss of power and legal authority by the States in favor of this international legal order.

If courts and tribunals can be pulled into the dynamics between the international community and civil society (the alliance between international bodies and NGOs), then this new legal, and eventually also political, order will be made dominant. Such a development will inevitably affect all areas of the law, because each legal system needs coherence.

The inevitable drive for a new coherence will be assured by the norms at the top of the new hierarchy (that is, the fundamental rights in international law) and by the creation or reinforcement of international institutions or authorities entrusted with defining their contents. One notices already a reinterpretation of existing norms in the light of new interpretations developed by UN agencies.[4]

## THE POLITICAL OBJECTIVES

A particularly instructive illustration of what was set forth in the previous section is offered by the campaign for an Earth Charter, formally mounted in 1994 by Maurice F. Strong, chairman of The Earth Council; Mikhail Gorbachev; and Green Cross International, with the support of the government of the Netherlands (Rockefeller 1995a). The objectives of the Earth Charter are described as follows:

> [T]here is now a need to consolidate and extend relevant legal principles in a new charter to guide state behavior in the transition to sustainable development. It would provide the basis for, and be subsequently expanded into, a Convention, setting out the sovereign rights and reciprocal responsibilities of all states on environmental protection and sustainable development.
>
> The Earth Charter will be designed as a soft law document. It is, however, important to remember that some documents like the Universal Declaration of Human Rights are initially accepted as soft law instruments but over the years acquire increasing binding force among those who have endorsed them. (Rockefeller 1995a)

The Earth Charter would have legal significance. It suggests an international convention that provides "an integrated legal framework for existing and future environmental and sustainable development law and policy." The concept of international environmental and sustainable development law is proposed as a new branch of all-encompassing law.

> The general objective of international environmental and sustainable development law is formation of a global partnership of all peoples and nations to ensure for present and future generations the well-being of humanity and the larger community of life by promoting equitable and sustainable development and by protecting and restoring the health and integrity of the Earth's biosphere, of which all life is a part and apart from which humanity cannot survive or realize its creative potential. This global alliance should be founded on commitment to an integrated framework of shared ethical principles and practical guidelines. (Rockefeller 1995b, I)
>
> Humanity is part of nature and the community of life, and all life depends for survival and well-being on the functioning of natural systems. (Rockefeller 1995b, III.2)
>
> Nature as a whole, the Earth, and all life forms should be respected. All persons have a fundamental responsibility to respect and care for the community of life. (Rockefeller 1995b, IV.2)

All human beings, including future generations, have a right to an environment adequate for their health, well-being, and dignity, and the responsibility to protect the environment. (Rockefeller 1995b,V.1)

All peoples have a right to their economic, social, political, and cultural development and a responsibility to adopt sustainable patterns of development. (Rockefeller 1995b,V.3)

This environment-centeredness creates the possibility for undefined and unlimited claims against any form of human activity that has an influence on the environment. Which rights exactly those are is not made clear, but they are called *fundamental*. Those rights will allow, for instance, as suggested in principle number 5 of the Benchmark Draft I,

> to share equitably the benefits of natural resource use and a healthy environment among the nations, between rich and poor, between males and females, between present and future generations, and internalize all environmental, social and economic costs. (Rockefeller 1995a, Benchmark Draft I)

One can easily see how such a provision could lead to undefined, very vague, and very general claims against a business. It could always be argued that for the sake of environmental protection some environmental cost should be internalized. Business will need to take measures to avoid what is deemed "damage to the environment." However, the concept of damage to the environment becomes very vague if it is no longer based primarily on human health concerns, but on abstract notions such as sustainable development or "the health and integrity of the Earth's biosphere."

The point is not that these objectives and principles are not worthwhile; quite the contrary. But again, we must draw attention to consequences that have little or nothing to do with the environment, but everything to do with the global power shift. By proposing the extreme legalization of a decision-making process, which is fundamentally political, the process is radically altered. By legalizing what is eminently political, the nature and core of the law are also affected.

What is proposed as Earth Charter threatens to destroy the very notion of law as we know it. In public law, the (legal) sovereignty of nations is restricted by and subject to so many restrictions of an unspecified nature that virtually nothing is left of the concept of sovereignty. It would seem that not only other States, but also individuals or groups, including advocacy groups for the "community of life" or the "integrity of the Earth's biosphere," would be granted jurisdiction.

Similar effects would manifest themselves in what today is still considered to be the private sphere. The very notion of fault or negligence would disappear as would the criterion to determine which behavior is legal and which is not. Not the content or nature of an act, but its perceived effects would determine whether it is legal. Effects on what? Nature as a whole, the Earth, the community of life, sustainable development, human rights? These all must be respected and protected. The content and nature of the effects are so wide open and interpretable that, as a result, the outcome of the proposed legal process will become unpredictable. Law is reduced to a mere power game, where "rights" oppose "rights," without the unifying principles and institutions that characterize the system called Law.

In this scenario, not only individual rights but also group rights would flourish; the private sphere would be politicized and the public sphere would be privatized.

## THE GREENING OF FOREIGN POLICY: A CONCLUSION

Making environmentalism one of the cornerstones of foreign policy leads to the reinforcement of the driving forces behind the new global consensus. This new consensus aims to replace the present international system by transforming international law, making it a tool for virtually eliminating the central role of States in the system. The central role would instead be assumed by global networks and partnerships, operating in the context of a rights-based legal system replacing, to a large extent, traditional democratic politics.

Those who disagree with the abovementioned agenda should start questioning the current expansion of international law, the legalization of society, and the role of the judicial system. They should question the current hierarchy between various branches of international law and domestic law. They should reflect upon restoring clearly defined centers of political decision making, which, unlike courts in this global system, can be influenced by building political majorities.

## ENDNOTES

1. The author is indebted to the work of Marguerite Peeters and the Brussels-based Interactive Information Services on many of the issues addressed in this paper.

2. The buildup of the various components of the new consensus happened through a series of special conferences, which each brought a building block: sustainable development (Rio 1992), the link between human rights and development (Vienna 1993), reproductive health and reproductive rights (Cairo 1994), the people-centered social contract (Copenhagen 1995), the gender perspective (Beijing 1995), the partnership with the actors of civil society (Istanbul 1996).

3. See, for example, UN Population Fund, *The State of World Population* (1997).

4. A project such as the European construction seems to be the perfect instrument for avoiding the risk that some Parliaments or Supreme Courts would reverse the priority of international law and would thereby endanger the international "consensus." The Treaty of Amsterdam, now in the process of ratification in the various Member States, provides that the European Union is bound by "human rights." As this provision is part of a European Union treaty, it will undoubtedly be the European Court of Justice in Luxembourg that will have the final say and impose its own interpretation of "human rights" on the institutions of the Member States. Taking account of the fact that the European Union considers international law to be a source of European law, this interpretation is bound to be determined by the international "consensus."

## REFERENCES

Rockefeller, Steven C. 1995a. Introduction. *Principles of Environmental Conservation and Sustainable Development.* 21 pars. Earth Charter Project. At <http://www.earthcharter.org/report/survey/intro_en.htm>.

Rockefeller, Steven C. 1995b. Summary of Principles. *Principles of Environmental Conservation and Sustainable Development.* Earth Charter Project. At <http://www.earthcharter.org/report/survey/summary_en.htm>.

United Nations. Population Fund. 1997. *The State of World Population.*

# CHAPTER 3

# Green Creep: The Increasing Influence of Environmentalism in U.S. Foreign Policy

*Brett D. Schaefer*

## INTRODUCTION

Americans have grown increasingly concerned with environmental issues over the past several decades (Esty 1994, 9). Highly publicized environmental disasters, health scares, and predictions of pending environmental doom have mobilized Americans to join and support groups that advocate greater protection for the environment. Environmental groups have used this popularity and financial support as a bludgeon to influence, at times even dominate, U.S. politics and policy. Although the effect of environmental issues on domestic policy is well documented, the critical issue of how they influence U.S. foreign policy has received less attention.

By characterizing the environment as an interdependent system—wherein actions in one area have an impact elsewhere—environmentalists argue that global environmental protection is not only prudent, but also necessary. Indeed, in the environmentalist mind-set, every other concern, including national security and economic prosperity, must yield to the overarching goal of environmental protection. A well-publicized example of this viewpoint is *Earth in the Balance*, in which Vice President Al Gore unequivocally states:

> We must make the rescue of the environment the central organizing principle for civilization. . . . Adopting a central organizing principle—one

agreed to voluntarily—means embarking on an all-out effort to use every policy and program, every law and institution, every treaty and alliance, every tactic and strategy, every plan and course of action—to use, in short, every means to halt the destruction of the environment and to preserve and nurture our ecological system. (Gore 1993, 274)

In fact, ample evidence shows that environmental policy has made significant inroads in all three key arms of U.S. foreign policy: diplomacy, trade, and defense. Environmental concerns have already become, if not central policy considerations, then major issues that are an integral part of standing policies and practices. Indeed, the Clinton administration considers environmental issues, such as ozone depletion, global warming, and forest management, "core national security objectives" (President 1997, ii).

Recent decades have yielded a blizzard of multilateral agreements, treaties, conventions, conferences, and protocols. As many as 650 international treaties containing environmental provisions are in force today. The United States has signed or put in force more than 150 international treaties dealing specifically with environmental issues or containing environmental provisions.

These treaties, agreements, and protocols affect U.S. foreign policy, as well as the daily lives of people in the United States, in very tangible ways. For example, trade agreements and organizations, including the World Trade Organization (WTO), that directly impact the ability of Americans to purchase necessary goods and services often now include environmental regulations as part of their missions and responsibilities. To understand the breadth and depth of that impact, we need to understand environmentalism's roots in America.

## ENVIRONMENTALISM IN THE UNITED STATES

Since the founding of the United States, America and the natural environment have been interdependent. At first this relationship was based on economics. People associated the natural environment with opportunity and prosperity. Untapped resources and unclaimed wilderness were cheap and plentiful and served as the basis for self-sufficiency and even wealth.

The perception of nature as an endless resource began to change in the middle to late nineteenth century. The effect of the human race on the environment was discernible and in many cases negative. Moreover, the Western frontier, which had represented an inexhaustible source of new land and untapped resources, was shrinking and officially closed in 1890 (Bandow 1986, 3).

The recognition of limited resources spawned two philosophies on the proper relationship between humans and the environment. The more prevalent philosophy at the turn of the century, conservationism, was based on the belief that natural resources should be managed for prudent use by people and protected to ensure that natural resources would be available to future generations.[1]

The second philosophy, preservationism, believed that natural resources should be protected from use altogether. Instead of regarding nature merely as a tool or resource valued in terms of how people might use it, preservationism regarded nature as having an inherent value beyond potential use. Indeed, in some instances, the preservationist philosophy grants the natural environment a value equal or superior to the needs and desires of humans. This viewpoint originated during the Enlightenment period of American philosophy championed by Henry David Thoreau and Ralph Waldo Emerson. Preservationism has evolved considerably in recent decades (Taylor 1998, 309–397).[2]

During the nineteenth century, the combination of scarcity of and greater reverence for nature led to increased action to prevent the despoiling of the environment. Although expansion of the government into timber, soil, and water management was predictable, the conservationist stance was preeminent and served as the foundation of American environmental policy. Examples of early environmental legislation include the Forest Reserve Act of 1891, which authorized the president to establish national timber reserves, and the Reclamation Acts of 1902, which authorized construction, operation, and maintenance of reclamation projects for arid and semiarid lands. Environmental protection and preservation became a federal government priority under President Theodore Roosevelt. In the early years of environmental policy, however, private individuals and organizations, such as the

National Wildlife Federation and the National Audubon Society, rather than the federal government commonly spearheaded conservation efforts (Adler 1995, ix).

In the later half of the twentieth century, the conservationist philosophy began to yield to the preservationist philosophy as the preeminent influence over environmental activism and policy. Spurred by publications with cataclysmic themes, such as Rachel Carson's crusade against pesticide in *The Silent Spring* (reprint edition, Houghton Mifflin, 1994) and Paul R. Ehrlich's Malthusian prediction in *The Population Bomb* (reprint edition, Buccaneer Books, 1997), those who advocated environmental preservation in the United States evolved into a modern activist lobby.

Without question, the inaugural Earth Day on April 22, 1970, marked the beginning of the modern era of environmentalism. A collaborative effort of dozens of environmental activists and organizations, Earth Day was intended to familiarize the public at large with—and capture broad-based support for—environmental issues. The plan was tremendously successful. Schools across the nation held Earth Day lectures and events, forty-two states passed resolutions in support of Earth Day, and the federal government saw widespread support for environmental issues (Adler 1995, 21–22).

The organizers of Earth Day were overwhelmingly preservationist in orientation. The success of the event propelled them to the forefront of the movement and relegated the conservationist activists and organizations to irrelevance or forced them to adapt to the new paradigm. As noted by environmental expert Jonathan Adler (1995), "The militants became the core participants in the next generation of environmental organizations and redefined the environmental agenda—so much so that the old-line organizations were pressured to change their approaches" (22).

In addition to the shift to preservationism as the dominant ideology of environmental activists, this new paradigm was significantly less geared to private-sector efforts. Instead, environmental groups focused their efforts on increasing political and legal influence to force environmental values upon society through government regulation. This shift is illustrated by the mushrooming of grassroots environmental groups and lobbying organizations just prior to and following Earth Day (Adler 1995, 23).[3] For example, the number of environmental lobbyists registered in Washington rose from only two in 1970 to 88 by 1985 (Adler 1995, 24).

The tactics of these groups switched to reflect this new strategy—away from encouraging wise use of resources through education and private sector land management and toward lobbying politicians to support environmental legislation and regulations, supporting politicians who have proenvironmental agendas, and using the courts to regulate through litigation. The growing political power of environmentalists and their success in achieving their goals is clearly illustrated by their legislative victories. More than a dozen major environmental laws were enacted by the end of the 1970s, including the creation of the Environmental Protection Agency and the Council on Environmental Quality (Adler 1995, 23, 42).

## ENVIRONMENTALISM IN U.S. FOREIGN POLICY INSTITUTIONS

As environmental issues gained stature in domestic politics in the twentieth century, environmentalists began to point out international aspects of environmental protection and to promote actions that would advance their agenda through U.S. foreign policy. Executive orders, congressional legislation, and political appointees have all been utilized to impose environmental standards on U.S. foreign policy departments and to ensure that those departments promote environmental protection in relations with foreign nations, international organizations, and treaty negotiations.

As noted by Secretary of State Madeleine Albright, "Not so long ago, many believed that the pursuit of clean air, clean water, and healthy forests was a worthy goal, but not part of our national security. Today environmental issues are part of the mainstream of American foreign policy" (U.S. Department of State 1998).

The State Department now embraces the idea of environmental diplomacy. Congressional decisions to grant to the administration fast-track trade negotiating authority now hinge on whether the administration should be allowed to include environmental provisions in trade agreements. The Department of Defense regards environmental protection as a national security issue and established a Deputy Under Secretary of Defense for Environmental Security in 1993. Clearly, environmentalism has a dramatic effect on U.S. foreign policy and the departments charged with conducting it—an influence that will only grow if left unchecked.

## ENVIRONMENTALISM AND THE STATE DEPARTMENT

Diplomacy is the first option in addressing potential threats to U.S. national interests and expressing U.S. concerns and priorities to foreign nations. The daily conduct of diplomacy through U.S. missions and representatives is essential in articulating U.S. interests and eliciting cooperation and support for those interests abroad.

Because diplomatic currency is finite—clearly, foreign countries and officials cannot be expected to endlessly support and promote U.S. concerns—it is critically important that the United States focus its diplomatic efforts on issues of paramount importance to the nation. Traditionally, these priorities had been opposing hostile domination of key geographic regions, supporting our allies, securing vital resources, and ensuring access to foreign economies (Holmes and Moore 1996, xi–xvii).

However, as environmental issues increased in domestic political influence, Congress and the executive branch began to project these issues into U.S. foreign policy. For example, in 1973, Congress passed legislation creating the Bureau of Oceans and International Environmental and Scientific Affairs (OES) at the Department of State (Graffey 1998, 405). The OES works with the White House, U.S. government agencies, Congress, American universities, and nongovernmental organizations to set U.S. foreign policy in global environment, science, and technology issues. OES implements this policy around the world through representation in bilateral and multilateral organizations and meetings and through cooperative agreements with foreign government agencies (U.S. Department of State 1998).

The Clinton administration implemented several policies designed to make environmental protection a State Department priority. For example, listed among the primary interests and strategic goals of the United States Strategic Plan for International Affairs, published by the State Department, are national security, protection of American citizens and U.S. borders, and global issues ("secur[ing] a sustainable global environment" and stabilizing world population are two of its three primary goals). Thus, the administration's strategic plan puts "a sustainable global environment" in the same strategic category as "eliminat[ing] the threat to the United States and its allies from weapons of mass destruction" (U.S. Department of State 1997). Former Under Secretary for Global Affairs Timothy Wirth reiterated this point when he stated that the "President and the Vice President believe strongly that managing the Earth's resources is inextricably linked to our ability to advance our national and global interests" (Wirth 1997). According to Wirth:

> In the past, environmental concerns were relegated to the periphery by diplomats more concerned with what were considered the "high policy" issues of the day, such as maintaining the arms balance, or preventing hostile alliances. All of this changed with the end of the Cold War. . . . [D]iplomats and foreign policy makers [realized] that America's national interests are undeniably bound to the quality of the earth's environment. . . . The link between the environment and U.S. national interests prompted Secretary Christopher in 1996 to . . . institutionalize the central role of environment in the daily conduct of our diplomacy. (Wirth 1997)

Secretary of State Albright confirmed that environmental issues are now a State Department priority. In her introductory statement to *Environmental Diplomacy*, she stated that environmental issues are "often at the heart of the political and economic challenges we face around the world" (Albright 1998). Further, she indicated that "we would not be doing our jobs as peacemakers and as democracy-builders, if we were not also good stewards of the global environment" (Albright 1998). In other words, Albright believes that failing to treat environmental issues as a priority undermines peace and the transition to representative government.

Vice President Gore's National Performance Review (NPR) initiative bolstered the State Department's green mission by redefining its responsibilities and reorganizing its structure to meet its new priorities. Under the guise of adapting the State Department to a post–Cold War world, the Clinton administration actively promoted environmental issues as a State Department priority and created a new under secretary position for Global Affairs in 1994 (PL 103-236, Section 161[b]). One of the responsibilities of the Under Secretary is to coordinate U.S. foreign relations on global issues (such as environment, oceans and science, and population) that are touchstones for international environmental groups and that are the objects of many international treaties and UN conferences.

The State Department released its first report on the environment and foreign policy on Earth Day 1997. The main thrust of this report was the announcement of a new State Department policy called "environmental diplomacy" (U.S. Department of State 1998). Environmental diplomacy is a comprehensive strategy for State Department action to promote environmental protection around the world through U.S. diplomatic efforts, international organizations, and multilateral treaties (U.S. Department of State 1998).

*United States Foreign Assistance*

Originally introduced as a temporary agency by President Kennedy in 1961, the United States Agency for International Development (USAID) has become a permanent agency charged with supervising and distributing U.S. economic development and humanitarian assistance around the world.

The original purpose of USAID was twofold: to promote economic growth in developing countries through assistance and to combat the expansion of communism during the Cold War. With the end of the Cold War, the first goal has gained preeminence. However, it has been altered to incorporate environmental protection (USAID 1998).[4] For instance, the Foreign Assistance Act has been amended over the years to require environmental impact assessments on all USAID projects, with emphasis on environmental concerns such as protecting tropical forests, biological diversity, and endangered species.

USAID has declared its intention to follow an environmental agenda—as outlined in Agenda 21—that is based on the concept of sustainable development, which was presented at the 1992 UN Conference on Environment and Development (UNCED)—the "Earth Summit."[5] According to USAID, their intention means that every activity of the organization must be considered with its potential environmental impact in mind. "Programs in every sphere of development—environment, economic growth, population and health, democracy—must be designed with conscious regard for their impact on the natural environment and their potential for improving environmental stewardship locally, nationally, regionally, and globally" (USAID 1998). Indeed, according to USAID, "Environmental sustainability is integral to USAID's overall goal. To meet this goal, environmental considerations shall be incorporated into results planning, achieving, and monitoring" (USAID 1998). In support of sustainable development in developing countries, U.S. foreign assistance focuses on encouraging broad-based economic growth, protecting the environment, reducing population growth, increasing health, and forging democracy.

USAID's plan to implement Agenda 21 focuses on both global and local environmental problems. Globally, USAID programs aim to reduce sources of greenhouse gas emissions and save the planet's biological diversity at the genetic, species, and ecosystem levels. Among other activities, USAID acts to implement Agenda 21 principles locally by combating "unsustainable exploitation of forests, wetlands, coastal zones, coral reefs, and other ecosystems that provide vital ecological services;" eliminating "environmentally unsound" production and use of energy; and promoting environmental protection through laws and regulations in developing countries (USAID 1998). In addition, USAID outlines plans for lobbying foreign governments to embrace environmental regulation and international efforts to combat global warming and protect biological diversity.

USAID creates specific programs to enhance its program goals. For example, in 1993, USAID created the Environmental Education and Communication Project, or GreenCOM, to help implement its environmental strategic objectives by working "in tandem with other projects in its portfolio, across sectors and across regions of the world" (USAID, "About GreenCOM" 1998). GreenCOM is jointly funded and managed by the Center for Environment and the USAID Center for Human Capacity Development of the Bureau for Global Programs, Field Support, and Research and USAID field missions (USAID 1998).

How far has USAID traveled from its original goal of promoting economic growth through economic assistance and market liberalization? In the agency's own words:

> Environmental problems reflect the imperfections of private markets. Adam Smith's "invisible hand" is not always a "green" hand. Government policies often distort markets and encourage excessive exploitation of natural resources. Public interventions to correct market failures and eliminate market distortions often are necessary to protect the environment. Effective public institutions that create and monitor an environment favorable to sustainable resource use are critical. This, in turn, requires active public participation in the setting of standards, monitoring, and enforcement. (USAID 1998)

Even though USAID's literature says "market-based approaches should be pursued wherever possible," the agency's stated policy of urging developing country bureaucrats to determine "what is economically rational and what is not" in pursuit of sustainable environmental policy clearly shows its bias against market solutions (USAID 1998).

GREENING THE TRADE AGENDA

Trade is an attractive vehicle for environmentalist legislation addressing global concerns. Trade is inherently international. Also, if the "carrot" of a cleaner environment that results from greater environmental regulation (according to the proponents of such efforts) is not sufficient incentive, then trade provides a ready "stick," in the form of trade sanctions or restrictions, for encouraging trade partners to abide by U.S. environmental standards. Because the United States is the world's largest market, accounting for 14 percent of world trade in 1997, it has a unique advantage in applying this tactic (Sweeney 1998, 532). An example of this effort, albeit an ultimately unsuccessful one, was the U.S. ban of Mexican tuna imports under the United States Marine Mammal Protection Act to prevent tuna harvesting techniques considered harmful to porpoises by environmentalists (Wilson 1997a, 2).

Application of these trade sanctions aggravates the relationship between the administration and Congress on trade policy. The U.S. Constitution, by granting Congress the power to "lay and collect . . . Duties" and to "regulate Commerce with foreign Nations" and then granting the president the responsibility of conducting foreign affairs, creates an internal conflict in trade negotiations. Any trade agreement with foreign nations requires the president to negotiate the agreement, but Congress must implement the agreement through legislation before the agreement enters into force. Obviously, this is a cumbersome process. Trade negotiations are made more difficult because trade partners cannot be assured that the agreement would pass unaltered by Congress, if it would be passed at all.

Actions taken during the Great Depression to address the economic crisis were key to establishing modern American trade policy. In a misguided effort to protect domestic industries and to promote a positive trade balance, Congress passed the Tariff Act of 1930—more commonly known as the Smoot-Hawley Tariff Act—which raised U.S. tariffs to unprecedented levels. Smoot-Hawley spurred retaliatory tariffs from twenty-five other countries, placing a stranglehold on international trade. The situation was further exacerbated by a series of competitive currency devaluations—the purposeful depreciation of a currency in an attempt to lower the cost of exports relative to products from other nations (Wilson 1994, 3).

Once it became apparent that the tariffs established by Smoot-Hawley deepened the global depression and lengthened its duration, Congress took steps to roll back trade barriers. The devastating experience of the Great Depression led Western governments, including the United States, to avoid a repetition of the 1930 trade wars and make trade liberalization the keystone of trade policy. In 1934 Congress authorized the president, for a predetermined time and within specific limitations, "to enter into foreign trade agreements with foreign governments . . . and to proclaim such modifications of existing duties and other import restrictions . . . as are required or appropriate to carry out any [such] trade agreement" (Pregelj 1998, 1).

It was also evident that one nation could not turn the tide alone. At the end of World War II, the United States and other developed nations met to discuss the 1930 trade wars and to determine actions to avoid repetition. The result of these discussions and the key to international trade liberalization was the General Agreement on Tariffs and Trade (GATT), which entered into force in 1948. The GATT established a set of principles to govern international trade, a forum to discuss trade issues, and a framework to settle trade-related disputes (Wilson 1994, 3).[6]

The benefits of the new focus on trade liberalization are legion. For example, world trade increased from less than $100 billion in the 1940s to more than $6.3 trillion in 1996 (Sweeney 1998, 535). This increase in trade contributed substantially to global economic growth. From 1965 to 1980, when annual growth in global exports averaged 6.6 percent, global GDP increased 4 percent annually, and with global export growth of 4.3 percent from 1980 to 1990, world GDP increased 3.2 percent (Wilson 1994, 4).

The exclusivity of trade liberalization as America's trade policy began to change with the Trade Act of 1974,[7] which expanded the authority of the executive branch to negotiate trade agreements with other nations or multilaterally. Formerly, the executive branch was authorized to negotiate tariff levels; the 1974 Trade Act authorized the president to negotiate nontariff barriers as well. Reminiscent of the 1934 debate, a 1974 Senate report summarized the justification for expanding the president's authority to enact trade agreements:

> Our negotiators cannot be expected to accomplish the negotiating goals . . . if there are no reasonable assurances that the negotiated agreements would be voted up or down on their merits. Our trading partners have expressed an unwillingness to negotiate without some assurances that the Congress will consider the agreements within a definite time frame. (Pregelj 1998, 3)

However, these acts also returned some trade-policy control to Congress. Congress reserved the right to ratify or confirm any trade negotiation, especially that involving nontariff barriers. This shift subjected trade policy toward a broader group of interests represented by Congress and increased pressures to use trade measures to address issues not previously associated with trade. One of these issues was the effect of trade on the environment and the possibility of using trade to advance environmental goals. Environmentalists had long criticized trade as harmful to the environment because of increased utilization of natural resources. At the same time, however, environmentalists began to perceive trade agreements as a means of enforcing environmental protection—especially in the absence of an international environmental organization to enforce universal standards.

Environmentalism's increasing influence in trade negotiations was evident during the six-year period from 1989 to 1994—a period marked both by the large number of trade agreements announced, negotiated, and passed, and by the rising influence of environmental policy in trade (Sweeney, Johnson, and O'Quinn 1997, 629–668).[8] Each of the three major trade issues of the 1990s thus far—the North American Free Trade Agreement (NAFTA), the Uruguay Round of the GATT (which established the World Trade Organization [WTO]), and fast-track trade negotiating authority for the U.S. president—has been influenced by and, to some extent, used to advance the environmental agenda.

## NAFTA

Ratified by Congress in 1993, the North American Free Trade Agreement created a free-trade zone among Canada, Mexico, and the United States. In addition to being the first free-trade agreement between "developed" countries (Canada and the United States) and a developing country (Mexico), NAFTA was the first trade agreement that fully joined trade and environment issues.

Wage disparities between Mexican and U.S. workers, in addition to well-publicized pollution along the U.S.-Mexican border, allowed environmentalists to argue that NAFTA would merely make Mexico a pollution haven for U.S. businesses. However, this additional pressure only added to monumental lobbying by environmental groups on the Bush and Clinton administrations to include environmental protection provisions in NAFTA, such as requiring treaty parties to meet automobile emissions standards, and make it the "greenest trade agreement ever negotiated" (Esty 1993, 50; Organization of American States 1998 ANNEX 913—A, Section 2, a, iii).

A clause in NAFTA ensures preeminence of international environmental agreements over trade. Article 104 states that, should a conflict arise between NAFTA and any multilateral environmental agreement (MEA) to which NAFTA signatories are parties, MEA would prevail (Wilson 1997a, 3). In addition, Clinton administration trade negotiators were careful to ensure that NAFTA protects the ability of a nation to implement ever more stringent environmental laws and regulations even if those laws and regulations negatively impact trade. For example, Article 713.3 of NAFTA states that "Nothing in Paragraph 1 shall be construed to prevent a Party from adopting, maintaining or applying, in accordance with other provisions of this Section, a sanitary or phytosanitary measure that is more stringent than the relevant international standard, guideline or recommendation" (Wilson 1997a, 5).

A side agreement to NAFTA established a Commission for Environmental Cooperation to deliberate environmental concerns. This agreement specifically requires NAFTA signatories to maintain and enforce laws and regulations to ensure strict environmental protection (Wilson 1997a, 3). Another NAFTA byproduct was the U.S.-Mexico bilateral agreement authorized in and funded through NAFTA-implementing legislation. The U.S.-Mexico bilateral agreement establishes a Border Environmental Cooperation Commission to plan and coordinate environmental infrastructure projects in local communities and the North American Development Bank to provide funds for environmental infrastructure projects (Wilson 1997a, 3; Wilson 1997b, 5).

## The General Agreement on Tariffs and Trade and the World Trade Organization

Since its founding in 1948 until the creation of the World Trade Organization (WTO), the General Agreement on Tariffs and Trade (GATT) was the primary multilateral agreement governing

international trade. The primary goal of the GATT was to eliminate trade barriers, which it accomplished admirably, reducing
average tariffs among GATT member countries from 40 percent
in 1948 to 5 percent in 1993 (Wathen 1993, 6). The GATT was
an extremely powerful agreement through which more than 100
nations, including the world's largest economies, agreed to coordinate their trade policies and abide by GATT rulings in trade
disputes (Wathen 1993, 6).

Although GATT did not explicitly prohibit countries from creating and implementing environmental laws, regulations, and
standards, it did bar environmental policies that served as barriers
to trade. Specifically, the GATT allowed for environmental laws
and regulations that protected human, animal, or plant life or
acted to conserve natural resources as long as they were justifiable,
applied equally to both domestic and foreign products and production processes, did not discriminate between countries, and
were not disguised trade barriers (Wilson 1994, 6).

These four caveats have often been used to restrict domestic
environmental regulation if it is determined that the regulation
discriminates against imported products, especially if the law or
regulation particularly affects imports or products of a particular
country or group of countries (Wilson 1994, 2). An example of
this conflict was the August 16, 1991, ruling that the U.S. ban on
Mexican tuna under the U.S. Marine Mammal Protection Act
was in violation of GATT (Wathen 1993, 3; Wilson 1994, 7).

During the most recently completed round of GATT negotiations in Punta del Este, Uruguay, from 1986 to 1994, GATT signatories agreed to create the World Trade Organization (WTO).
The WTO replaced GATT by incorporating the GATT agreement
into the WTO agreement. The WTO has a much wider sphere of
authority than GATT. Whereas the GATT dealt only with trade in
goods, the WTO covers trade in goods, services, and intellectual
property issues. According to the WTO Internet site:

> The WTO is the only international body dealing with the rules of
> trade between nations. At its heart are the WTO agreements, the legal
> ground-rules for international commerce and for trade policy. The
> agreements have three main objectives: to help trade flow as freely as

possible, to achieve further liberalization gradually through negotiation, and to set up an impartial means of settling disputes. (World
Trade Organization 1998)

Because proponents of environmental protection view trade as
anti-environment, a primary goal of environmentalists has long
been to gain exception for environmental laws and regulations in
the GATT and other trade agreements. This goal was advanced to
a large extent with the creation of the WTO. Whereas the GATT
does not even mention the word *environment,* the preamble of the
WTO Agreement includes direct references to sustainable development and to the need for protecting and preserving the environment. Indeed, the WTO has created a Committee on Trade and
Environment to bring environmental issues into the mainstream of
WTO discussions and considerations. According to this committee, "The multilateral trading system has the capacity to further
integrate environmental considerations and enhance its contribution to the promotion of sustainable development without under-
mining its open, equitable and non-discriminatory character"
(World Trade Organization 1998).

Specific WTO agreements that make concessions on environmental regulation abound. For example, the Agreements on
Technical Barriers to Trade and on Sanitary and Phytosanitary
Measures explicitly exempt measures to protect humans, animal
and plant life, health, and the environment. The WTO Agreement
on Agriculture exempts direct payments under federal environmental programs from WTO members' commitments to reduce agricultural subsidies. The Agreement on Subsidies and Countervailing
Measures exempts government subsidies of up to 20 percent of the
cost of adapting existing facilities to new environmental legislation
(World Trade Organization 1998).

### Fast Track and the Clinton Administration
In the Trade Act of 1974, which first created fast-track authority, Congress expanded the power of the president not just to reduce duties (tariffs), but also to enter into agreements to reduce
nontariff trade barriers, including environmental regulations
(subject to congressional confirmation). Fast-track authority fa-

cilitates trade negotiations by limiting congressional debate on trade agreements negotiated by the president and by prohibiting congressional amendments on the implementation of legislation contained in the agreement. More specifically, under fast track, Congress agrees to vote straight up or down on trade legislation within sixty days of it being submitted by the president and to allow no amendments (Wathen 1993, 13). With fast-track authority in place, U.S. trade partners can be certain that the principles established in negotiations with the president will remain unaltered by Congress in the approval process. In all, fast track has achieved its goal of facilitating trade agreements—as evidenced by the three free trade agreements and two comprehensive trade packages implemented since 1974.[9]

Congress has granted every president fast-track authority since that authority was first enacted in 1974. The most recent version of fast track, the Omnibus Trade and Competitiveness Act of 1988, expired on April 1, 1993, but was extended through April 15, 1994, to allow for completion of the Uruguay Round of GATT negotiations. Although President Clinton has asked Congress to extend fast-track authority, Congress has refused to grant the request, in part, because of the president's insistence on including labor and environmental protection language in the authority (Sweeney 1998, 536; Fletcher 1997, 1).[10] For instance, the administration listed as its three major objectives for fast track to "break down unfair and foreign trade barriers and create good American jobs," "promote and advance worker rights," and "promote responsible environmental protections" (Fletcher 1997, 2).

The president's September 17, 1997, proposal for fast track, the Export Expansion and Reciprocal Trade Agreements Act of 1997, included three specific references to the environment to implement the administration's stated goals. The president's proposal would:

1.    allow him to address foreign government environmental policies and practices;

2.    establish the U.S. position as supportive of sustainable development and charge the president to "ensure that trade and environmental protection are mutually supportive;" and

3.     require U.S. trade negotiators to take U.S. environmental laws, regulations, and levels of protection into account. (Fletcher 1997, 1–2)

Although opposition to the Clinton fast-track proposal was not based solely on the inclusion of environmental provisions as a part of fast-track negotiating authority, the president's intractable stance was partly responsible for the virtual standstill in U.S. trade policy since 1994.

## ENVIRONMENT AND EXPORT PROMOTION

Other trade targets for environmental groups are the Overseas Private Investment Corporation (OPIC) and the Export-Import Bank of the United States (Ex-Im Bank)—two federal agencies tasked with aiding U.S. businesses in overseas markets. OPIC insures overseas investments by U.S. businesses against losses due to expropriation, political instability, and such unforeseen contingencies as currency inconvertibility. It also issues investment guarantees and direct loans to U.S. businesses for international investments and manages international investment funds in high-risk developing countries (OPIC 1998; Schaefer 1996; Schaefer 1997). The Ex-Im Bank guarantees loans for U.S. exporters, provides loans to or guarantees the repayment of loans to foreign purchasers of U.S. goods and services, and issues insurance against nonpayment by foreign buyers for political or commercial risk (Ex-Im Bank 1996).

Environmental groups have long criticized the allegedly harmful effects on the environment caused by the projects financed or insured by OPIC and the Ex-Im Bank. In response to this criticism, Congress has imposed environmental restrictions on the agencies. Since 1985, OPIC has been required to assess the environmental effect of proposed projects. If projects pose a "major or unreasonable hazard to the environment, health or safety" or result in "significant degradation of a national park or similar protected area," OPIC is required to deny funding (OPIC 1998). In 1992, Congress amended the charter of the Ex-Im Bank, requiring an environmental review to ensure that Ex-Im Bank projects are "environmentally responsible." Proposed projects must be reviewed to examine their environmental effects on air quality, water use and quality, management of hazardous and toxic materials and waste, natural hazards, ecological effects, and noise. If projects are found to have "adverse environmental effects," the Bank is required to decline financing (Ex-Im Bank 1999).

Nongovernmental organizations (NGOs) with environmental agendas successfully forced OPIC and the Ex-Im Bank to withdraw their support for certain ventures. In 1995, OPIC withdrew its political risk coverage of Freeport McMoRan's copper mining operations in Irian Jaya, Indonesia, after environmental groups condemned the project (FOE 1998). The Ex-Im Bank refused to support U.S. business participation in the world's largest construction project—China's Three Gorges Dam—because its environmental concerns had "not been adequately addressed" (Murkowski 1998, A17).

Under pressure from environmental NGOs, President Clinton revealed new environmental guidelines for OPIC at the 1997 Earth II Summit in June 1997. The new guidelines included imposing U.S. federal or World Bank standards on OPIC projects, NGO environmental auditing of OPIC projects, tracking greenhouse gas emissions resulting from OPIC projects, and submitting an annual report to Congress on OPIC's compliance with environmental treaties, laws, and policies (FOE 1998). For example, OPIC recently declared that it would no longer support "projects in or impacting United Nations World Heritage Sites"—areas, such as Yellowstone National Park, that are identified by the United Nations to have unique environmental or cultural significance.[11]

Environmental values are now so embedded in OPIC and the Ex-Im Bank that the agencies themselves are the biggest allies of the environmental groups. U.S. businesses criticized environmental restrictions on OPIC and Ex-Im Bank funding, claiming that the restrictions hurt the businesses in the global market because other countries were not abiding by the same standards. In a recent *Washington Post* op-ed, chairman and Ex-Im Bank president James Harmon emphatically argued against relaxing environmental restrictions, even if those restrictions would aid U.S. businesses. Senator Frank Murkowski (R-AK) proposed an

amendment allowing the Ex-Im Bank to finance American businesses for a project normally barred from Ex-Im Bank assistance
because of environmental concerns if other Group of Seven export agencies supported their businesses for the same project.
Harmon criticized that the Murkowski amendment would

> surrender U.S. leadership internationally on the environment. . . . What
> the U.S. exporter needs now is for all the industrialized countries to
> agree on the importance of the environment. . . . Congress was right to
> urge us to adopt environmental guidelines in 1992. I believe it would
> be wrong for Congress, the Ex-Im Bank and U.S. business to retreat
> now. (Harmon 1998, A19)

## No Defense for the Military

The U.S. Constitution commands the president and Congress to
"provide for the common defence." Traditionally, this mission has
been the sole concern of the U.S. military. During the nearly fifty
years of Cold War policy, the national security strategy of the
United States was based on one overriding principle: Contain the
power of the Soviet Union and its allies around the world. This
principle is exemplified in Department of Defense Directive
5100.1, issued on September 25, 1987, which defines the functions and responsibilities of the Department of Defense and its
major components under this national strategy.

> The Department of Defense shall maintain and employ Armed Forces to:
>
> 1.   Support and defend the Constitution of the United States
> against all enemies, foreign and domestic.
>
> 2.   Ensure, by timely and effective military action, the security of
> the United States, its possessions, and areas vital to its interest.
>
> 3.   Uphold and advance the national policies and interests of the
> United States. (Department of Defense 1987, Section 3)

Despite an apparently clear purpose, the U.S. military has
nonetheless fallen victim to the environmental agenda. The
process of greening the Department of Defense began in 1970
when President Richard Nixon called for a "total mobilization" of
federal government resources to protect the environment (Hicks

and Daggett 1996, 3). Throughout the 1970s, 1980s, and 1990s Congress increased environmental regulation domestically and enacted a series of laws requiring federal agencies, including the Department of Defense, to comply with environmental regulation (Hicks and Daggett 1996, 3–4, 14). For instance, environmental laws require the U.S. military to change military operations, procedures, and use on much of the 25 million acres under U.S. military control to preserve endangered species (Maze 1998).

The Defense Department's environmental requirements gradually increased through the 1980s. For example, the Defense Environmental Restoration Account in 1984 set Department of Defense funds aside for environmental cleanup, and President Reagan's Executive Order 12580 required federal agencies to comply with federal cleanup standards (Hicks and Daggett 1996, 4). The cost of these mandates has been steep. From 1984 to 1994, Department of Defense spending on environmental programs, such as conservation of resources on military bases and environmental research, has increased twentyfold—from $250 million to $5 billion—and now accounts for approximately 2 percent of the Department of Defense budget (Hicks and Daggett 1996, 2).

The conviction of three Department of Defense civilian employees for "illegal waste storage and disposal" further increased public and congressional criticism of Department of Defense environmental programs. In response, then-Secretary of Defense Dick Cheney issued a policy statement to the Secretaries of the Military stating that "the Department of Defense [will] be the Federal leader in agency compliance and protection. We must demonstrate commitment with accountability for responding to the Nation's environmental agenda" (Hicks and Daggett 1996, 3). In addition to placing a greater emphasis on environmental policy, Cheney established the position of Deputy Assistant Secretary of Defense (Environment).

The greening process was accelerated by the demise of the Soviet Union and the end of the Cold War. During the Cold War, the president, Congress, and the American people were in general agreement on the focus of the Defense Department. When the Cold War ended, however, this clear purpose and consensus dissipated, leaving the U.S. military without a clear focus. As a result, many issues not considered priorities during the Cold War, including environmental protection, became military priorities as national security interests.

Indeed, environmental concerns in the Department of Defense reached unprecedented heights under the Clinton administration. Immediately upon assuming office in 1993, President Clinton elevated the Department of Defense's environmental officer from a Deputy Assistant Secretary to a Deputy Under Secretary of Defense (Environmental Security) (Hicks and Daggett 1996, 4). Under Clinton not only does the Department of Defense now have five categories of environmental programs, but also environmental concerns have been classified as national security interests.[12]

According to President Clinton's preface to the 1997 National Security Strategy, "core national security objectives" include countering environmental damage. Specifically, protecting U.S. national security interests means, in part, "protecting the global environment—managing our forests, stopping the spread of toxic chemicals, working to close the hole in the ozone layer, reducing the greenhouse gases that challenge our health as they change our climate" (President 1997, ii).

The Clinton administration justifies the inclusion of environmental protection as a national security priority because "decisions today regarding the environment and natural resources can affect our security for generations; consequently, our national security planning is incorporating environmental analyses as never before" (President 1997, 11). The administration has already gone beyond analysis, however. The National Security Strategy clearly outlines the administration's intent to "forge an international consensus to address the challenge of global climate change" and actively enforces U.S. military compliance with international environmental treaties (President 1997, 18–19).

Even the former Chairman of the Joint Chiefs of Staff, General John M. Shalikashvili, acknowledged environmental concerns as a legitimate security concern, albeit in a much smaller role than the Clinton administration outlines. General Shalikashvili maintains that the national military objectives are "to defend and protect U.S. national interests, . . . to promote peace and stability and, when necessary, to defeat adversaries." The National Military Strategy does acknowledge, however, that "threats to the environment [have] the potential to put U.S. interests at risk" and acknowledges a role for the military (U.S. Joint Chiefs of Staff "National Military Strategy of the United States of America" 1997).

## INTERNATIONAL ENVIRONMENTALISM

Concern about international environmental problems and about using international organizations and legal instruments to address these problems is not new. On the contrary, there is a long history of international law cases dealing with transboundary pollution and the large number of international agreements containing environmental or conservationist provisions (Pearson 1993, 29). Environmental treaties prior to the late 1960s, however, were generally simple proclamations, without international standards or enforcement provisions, and largely dependent on each nation to adopt, implement, and enforce protections as outlined in each treaty.[13] In other words, environmental concerns were discussed and actions were taken; however, these concerns were not judged serious enough to require forceful action (Pearson 1993, 29).

Beginning in the 1960s, however, environmentalists began to raise such issues as international pollution, species extinction, and potential environmental harm on a global scale. According to environmental credo, the basis for this new emphasis was that environmental concerns transcend political divisions and geographic boundaries and are, therefore, beyond the power of any one nation to address.

Environmental groups were particularly effective in eliciting the cooperation of the United Nations in announcing and advancing the principles of environmental protection onto a global stage. Indeed, by the late 1960s, the United Nations had become a regular forum for environmental concerns. Certain UN organizations had become focused on particular issues, such as the World Health Organization's investigation into air pollution (Luard 1979, 63). Thus, it is not surprising that the first serious international conference addressing environmental concerns—the 1972 Conference on the Human Environment in Stockholm, Sweden—was orchestrated and sponsored by the United Nations. The conference covered nearly every environmental concern that was an issue at the time, including endangered species, preservation of territory possessing unique natural and archaeological value, pollution, conservation of natural resources, and a system to monitor environmental damage (Luard 1979, 63).

The UN Conference on the Human Environment led member governments to create and financially support a cadre of new UN agencies that would dedicate all or a portion of their efforts to environmental issues (Sheehan 1998, 11).[14] Chief among these new agencies was the United Nations Environment Program (UNEP). As the self-described "environmental conscience of the United Nations system," UNEP champions the view that environmental issues cannot be considered in isolation. Instead, UNEP sees the environment as "a system of interacting relationships that extends through all sectors of activity"[15] and its role as one of encouraging sustainable development. Other UN organizations and programs focusing on the environment include the United Nations Development Program (UNDP) and the United Nations Educational, Scientific and Cultural Organization (UNESCO). UNESCO oversees seven programs that focus on "environment and sustainable development" and the World Heritage Program. The UNDP also oversees seven environmental programs, including partial oversight of the Global Environment Facility (GEF).[16]

As evidenced by the 1992 United Nations Conference on Environment and Development (UNCED or the Earth Summit) in Rio de Janeiro, Brazil, environmental issues on the world stage have only grown since 1972. Almost every sovereign nation, including more than 100 heads of state, attended the Earth Summit for the sole purpose of discussing environmental protection, economic development, and the relationship between the two. Among other conclusions, UNCED conferees proclaimed that transboundary and global environmental problems require immediate, often punishing, action by all countries. Immediate action was deemed necessary because environmental deterioration threatens the "ecosystems on which we depend for our well-being" (UNCED 1992, Preamble, Section 1, Article 1).

Because the consequences of transboundary environmental threats, such as global warming, are thought to be so severe, the conferees found that immediate action was necessary even though there was no conclusive scientific evidence of the threat. Specifically, UNCED participants agreed that "where there are threats of serious or irreversible damage, lack of full scientific certainty shall not be used as a reason for postponing cost-effective measures to prevent environmental degradation" (United Nations 1992, Principle 15). In sum, even in the face of scientific doubt or uncertainty, immediate action must be taken because the survival of humanity is at stake and outweighs any potential cost.

In support of this conclusion, UNCED urged the adoption of MEAs to regulate and eventually eliminate transboundary and global environmental threats. As a part of this approach, UNCED acknowledged that a multilateral trading system would make a key contribution to national and international efforts to better protect and conserve environmental resources and promote sustainable development.

The link between trade and MEAs has a long history. For example, the Convention on International Trade in Endangered Species of Wild Fauna and Flora in 1975 established a ban on trade of specific species between signatory nations. However, the Montreal Protocol on Substances that Deplete the Ozone Layer went further—environmental issues rose to the stature of international trade when trade sanctions were used to enforce the protocol's elimination of chlorofluorocarbons. International environmental activists eagerly adopted this enforcement mechanism and have used it in nearly every subsequent treaty. Two examples are the Convention on Climate Change and the Biodiversity Convention, both of which utilize trade restrictions, inspections, international bureaucracies, and enforcement sanctions to enforce treaty provisions.

The environmental agenda has so permeated the United Nations that it is difficult to find an agency or program within the UN system that does not highlight its actions in support of the environment. Every international development organization, including the International Monetary Fund and the World Bank, has rules requiring environmental impact statements for their actions.

Traditional UN organizations trumpet their dedication to environmental protections and sustainable development, such as the International Labor Organization's (ILO) Working Conditions & the Environment program and the Sustainable Development Department of the Food and Agriculture Organization (FAO). In addition, environmental groups have targeted seemingly unrelated environmental concerns, such as the International Criminal Court, as possible vehicles for expanding their agenda.

Even UN departments that serve no purpose or that have fulfilled their original purpose have found new justification in support of environmental causes. For example, the UN Charter established the Trusteeship Council, one of the main organs of the United Nations charged with supervising the administration of newly independent territories placed in UN trusteeship until they achieve self-government. When Palau—the last remaining UN trust territory—achieved independence and established a functioning self-government on November 1, 1994, the Trusteeship Council had no further responsibilities, and a resolution was adopted on May 25, 1994, to drop the obligation to meet annually. Instead of dissolving the Council, however, "the Secretary-General has proposed that [the Trusteeship Council] be restructured as the forum through which Member States exercise their collective trusteeship for the integrity of the global environment and common areas such as the oceans, atmosphere and outer space" (Petrovsky 1997).

## THE EFFECT OF INTERNATIONAL ENVIRONMENTALISM ON U.S. FOREIGN POLICY

Environmentalists have been wildly successful in creating and implementing MEAs, which have become the preferred method for addressing environmental concerns. Estimates on the number of environmental treaties range from 140 to 650, depending on whether bilateral agreements or treaties containing environmental components but not centrally focused on environment, such as the World Trade Organization, are considered.[17] Complementing MEAs are environmental provisions added to international

treaties with little direct connection to environmental issues and
environmental guidelines adopted by international organizations
and institutions.[18] These international environmental laws and
regulations directly affect and, through international treaties and
agreements, bind U.S. foreign policy.

The United States has been a primary target of MEAs—examination of the number and frequency of MEAs and international agreements containing environmental provisions signed by and entering
into force in the United States shows a clear increase. Between 1940
and 1996, the United States became a signatory to 112 international
treaties and agreements that contain environmental provisions—an
average of more than two per year.[19] More than twice as many of
these treaties were signed by the United States after 1970 (78) as
were signed between 1940 and 1970 (34). (See Figure 1.) The pattern is similar for treaties entering into force annually for the United
States. Between 1940 and 1970, forty-three international treaties focusing on environmental protection or containing environmental
provisions entered into force in the United States. Since 1970, sev-
enty-five have entered into force. (See Figure 2.)

International environmental laws, regulations, and policies outlined and mandated in MEAs often have direct, and in many
cases, costly effects on the United States. Indeed, environmental
priorities and mandates contained in MEAs, such as the Montreal
and Kyoto Protocols, can impose costly economic conditions or
curtail America's ability to protect its interests.

### The Montreal Protocol

The 1987 Montreal Protocol on Substances that Deplete the
Ozone Layer, which was ratified or signed by 165 countries, is
dedicated to reducing the production and use of gases identified by
the treaty as active agents in eroding the atmosphere's ozone layer.
In particular, the Montreal Protocol seeks to eliminate the production and use of chlorofluorocarbons (CFCs), which are identified as the primary anthropogenic agents in ozone depletion
(Ozone Secretariat 1989).

The Montreal Protocol currently lists more than ninety specific
chemical compounds and six product categories that use controlled

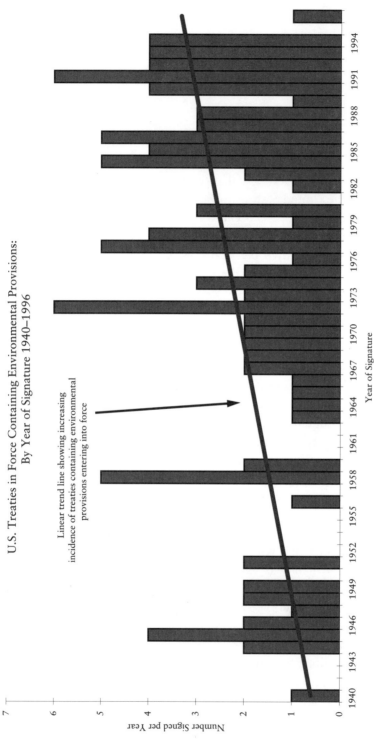

U.S. Treaties in Force Containing Environmental Provisions:
By Year of Signature 1940–1996

Linear trend line showing increasing
incidence of treaties containing environmental
provisions entering into force

Year of Signature

Number Signed per Year

FIGURE 1  Source for treaty charts: Environmental Treaties and Resource Indicators
(ENTRI) at <http://sedac.ciesin.org/entri>, based on data provided by The World
Conservation Union (IUCN); the United Nations Environment Program (UNEP); Freedom
House; the Fletcher School of Law and Diplomacy; the World Resources Institute; the British
Columbia Ministry of Environment, Land, & Parks; and the Cooperative Research Centre
for Antarctica and the Southern Ocean (ACRC). ENTRI is jointly funded by the Center for
International Earth Science Information Network (CIESIN) and Socioeconomic Data and
Applications Center (SEDAC) within the Columbia Earth Institute at Columbia University
and the National Aeronautics and Space Administration (NASA).

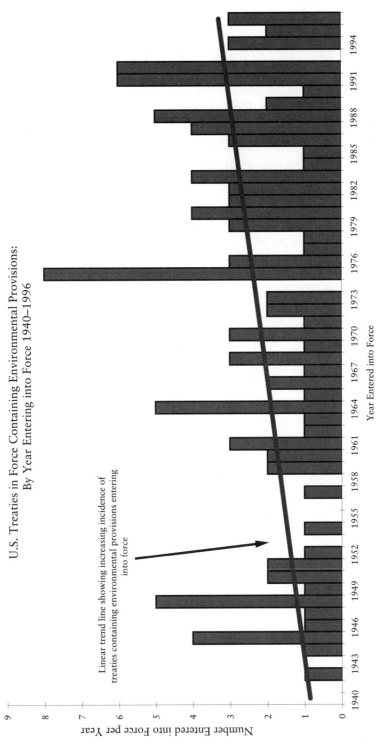

U.S. Treaties in Force Containing Environmental Provisions:
By Year Entering into Force 1940–1996

Linear trend line showing increasing incidence of
treaties containing environmental provisions entering
into force

Year Entered into Force

Number Entered into Force per Year

FIGURE 2   Source for treaty charts: Environmental Treaties and Resource Indicators (ENTRI) at <http://sedac.ciesin.org/entri>, based on data provided by The World Conservation Union (IUCN); the United Nations Environment Program (UNEP); Freedom House; the Fletcher School of Law and Diplomacy; the World Resources Institute; the British Columbia Ministry of Environment, Land, & Parks; and the Cooperative Research Centre for Antarctica and the Southern Ocean (ACRC). ENTRI is jointly funded by the Center for International Earth Science Information Network (CIESIN) and Socioeconomic Data and Applications Center (SEDAC) within the Columbia Earth Institute at Columbia University and the National Aeronautics and Space Administration (NASA).

substances, including fire extinguishers and air-conditioning equipment (Ozone Secretariat 1997, Annexes A–E). The 1990 London amendments set the phaseout date for developed countries as 2000, and 2010 for developing countries. The 1992 Copenhagen amendments called for elimination of CFC production by 1996 (Esty 1994, 279–280). The 1997 Montreal amendments require all signatories to ban the import and export of controlled substances and establish a "system for licensing the import and export of new, used, recycled and reclaimed controlled substances" (Ozone Secretariat, *The Montreal Protocol on Substances that Deplete the Ozone Layer*, Article 4, sections 1–2, Articles 4A, 4B as amended at ninth meeting of parties Sept. 1997).

To enforce and induce countries to restrict and phase out ozone-depleting substances, the Protocol calls for trade sanctions by treaty signatories against nonsignatory countries. Estimates place the total cost of the Montreal Protocol on the United States as high as $100 billion, including cumulative losses through costly technology to replace CFCs, closed businesses, lost jobs, and trade prohibitions (Lieberman 1995).[20]

### The Convention on Biological Diversity

Biological diversity is defined as the "sum total of the plants, animals, fungi and microorganisms in the world, or a particular area; all of their individual variation; and all of the interaction between them" (Edwards 1995, 214). Preservation of biological diversity was first raised as an international issue at the 1972 UN Conference on the Human Environment, and it was one of UNEP's key issues at its 1973 founding. UNEP first proposed international action in 1988, convening the Ad Hoc Working Group of Experts on Biological Diversity. The working group found "biological diversity [to be] a global asset of tremendous value to present and future generations" and recommended immediate action because the "threat to species and ecosystems has never been so great as it is today" (Convention on Biological Diversity, "An Introduction to the Convention on Biological Diversity" 1998). The working group determined that the best way to address the threat was to establish an MEA to protect biological diversity.

The Biological Diversity Treaty was presented at the 1992 Earth Summit and entered into force on December 29, 1993. The treaty is signed or ratified by 168 countries, although the United States has not yet ratified it. The treaty is a legal instrument that outlines the rights and obligations of every signatory. These rights and obligations include significant financial contributions or mandatory transfer of technical and scientific information and research. Specifically, the treaty charges developed country signatories to provide financial assistance in support of treaty goals to developing country signatories and requires transfer of ecologically sound technologies from developed to developing nations (Convention on Biological Diversity 1992, Articles 15, 16, 20, 21, 25).

The treaty also establishes an international regulatory framework to examine, regulate, and, in some cases, prevent development of biotechnology, such as genetically specialized crops and bacteria. Because biotechnology is a field of expertise in which the United States has a significant competitive advantage, the treaty, if ratified, would impose a direct economic penalty to the United States. An even greater cost, however, would result from lost methods that could increase crop yields through bioengineered crops or address environmental damage through biotechnology, such as specialized bacteria to break down toxic waste (see Miller, this volume).

### UN Framework Convention on Climate Change and the Kyoto Protocol

Despite disagreement within the scientific community on the theory of global warming and its potential impact (Antonelli, Schaefer, and Annett 1997, 4–6), two treaties address global warming: the United Nations Framework Convention on Climate Change (UNFCCC) and the Kyoto Protocol to the UNFCCC. The UNFCCC, which was finalized and presented for signature at the 1992 UNCED conference, seeks to stabilize "greenhouse gas concentrations in the atmosphere at a level that would prevent dangerous anthropogenic interference with the climate system" (United Nations 1992). This goal was to be achieved through largely voluntary actions by signatory countries.

Environmentalist groups criticized the effectiveness of the UNFCCC and urged countries to amend the treaty to include mandatory emissions reductions and measures to enforce treaty compliance. In response to such criticisms, more than 160 countries negotiated and agreed to the Kyoto Protocol on December 10, 1997, in Japan. The protocol sets strict, enforceable standards for greenhouse gas emissions for industrialized countries like the United States, Great Britain, and Japan, with possible sanctions if they do not comply. In addition, industrialized countries must transfer technology and provide financial resources to developing countries to help reduce emissions (Antonelli and Schaefer 1998, 4). The protocol establishes at least six new international bureaucracies to supervise the parties to the treaty, to monitor and verify emissions reports, and to enforce treaty guidelines. Essentially, the Kyoto Protocol will create an international version of the U.S. Environmental Protection Agency, with the potential power to regulate Americans and their economic activity (Antonelli and Schaefer 1998, 5–6).

The estimated cost of the Kyoto Protocol to the United States alone is $3.3 trillion in economic output, millions of jobs lost, and a dramatic increase in the cost of living (Antonelli, Schaefer, and Annett 1997, 11–16). In addition, the Kyoto Protocol will institute a new foreign aid bureaucracy to transfer American tax dollars to developing countries participating in the treaty (Antonelli and Schaefer 1998, 4). The greatest potential cost, however, is the protocol's effect on U.S. national security and the U.S. military. For example, the Kyoto Protocol would penalize the United States for greenhouse gas emissions created through military activity. Only emissions resulting from U.S. forces participating in multilateral operations with UN approval would be exempt. The current version of the treaty fails to provide an exemption for unilateral U.S. military action or make allowance for emissions resulting from training exercises. By potentially restricting training and troop readiness and imposing economic penalties, the Kyoto Protocol could severely curtail America's ability to protect its national interests. For example, unilateral U.S. military actions in the 1986 bombing of Libya and the 1983 liberation of Grenada were condemned by UN members and most likely would not have received a military exemption from the UN Security Council, whose member nations often oppose U.S. interests (Antonelli and Schaefer 1998, 6).

### International Criminal Court

Even international agreements that bear little overt relation to environmental issues have become targets for environmental regulation. For example, the International Criminal Court (ICC) is designed to address the crime of aggression, crimes against humanity, war crimes, and genocide. The ICC is empowered to investigate, try, and punish those convicted of such crimes. Most analysis of the ICC focuses on the larger issues—such as the inclusion of the crime of aggression in the ICC and the potential effect on sovereignty. However, the ICC significantly extends the environmental agenda by including environmental destruction as a war crime. Specifically, the Rome Statute of the International Criminal Court lists as a crime "Intentionally launching an attack in the knowledge that such attack will cause . . . widespread, long-term and severe damage to the natural environment which would be clearly excessive in relation to the concrete and direct overall military advantage anticipated" (International Criminal Court 1998, Article 8, section b, part iv).

The inclusion of environmental damage as a war crime in the ICC statute formalizes a long-sought goal of environmentalists: "to help stem the tide of ecological catastrophe in war" by "plac[ing] enforceable limits on unjustified environmental damage" through international law (Parsons 1998, 443).[21] Although a number of existing international agreements address environmental damage during war, including the Protocol Additional to the Geneva Convention of August 12, 1949, and Relating to the Protection of Victims of International Armed Conflicts, these agreements lack widespread support and enforcement mechanisms (Parsons 1998, 446–459). By including environmental destruction as a "war crime" within the jurisdiction of the ICC and making it punishable by the Court, however, environmentalists may have succeeded in addressing these perceived weaknesses.

The ICC would have authority to charge and sentence U.S. military officials with the "war crime" of environmental damage resulting from U.S. military actions. The destructive nature of war makes environmental damage a foregone conclusion. The only judgment lies in whether the damage is judged "clearly excessive" by ICC prosecutors, investigators, and judges—some of whom may well be enemies of the United States. If the environmental damage is judged "clearly excessive," every U.S. official involved in the operation, up to and including the President of the United States, could be charged, tried, convicted, and sentenced for protecting U.S. interests. An obvious example of this possibility would be the use of defoliant in support of war efforts, such as during the Vietnam War, but investigations into environmental damage caused by conventional combat, such as the bombings and invasion of Iraq during the Persian Gulf War, are also possible.

The potential exercise of this clause is magnified by the fact that the ICC, under certain circumstances, claims jurisdiction over every nation—even those not party to the ICC (International Criminal Court 1998, Articles 12 and 13). Thus, even if the United States refuses to become a party to the ICC, it could be subject to ICC investigations and rulings.

## INTERNATIONAL DEVELOPMENT ORGANIZATIONS

Public relations campaigns have forced multilateral development banks to incorporate environmental concerns into their projects, including allowing environmental NGOs to evaluate project plans and hiring and contracting environmental groups as consultants (The Asian Development Bank 1998). Environmental lobbying in the United States and other countries has engendered support for environmental restrictions on the activities of every international development bank. In the United States, pressure from environmental lobbyists led the United States to amend the Bretton Woods Agreements Act, which governs U.S. participation in the International Monetary Fund and the World Bank. The amendment requires the Secretary of the Treasury to instruct the U.S. Executive Director of the IMF to

> seek policy changes by the Fund, through formal initiatives and through bilateral discussions, which will result in:

    1.  the initiation of a systematic review of policy prescriptions implemented by the Fund, for the purpose of determining . . . environmental impacts of such policy prescriptions

    2.  the establishment of procedures which ensure the inclusion . . . of policy options which eliminate or reduce the potential adverse impact on the well being of the poor or the environment resulting from such programs. (22 U.S.C. Sc. 286kk)

Environmentalist groups continue to pressure U.S. politicians to impose greater environmental requirements on international financial institutions. By its own admission, the Clinton administration advocates "environmentally sound private investment and responsible approaches by international lenders," and brags that, partly due to their efforts, multilateral development banks "are now placing increased emphasis upon sustainable development in their funding decisions" (President 1997, 18–19). Not only do these requirements have a direct effect on U.S. businesses, which face greater environmental regulations as a result of IMF and World Bank demands for environmental protections, but also the greater regulations and red tape have a dampening effect on foreign investment and growth in developing countries.

*The World Bank*

The World Bank has long been a common target of environmental groups, who claim that the bank has focused too much on industrialization without considering the environmental effect of its policies (Sheehan 1998, 144–148). In response to the public relations pressure of environmentally oriented member nations, the World Bank has tried to placate such concerns. It publicly embraces the concept of sustainable development as the basis of its development philosophy, noting that "environmental protection is a key component of sustainable development. Without this, long-term development is undermined" (World Bank Group 1998). Consequently, the World Bank has shifted its emphasis from exclusively funding large construction projects that draw environmental criticism, such as dams and power plants, to funding reforestation, pollution control, land management, and other projects to help combat environmental problems.

The World Bank has also attempted to improve its environmental image through participation in the GEF. Managed by the UN Development Program, the UN Environment Program, and the World Bank, the GEF gives assistance to developing countries and encourages them to undertake the additional costs involved in making development projects more environmentally friendly. Specifically, the GEF extends subsidized loans and grants to developing countries to help them address biological diversity, climate change, international waters, and ozone layer depletion (GEF 1998; Schaefer 1998b; Semans 1996).

### The International Monetary Fund

In 1997 and 1998 environmental groups were at the forefront of opposition to IMF funding, alleging that IMF policies directly led to environmentally harmful practices, such as promoting unsustainable harvesting of timber, encouraging countries to weaken environmental laws, and reducing funding for government environment bureaucracies or programs.[22] In a September 10, 1998, letter entitled "Oppose the Expansion of the International Monetary Fund!" 140 U.S. and international environmental groups, labor unions, and development organizations urged the U.S. Congress to deny the Clinton administration's requested $17.9 billion IMF replenishment because

> IMF policies encourage and frequently require the lowering of environmental standards and the reckless exploitation of natural resources in debtor countries. The export of natural resources to earn hard currency to pay foreign debts under IMF mandates damages the environment while providing no benefit to poor and working people in debtor countries. (Preamble Center 1997)

Congress has responded to the criticism. The Foreign Operations, Export Financing, and Related Programs Appropriations bill for FY 99, recently reported to the U.S. House of Representatives, contains three provisions requiring greater environmental scrutiny by the IMF (PL 103-236, Sections 1503.a.11, 1503.b.e.2.E, 1704.a.7). Moreover, amendments abound to further increase environmental restrictions on the IMF. For instance, Representative George Miller (D-CA) has offered an amendment to the IMF funding that would require the fund to analyze the environmental effect of its policies on recipient countries and the global environment before distributing assistance; create a new accounting system to incorporate depletion of natural resources into national accounting; and support any environmental law in force in recipient countries.[23]

## INTERNATIONAL ENVIRONMENTALISM AND THE CLINTON ADMINISTRATION

As the president's proposal for including environmental issues in fast-track authority shows, the Clinton administration's unprecedented support for international environmental policies can only be expected to increase through 2000. In his 1998 State of the Union address, Clinton proclaimed: "Our overriding environmental challenge tonight is the worldwide problem of climate change, global warming, the gathering crisis that requires worldwide action" (Clinton 1998).

The State Department has been the primary instrument for generating congressional support for and inserting U.S. environmental priorities into MEAs. Because "environmental concerns transcend political divisions and geographic boundaries," the State Department insists that these concerns can be addressed effectively only if the nations of the world and international organizations work together. This belief is clearly expressed in the State Department's (1998) *Environmental Diplomacy*:

> It will take more than governments to combat environmental threats. Global institutions, including a World Bank which factors environmental implications into its lending decisions, private businesses and industries, and non-governmental organizations must all be involved in the search for and implementation of solutions. Additionally, we must reform key United Nations structures to help organize and coordinate international actions.

Indeed, the Department of State acknowledges efforts to "adapt the Department to the increasing globalization of many foreign policy matters and reflect the growing importance of developing options for multilateral approaches in the conduct of foreign relations" (Department of State 1998).

Support for MEAs and multilateral action has been reinforced from several other U.S. foreign policy arms. For example, the White

House's National Security Strategy states that the United States has "a full diplomatic agenda, working unilaterally, regionally and multilaterally to forge agreements to protect the global environment" (President 1997, 11). Former U.S. Ambassador to the United Nations and current Secretary of Energy Bill Richardson actively urged U.S. ratification of three MEAs: global warming, biological diversity, and desertification. According to Richardson, "If we are to succeed in ensuring environmental security in the face of great challenges to the sustainability of our planet, the United States must firmly commit itself to serving as an international leader in devising and abiding by practical and appropriate multilateral approaches for preserving the environment" (Richardson 1998).

Clearly, under the Clinton administration, the United States will work through multilateral treaties and organizations to achieve its environmental goals. This should raise concern among Americans because the goals of environmentalist groups run counter to the freedoms valued by most Americans. For example, most advocates of international environmental laws and protection embrace the idea that individual human rights must be proscribed in favor of collective human interests and that those "human interests and welfare are now seen to be so clearly linked to, and dependent upon, the environment" (Taylor 1998, 326). This conclusion has led several environmental activists to propose radical changes to existing international law, including:

1.  prescribing the right to use and enjoy private property in order to prevent harm to the natural environment;

2.  altering existing human rights documents (such as the Universal Declaration for Human Rights, the International Covenant on Civil and Political Rights, and the International Covenant on Economic, Social and Cultural Rights) to include environmental protection as a human right; and

3.  broadening the definition of current language contained in existing international agreements (such as "general welfare" and "duties to the community") to include environmental protection as contributing to the general welfare and including the ecosystem as part of the "community."

Such action would have dramatic effects on national sovereignty. It would essentially cede individual rights to environmental policy as dictated by an international treaty. International tribunals or courts would investigate, judge, and issue instructions for implementing environmental policy to governments. Efforts to achieve this goal also directly counter free-market understanding of property rights and the right of the individual to use private property.

## CONCLUSION

Clearly U.S. foreign policy has been dramatically influenced by environmental concerns, often to the detriment of traditional priorities and national interests. Indeed, the three primary arms of U.S. foreign policy now spend valuable time and resources abiding by environmental restrictions. Specifically:

•  The Department of State has morphed from a representative of U.S. foreign policy priorities in international treaty negotiations to an advocate of international environmental treaties.

•  The Clinton administration's insistence on including environmental protections in fast-track negotiating authority has brought U.S. trade negotiations to a virtual standstill.

•  As the Department of Defense's expenditures on environmental programs have increased, its activities have been curtailed, and it has shifted its focus from traditional security concerns to environmental concerns.

Likewise the United Nations and other international organizations have accepted the dominance of an environmental agenda. The policies of these organizations, many times influenced by U.S. environmental lobbyists and legislation, in turn impact America's ability to defend its interests and increase prosperity.

Common sense dictates that environmental laws, regulations, or policies having a negative impact on the ability of U.S. foreign policy organs to address national interests should be avoided. Likewise, international agreements, treaties, or actions should be governed by necessity and proven threat, not suspicion; and proposed solutions should demonstrably address a proven problem. Regrettably, common sense seems to have been abandoned in the fervor to combat perceived environmental threats through laws, regulations, and policies.


## ENDNOTES

1. A far more comprehensive overview of the early history of environmentalism in America can be found in Jonathan Adler's (1995) *Environmentalism at the Crossroads: Green Activism in America.*

2. The perception of an intrinsic worth to nature has increasingly dominated environmental law cases and philosophy, both of which are championed by the concepts of "ecological rights" and "environmental rights." Environmental rights essentially confer legal rights, duties, and obligations on the environment in order to protect it from exploitation and preserve it for future generations. Slightly different, ecological rights seek to limit human rights and individual freedoms to ensure that individuals act in an environmentally sound manner. As noted by University of Auckland, New Zealand, law professor Prudence E. Taylor (1998), the desired goal of ecological rights advocates is to create "a transition from anthropocentric (human-centered), toward eco-centric (humanity as an integral part of nature) ethics and law" (310). Indeed, many environmental groups see law as the primary method for imposing ecocentrism as a dominant policy.

3. Eleven of the most influential and radical environmental groups (including Friends of the Earth, Greenpeace, U.S. Public Interest Research Group, and Zero Population Growth) were created between 1968 and 1971.

4. As with the State Department, USAID is required to meet U.S. law requirements governing its actions. In the case of USAID, this involves a hugely bureaucratic process to meet environmental guidelines. The agency is required to conduct an Initial Environmental Examination, Environmental Assessment, and Environmental Impact Statement on every project proposal. Before the project is approved or receives funding, a Threshold Decision must be made on whether to approve a project based on anticipated environmental impact. If a positive Threshold Decision is made, then a Scope of Environmental Assessment or Impact Statement, which identifies "the significant issues relating to the proposed action" and determines "the scope of the issues to be addressed in the Environmental Assessment or Environmental Impact Statement," is conducted. The Scope Statement must be circulated and reviewed by selected federal agencies. An Environmental Assessment and an Environ-

mental Impact Statement on the project, which must be "reviewed as an integral part of the Project Paper or equivalent document" and approved by the Bureau Environmental Officer and the Agency's Environmental Coordinator, are then required. After funding is authorized for the project, an Environmental Review must be conducted. In addition, the Agency's Environmental Coordinator and local environmental officers are required to monitor and report on the project's environmental impact during the life of the project.

5. Nations attending UNCED also agreed to supply greater amounts of foreign aid in support of sustainable development. As stated in Agenda 21, "The developmental and environmental objectives of Agenda 21 will require a substantial flow of new and additional financial resources to developing countries, in order to cover the incremental costs for the actions they have to undertake to deal with global environmental problems and to accelerate sustainable development." (Agenda 21 Preamble, United Nations Conference on Environment and Development, http://ches.ing.ula.ve/GAIA/AG21/preamble.html.)

6. Subsequent GATT negotiations dramatically increased trade liberalization, including lowering tariffs and addressing nontariff barriers and subsidies.

7. The Trade Act of 1974 and the Omnibus Trade and Competitiveness Act (OTCA) expanded Congress' role in negotiating and implementing trade agreements and established the fast-track negotiating authority, which allows the president to negotiate and implement trade agreements beyond tariffs to include agreements on nontariff barriers as well.

8. For example, the Asia-Pacific Economic Cooperation (APEC) forum was launched in 1989; the Bush administration announced the Enterprise of the Americas Initiative (EAI) and embraced a proposal by then-Mexican President Carlos Salinas de Gortari to negotiate the North American Free Trade Agreement (NAFTA), the world's first free-trade agreement between an industrialized country and a developing nation in 1990; NAFTA was ratified by Congress in November 1993; the Uruguay Round Agreements, negotiated under the auspices of GATT, were completed in 1994; Congress ratified the Uruguay Round Agreements that created the World Trade Organization (WTO) in 1994; the Clinton administration committed America to creating an APEC free-trade area by 2020 and a Free Trade Area of the Americas (FTAA) by 2005.

9. Fourteen agreements during the Tokyo round of GATT negotiations signed on June 30, 1979 (enacted July 26, 1979); the U.S.-Israel Free Trade Area Agreement of April 22, 1985 (enacted June 11, 1985); the U.S.-Canada Free Trade Agreement of January 2, 1988 (enacted September 28, 1988); the North American Free Trade Agreement of December 17, 1992 (enacted December 8, 1993); and fifty-four agreements, declarations,

and decisions resulting from the Uruguay Round of the GATT signed on April 15, 1994 (enacted December 8, 1994).

10. Other factors, including increasing antitrade sentiments in Congress, also contributed to the failure of Congress to grant the president fast-track authority.

11. The World Heritage Program was created by the 1972 United Nations Convention Concerning the Protection of the World Cultural and Natural Heritage. Governments register areas of unique historic, cultural, or environmental character "whose outstanding values should be preserved for all humanity and to ensure their protection through a closer cooperation among nations" with the program. ("Defining Our Heritage," World Heritage Program, http://www.unesco.org/whc/nwhc/pages/doc/main.htm.)

12. The five categories are environmental restoration, environmental compliance, environmental prevention, environmental technology, and environmental conservation.

13. Examples of these early treaties include agreements to protect flora and fauna or sanitary (relating to animals) and phytosanitary (relating to plants) measures to protect humans, animals, and plants from diseases, pests, or contaminants.

14. Other UN programs and studies included the Global Environmental Monitoring System and an International Referral System for tracking and reporting the state of the global environment. In addition to international environmental action, the UN Conference on the Human Environment led national governments to take these issues more seriously, and debate began on how to address environmental problems. Pledges made by government officials attending the UN Conference on the Human Environment in 1972 eventually resulted in the creation of environmental agencies in 114 countries.

15. United Nations Environmental Program Internet site at <http://www.unep.org/unep/about.htm>.

16. Jointly overseen by the World Bank, UNEP, and UNDP, the Global Environment Facility provides subsidized loans and grants to developing countries. These subsidized loans and grants are designed to pay for extra expenses incurred by those countries in supporting biological diversity and combating climate change, ozone depletion, and pollution in international waters. The GEF was provided with $730 million when it was established in 1991. Negotiations that concluded in March 1994, referred to as GEF-1, resulted in an additional $2 billion pledge by thirty-four nations, of which the U.S. portion, pledged by the Clinton administration, was $430 million (21.5 percent). Congress has appropriated only $227.5 million of this obligation, including $35 million and $48 million in 1997 and 1998, respectively. The administration is cur-

rently negotiating another $2 billion replenishment of the Global Environment Facility, GEF-2, which would commit the United States to another $430 million over the next four years. In anticipation of this replenishment, the administration's budget proposal for FY 99 requests $300 million for the GEF—$192.5 million to eliminate the current arrears and $107.5 million for the first installment of GEF-2.

17. The Environmental Treaties and Resource Indicators (ENTRI) database at <http://sedac.ciesin.org/entri> lists 430 multilateral environmental treaties. Ken Conca (professor, University of Maryland Department of Government and Politics) maintains that more than 650 environmental treaties are in force, although many of these are bilateral. Conca also cites Peter Haas, Robert Keohane, and Marc Levy, who reported in *Institutions for the Earth: Sources for Effective International Environmental Protection* that more than 140 multilateral environmental treaties were in effect by the early 1990s.

18. In a circular relationship, environmental NGOs lobby U.S. and foreign governments to adopt environmental laws and regulations. Government representatives to international organizations and conferences, bound by domestic laws and instructions, then cooperate with environmental NGOs to create international laws and regulations to enforce environmental protection. These international protection measures then reinforce national protection measures.

19. A full list of these treaties, agreements, conventions, instruments, and so on is provided in the Appendix.

20. Most estimates of the cost are much lower.

21. Although the current language is very defined and restricted to military action, it is not inconceivable that the jurisdiction of the court over environmental matters would be extended to cover all environmental damage deemed excessive when the ICC statute is eligible for revision seven years after implementation.

22. Examples of these allegations can be found at the Friends of the Earth Internet site <http://www.foe.org/ga/imf.html>. Papers include "IMF Bailouts: How Do They Impact on the Environment?", "How Do IMF Policies and Programs Hurt the Poor and the Environment?", and "Structural Adjustment and the Environment: Promoting Efficiency or Exploiting Natural Resources?".

23. Environmental influence in multilateral banks and financial institutions does not end with the World Bank and IMF. Other development banks that have yielded to environmental pressure include the Asian Development Bank and the Inter-American Development Bank. For instance, the Internet site of the Inter-American Development Bank, the oldest regional development bank, states that the Bank "monitors the environmental impact of all its operations and directly finances a growing

number of projects specifically designed to protect natural resources. In 1996, the Bank approved 12 environmental loans totaling $746 million" (Inter-American Development Bank). The Asian Development Bank includes environmental protection as one of its primary objectives (Asian Development Bank). The bottom line is that the influence of environmental NGOs is pervasive and extends to every international development bank. Developing countries are forced to abide by the environmentalist agenda if they wish to receive financial assistance from multilateral development institutions.

## REFERENCES

Adler, Jonathan. 1995. *Environmentalism at the Crossroads: Green Activism in America*. Washington, D.C.: Capitol Research Center.

Albright, Madeleine. 1997. Letter from Secretary of State Madeleine K. Albright. *Environmental Diplomacy: The Environment and U.S. Foreign Policy*. United States Department of State. At <http://www.state.gov/www/global/oes/earth.html albright> (September 1998).

Antonelli, Angela, and Brett D. Schaefer. 1998. From Fear to Folly: Why the Kyoto Treaty Is a "Very Bad Deal." *Backgrounder Update* (Heritage Foundation) 289 (7 January).

Antonelli, Angela, Brett D. Schaefer, and Alex Annett. 1997. The Road to Kyoto: How the Global Climate Treaty Fosters Economic Impoverishment and Endangers U.S. Sovereignty. *Backgrounder* (Heritage Foundation) 1143 (6 October).

Asian Development Bank. Environmental Protection. Manila, Philippines. At <http://www.adb.org/About/Objectives/envprtct.asp> (As of September 1999).

———. Cooperation Between the ADB and NGOs. At <http://www.adb.org/Work/Social_Devt/coop-01.asp> (As of September 1999).

Bandow, Doug, ed. 1986. Protecting the Environment: A Free Market Strategy. *Critical Issues*. Washington, D.C.: The Heritage Foundation.

Clinton, William J. 1998. *State of the Union Address*.

Conca, Ken. 1995. Global Environmental Governance: Causes, Components, and Consequences. *Occasional Paper* 6. College Park: University of Maryland, Harrison Program on the Future Global Agenda. At <http://www.bosos.umd.edu/harrison/papers/paper06.htm>.

Convention on Biological Diversity. 1992. *Homepage*. "An Introduction to the Convention on Biological Diversity." At <http://www.biodiv.org/bio.bio-intr.html> (September 1998).

Convention on Biological Diversity. Background on the Convention. At <http://www.biodiv.org/conv/background.html> (As of September 1998).

Edwards, Stephen R. 1995. Conserving Biodiversity: Resources for Our Future. In *The True State of the Planet,* edited by Ronald Bailey. Washington, D.C.: Competitive Enterprise Institute.

Environmental Treaties and Resource Indicators (ENTRI). Database. At <http://sedac.ciesin.org/entri> (September 1998).

Esty, Daniel C. 1993. Integrating Trade and Environmental Policy Making: First Steps in the North American Free Trade Agreement. In *Trade and the Environment: Law, Economics, and Policy,* edited by Durwood Zaelke, Paul Orbuch, and Robert F. Housman. Washington, D.C.: Center for International Environmental Law.

———. 1994. *Greening the GATT: Trade, Environment, and the Future.* Washington, D.C.: Institute for International Economics.

Export-Import Bank of the United States. 1996. A Brief History of the Export-Import Bank of the United States. At <http://www.exim.gov:80/envpol.html> (September 1998).

———. 1999. Ex-Im Bank Environmental Requirements. At <http://www.exim.gov:80/envpol.html> (September 1998).

Fletcher, Susan R. 1997. Environment in Fast Track Authority: Summary of the Clinton Administration Proposal. Washington, D.C.: Congressional Research Service.

Friends of the Earth (FOE). Freeport McMoRan in Indonesia: An Environmental and Human Rights Debacle. Washington, D.C. At <http://www.foe.org/> (As of September 1998).

———. How Do IMF Policies and Programs Hurt the Poor and the Environment? Washington, D.C. At <http://www.foe.org/> (September 1998).

———. IMF Bailouts: How Do They Impact on the Environment? Washington, D.C. At <http://www.foe.org/> (September 1998).

———. NGO Concerns About OPIC. Washington, D.C. At <http://www.foe.org/> (September 1998).

———. OPICs New Environmental Policies. Washington, D.C. At <http://www.foe.org/> (September 1998).

———. Structural Adjustment and the Environment: Promoting Efficiency or Exploiting Natural Resources? Washington, D.C. At <http://www.foe.org/> (September 1998).

Global Environmental Facility (GEF). Introduction to the Global Environment Facility. Washington, D.C. At <http://www.gefweb.org/intro/intq9.htm> (September 1998).

———. The Global Environmental Facility: Frequently Asked Questions. Washington, D.C. At <http://www.gefweb.org/intro/revqa.htm> (September 1998).

Gore, Albert. 1993. *Earth in the Balance: Ecology and the Human Spirit.* New York: Penguin.

Graffey, Collen P. 1998. Water, Water, Everywhere, Nor Any Drop to Drink: The Urgency of Transnational Solutions to International Riparian Disputes. *The Georgetown International Environmental Law Review* 10, 2. Winter: 399–440.

Harmon, James A. 1998. Preaching Green: Subsidizing Dirty. *The Washington Post*, 1 September, A19.

Hicks, Kathleen H., and Stephen Daggett. 1996. Department of Defense Environment Programs: Background and Issues for Congress, 96–218F. Washington, D.C.: Congressional Research Service.

Holmes, Kim R., and Thomas G. Moore, eds. 1996. *Restoring American Leadership: A U.S. Foreign and Defense Policy Blueprint.* Washington, D.C.: The Heritage Foundation.

Inter-American Development Bank. 1998. Policies and Objectives: What Is the Bank Doing to Protect the Environment? Washington, D.C. At <http://www.iadb.org/exr/english/basi/basic2.htm#what17> (September 1998).

International Criminal Court. 1998. *Rome Statute of the International Criminal Court.* At <http://www.un.org/icc> (September 1998).

International Labor Organization. 1998. ILO Programmes Home Pages. At <http://www.ilo.org/public/english/depts/depts.htm> (September 1998).

Lieberman, Ben. 1995. Ozone Depletion's Lesson. *CEI Update.* Competitive Enterprise Institute. Washington, D.C. At <http://www.cei.org/update/1998/0998-bl.html> (September 1998).

Luard, Evan. 1979. *The United Nations: How It Works and What It Does.* New York: St. Martin's Press.

Maze, Rick. 1998. Nurturing Nature/The Military Is Providing Habitats for Endangered Species. *Army Times.* At <http://www.mco.com/mem/archives/army/1997/army1_891295526.html>.

Murkowski, Frank. 1998. Too Green. *The Washington Post,* 16 September, A17.

Organization of American States. 1995–1999. *North American Free Trade Agreement.* At <http://www.sice.oas.org/trade/nafta/naftatce.stm> (September 1998).

Overseas Private Investment Corporation (OPIC). OPIC's Environmental Handbook: A Message from OPIC president George Muñoz. Washington, D.C. At <http://www.opic.gov> (As of September 1999).

———. What is OPIC? Washington, D.C. At <http://www.opic.gov> (As of September 1999).

Ozone Secretariat. *The Montreal Protocol on Substances that Deplete the Ozone Layer.* United Nations Environment Program. At <http://www.unep.ch/ozone/treaties.htm> (As of September 1998).

Parsons, Rymn James. 1998. The Fight to Save the Planet: U.S. Armed Forces, "Greenkeeping," and Enforcement of Law Pertaining to Environmental Protection During Armed Conflict. *The Georgetown International Environmental Law Review* X, 2 (Winter): 441–500.

Pearson, Charles S. 1993. The Trade and Environment Nexus: What Is New Since '72? In *Trade and the Environment: Law, Economics, and Policy,* edited by Durwood Zaelke, Paul Orbuch, and Robert F. Housman. Washington, D.C.: Center for International Environmental Law.

Petrovsky, Vladimir. 1997. Statement at the 50th Anniversary of the World Federalist Movement and Its Special Joint Conference with the Union of European Federalists, September 19. Montreux, France. At <http://193.135.136.30/frames/montreux.htm>.

Preamble Center. 1997. 140 Environmental Groups, Labor Unions, and Development Organizations, U.S. and International, Ask Congress to Oppose IMF Expansion. *News from Preamble,* September 10. Washington, D.C.: Preamble Center.

Pregelj, Vladimir N. Updated June 30, 1998. CRS Report for Congress #97016. Trade Agreements: Renewing the Negotiating and Fast-Track Implementing Authority. Washington, D.C.: Congressional Research Service.

President. 1997. *A National Security Strategy for a New Century*. White House, May.

Richardson, Bill. 1998. Environmental Challenges Facing the World in the 21st Century. Speech delivered to the American Museum of Natural History, April 29. At <http://www.undp.org/missions/usa/98_80.htm> (September 1998).

Schaefer, Brett D. 1996. OPIC-ing the Taxpayer's Pocket. *Executive Memorandum* 458. Washington, D.C.: The Heritage Foundation.

———. 1997. The Overseas Private Investment Corporation: Myths and Realities. *Roe Backgrounder* 1127. Washington, D.C.: The Heritage Foundation.

———. 1998a. Understanding the Limits of Globalism: Global Environmentalism. In *Issues '98: The Candidate's Briefing Book*, edited by Stuart M. Butler and Kim R. Holmes. Washington, D.C.: The Heritage Foundation.

———. 1998b. Unratified Environmental Treaties Deserve No U.S. Funding. *Executive Memorandum 552*. Washington, D.C.: The Heritage Foundation.

Semans, Truman T. 1996. Memorandum to Staff Member of Congressman Tom DeLay. Office of Multilateral Development Banks. Department of the Treasury. (Available upon request)

Sheehan, James M. 1998. *Global Greens: Inside the International Environmental Establishment*. Washington, D.C.: Capital Research Center.

Sustainable Development (SD) Dimensions. 1998. UN Food and Agriculture Organization. *Environmental Policy, Planning and Management*. At <http://www.fao.org/WAICENT/FAOINFO/SUSTDEV/EPdirect/EPhomepg.htm> (September 1998).

Sweeney, John P. 1998. International Trade: Creating Wealth and Jobs for Americans. In *Issues '98: The Candidate's Briefing Book*, edited by Stuart M. Butler and Kim R. Holmes. Washington, D.C.: The Heritage Foundation.

Sweeney, John P., Bryan T. Johnson, and Robert O'Quinn. 1997. Building Support for Free Trade and Investment. In *Mandate for Leadership IV: Turning Ideas into Actions*, edited by Stuart M. Butler and Kim R. Holmes. Washington, D.C.: The Heritage Foundation.

Taylor, Prudence E. 1998. From Environmental to Ecological Human Rights: A New Dynamic in International Law? *The Georgetown International Environmental Law Review* X, 2 (Winter): 309–396.

United Nations. Conference on Environment and Development (UNCED). 1992. *Agenda 21*. At <http://sedac.ciesin.org/pidb/texts/a21/a21-contents.html> (September 1998).

United Nations. 1992. Report of the Intergovernmental Negotiating Committee for a Framework Convention on Climate Change on the Work of the Second Part of Its Fifth Session Held at New York from 30 April to 9 May 1992. Doc. A/AC.237/18. Part II. At <http://www.unep.ch/unfccc/fca6.html> (September 1998).

United Nations. 1992. *Report of the United Nations Conference on Environment and Development*. At <gopher://gopher.un.org:70/00/conf/unced/English/re_vol1.txt>.

U.S. Agency for International Development (USAID). About GreenCOM. Environmental Education and Communication Project. Washington, D.C. At <http://www.info.usaid.gov/environment/greencom/aboutgreen2.htm> (As of September 1998).

———. Major Functional Series 200: USAID Program Assistance ADS 204 Environmental Procedures. Washington, D.C. At <http://www.info.usaid.gov/pubs/ads/200/204.htm> (As of September 1998).

———. 22 CFR 216 Agency Environmental Procedures. Washington, D.C. At <http://www.info.usaid.gov/environment/22cfr216.htm> (As of September 1998).

———. USAID's Strategies for Sustainable Development: Protecting the Environment. Washington, D.C. At <http://www.info.usaid.gov/environment/strategy.htm> (As of September 1998).

U.S. Department of Defense. 1987. Directive 5100.1. *Functions of the Department of Defense and Its Major Components.* At <http://web7.whsosd.mil/text/d51001p.txt> (As of September 1998).

U.S. Department of State. Bureau of Oceans and International Environmental and Scientific Affairs. At <http://www.state.gov/www/global/oes/index.html> (As of September 1998).

———. Structure and Organization. Washington, D.C. At <http://www.state.gov/www/about_state/dosstruc.html> (As of September 1998).

———. *Environmental Diplomacy: The Environment and U.S. Foreign Policy, Challenges for the Planet.* At <http://www.state.gov/www/global/oes/earth.html> (As of September 1998).

———. 1997. *United States Strategic Plan for International Affairs.* Washington, D.C. At <http://www.state.gov/www/global/general_ foreign_policy/ dosidex. html>.

U.S. House. 1999. *Foreign Operations, Export Financing, and Related Programs Appropriations for FY 1999.* H.R. 4569. 105th Cong., 2d session.

U.S. Joint Chiefs of Staff. 1997. National Military Strategy of the United States of America. Washington, D.C.

U.S. Public Law 103-236. 103d Cong. 2d sess., 4/30/94. *Foreign Relations Authorization Act for Fiscal Years 1994 and 1995* (108 Stat. 402).

Wathen, Tom. 1993. A Guide to Trade and the Environment. In *Trade and the Environment: Law, Economics, and Policy,* edited by Durwood Zaelke, Paul Orbuch, and Robert F. Housman. Washington, D.C.: Center for International Environmental Law.

Wilson, Arlene. 1994. GATT, Trade Liberalization, and the Environment: An Economic Analysis. Washington, D.C.: Congressional Research Service.

———. 1997a. Fast Track Trade Authority: Which Environmental Issues Are "Directly Related to Trade"? Washington, D.C.: Congressional Research Service.

———. 1997b. Fast-Track Trade Authority Proposals: Which Environmental Issues Are Included in the Principal Negotiating Objectives? Washington, D.C.: Congressional Research Service.

Wirth, Timothy E. 1997. Remarks at the Forum on International Geosciences, November 17. National Academy of Sciences. Washington, D.C. At <http://www.state.gov/www/global/oes/971117tw.html> (January 1998).

World Bank Group. The World Bank's Role: Environmentally Sustainable
    Development. Washington, D.C. At <http://www.worldbank.org/html/extdr/
    backgrd/ibrd/role.htm> (As of September 1998).
World Trade Organization (WTO). About the WTO. Geneva, Switzerland. At
    <http://www.wto.org/wto/about/facts0.htm> (September 1998).
———. Trade and Environment in the WTO: Background to WTO Work on
    Trade and Environment. At <http://www.wto.org/wto/environ/environ1.htm>
    (As of September 1998).

# APPENDIX

| U.S. Treaties in Force Containing Environmental Provisions | Date of Signature by the United States |
|---|---|
| Agreed Measures for the Conservation of Antarctic Fauna and Flora | |
| Agreement amending the Agreement Establishing the South Pacific Commission (SPC) | October 6, 1964 |
| Agreement concerning Interim Arrangements relating to Polymetallic Nodules of the Deep Sea Bed | September 2, 1982 |
| Agreement establishing the Asian Development Bank (ADB) | December 4, 1965 |
| Agreement establishing the Inter-American Development Bank | October 14, 1959 |
| Agreement establishing the South Pacific Commission | February 6, 1947 |
| Agreement establishing the South Pacific Regional Environment Programme (SPREP) | June 16, 1993 |
| Agreement extending the territorial scope of the South Pacific Commission | November 7, 1951 |
| Agreement for the Establishment of the Asia Pacific Fishery Commission | |
| Agreement for the Implementation of the Provisions of the United Nations Convention on the Law of the Sea relating to the Conservation and Management of Straddling Fish Stocks and Highly Migratory Fish Stocks | January 16, 1996 |
| Agreement of the International Bank for Reconstruction and Development | December 27, 1945 |
| Agreement of the International Monetary Fund | December 27, 1945 |

| Date Entered into Force | Description of the Treaty or Its Environmental Aspects |
|---|---|
| November 1, 1982 | Within the framework of the Antarctic Treaty; protect Antarctic fauna and flora and promote scientific study and rational use of those resources. |
| July 15, 1965 | Amends the SPC. |
| September 2, 1982 | Identifies and resolves conflicts arising from filing and processing applications to harvest deep seabed resources. |
| August 22, 1966 | The ADB is a multilateral development finance institution engaged in promoting sustainable economic development in the Asian and Pacific region. |
| December 30, 1959 | The Inter-American Development Bank was established to accelerate economic development in Latin America and the Caribbean. The Bank's operations cover the entire spectrum of economic and social development, including environmental and public health. |
| July 29, 1948 | The SPC was established to encourage international cooperation in promoting the sustainable economic and social welfare in non–self-governing territories in the South Pacific region. |
| | Establishes the SPREP as an intergovernmental organization to provide assistance and coordinate action to protect and improve the environment. |
| November 7, 1951 | Extends the SPC to Guam and Pacific Island. |
| November 9, 1948 | Promotes proper utilization of living aquatic resources by developing and managing fishing and culture operations. |
| | Ensures the long-term conservation and sustainable use of straddling and highly migratory fish stocks. |
| December 20, 1945 | Created the World Bank to facilitate investment of capital for productive purposes, to promote private foreign investment and long-range balanced growth of international trade and the maintenance of equilibrium in balances of payments, and to arrange and provide loans for sustainable development. |
| December 20, 1945 | The IMF provides monetary assistance for countries in financial distress. IMF assistance must meet environmental standards. |

*(appendix continues)*

| *U.S. Treaties in Force Containing Environmental Provisions* | *Date of Signature by the United States* |
|---|---|
| Agreement on an International Energy Program | |
| Agreement on Conservation of Polar Bears | November 15, 1973 |
| Agreement on the Rescue of Astronauts, the Return of Astronauts and the Return of Objects Launched into Outer Space | April 22, 1968 |
| Agreement on the Resolution of Practical Problems with Respect to Deep Seabed Mining Areas | |
| Agreement regarding Monitoring of the Stratosphere | May 5, 1976 |
| Agreement relating to the Implementation of Part XI of the United Nations Convention on the Law of the Sea of 10 December 1982 | July 29, 1994 |
| Agreement to Promote Compliance with International Conservation and Management Measures by Fishing Vessels on the High Seas | |
| Amendment to the Convention on International Trade in Endangered Species of Wild Fauna and Flora (art. XI) | |
| Amendment to the Montreal Protocol on Substances that Deplete the Ozone Layer | |
| Amendment to the Montreal Protocol on Substances that Deplete the Ozone Layer | |
| Amendments to Annexes to the Convention on the Prevention of Marine Pollution by Dumping of Wastes and Other Matter concerning Incineration at Sea | |
| Amendments to the Annexes to the Convention on the Prevention of Marine Pollution by Dumping of Wastes and Other Matter | |
| Amendments to the Convention on the Prevention of Marine Pollution by Dumping of Wastes and Other Matter concerning Settlement of Disputes | |
| Antarctic Treaty | December 1, 1959 |

| Date Entered into Force | Description of the Treaty or Its Environmental Aspects |
|---|---|
| February 15, 1980 | Reduces dependence on oil energy conservation efforts and promotes development of alternative sources of energy. |
| November 1, 1976 | Aims to achieve protection of the polar bear through further conservation and management measures. |
| December 3, 1968 | Calls for the rendering of all possible assistance to aid astronauts in the event of accident, distress, or emergency landing; to return astronauts promptly and safely; and to return objects launched into outer space. |
| August 14, 1987 | Resolves U.S. disputes with Resolution and establishes environmental standards for deep seabed mining. |
| May 5, 1976 | Multilateral agreement to monitor pollution levels in the stratosphere and the pollution's impact. |
| July 28, 1996 | New legal regime for sea and oceans; includes material rules concerning environmental standards as well as enforcement provisions dealing with pollution of the marine environment. |
|  | International agreement, within the framework of the Food and Agriculture Organization, to regulate the fishing vessels on the high seas. |
| April 13, 1987 | Protects certain endangered species from overexploitation by means of a system of import/export permits. |
| August 10, 1992 | Strengthens control procedures under the Montreal Protocol on Substances that Deplete the Ozone Layer, extends coverage to new substances, and establishes financial mechanisms for the protocol. |
| June 14, 1994 | Technical modifications of some articles of the Montreal Protocol. |
| March 11, 1979 | Controls pollution of the sea by dumping and encourages similar regional agreements. |
| March 11, 1981 |  |
| June 23, 1961 | Ensures that Antarctica is used for peaceful purposes and scientific research rather than as a scene or object of international discord. |

(appendix continues)

94

| U.S. Treaties in Force Containing Environmental Provisions | Date of Signature by the United States |
|---|---|
| Articles of Agreement of the International Development Association (IDA) | |
| Charter of the Organization of American States (OAS) | April 30, 1948 |
| Charter of the United Nations | October 24, 1945 |
| Constitution of the Food and Agriculture Organization of the United Nations (FAO) | |
| Constitution of the International Labour Organization (ILO) | |
| Constitution of the United Nations Educational, Scientific and Cultural Organization (UNESCO) | September 30, 1946 |
| Constitution of the United Nations Industrial Development Organization (UNIDO) | January 17, 1980 |
| Constitution of the World Health Organization (WHO) | July 22, 1946 |
| Convention concerning Minimum Standards in Merchant Ships (No. 147) | |
| Convention concerning the Protection of the World Cultural and Natural Heritage | |
| Convention establishing a marine scientific organization for the North Pacific Region (PICES) | May 28, 1991 |
| Convention for the Conservation of Antarctic Seals | June 28, 1972 |
| Convention for the Conservation of Salmon in the North Atlantic Ocean | |

| Date Entered into Force | Description of the Treaty or Its Environmental Aspects |
| --- | --- |
| September 24, 1960 | The IDA provides development assistance, at no interest and for a long repayment period, to developing countries that cannot afford development loans at ordinary rates of interest and in the time span of conventional loans. All loans must meet environmental standards. |
| June 19, 1951 | The OAS is the world's oldest regional organization, dating back to 1889. In addition to ongoing environmental programs, the OAS secretariat had primary responsibility for the second Summit on Sustainable Development. |
| October 24, 1945 | Among its many stated purposes, the UN coordinates and promotes environmental regulation through treaties, conferences, and funding. |
| October 16, 1945 | The FAO promotes sustainable agricultural policies. |
| February 18, 1980 | The ILO monitors international labor standards, including working environment and pollution. |
| November 4, 1946 | UNESCO promotes the idea of sustainable development and maintains numerous environmental programs. |
| June 21, 1985 | UNIDO promotes sustainable development in developing countries and encourages industrial cooperation. |
| June 21, 1948 | WHO studies and funds programs to promote health, including environmental protection issues. |
| June 15, 1989 | Establishes minimum standards of conduct for merchant ships. |
| December 17, 1975 | Collective protection of the cultural and natural heritage of outstanding universal value and unique nature. |
| March 24, 1992 | Establishes an intergovernmental organization to promote and facilitate such scientific cooperation and avoid duplication of effort in studying marine resources in the North Pacific. |
| March 11, 1978 | Promotes and achieves protection, scientific study, and rational use of Antarctic seals and maintains a satisfactory balance within the ecological system of the Antarctic. |
| October 1, 1983 | Promotes conservation, restoration, enhancement, and rational management of salmon stock in the North Atlantic Ocean through international regulation, acquisition, and analysis and dissemination of appropriate scientific information. |

*(appendix continues)*

| U.S. Treaties in Force Containing Environmental Provisions | Date of Signature by the United States |
|---|---|
| Convention for the Establishment of an Inter-American Tropical Tuna Commission | |
| Convention for the International Council for the Exploration of the Sea | |
| Convention for the Prohibition of Fishing with Long Driftnets in the South Pacific | November 14, 1990 |
| Convention for the Protection and Development of the Marine Environment of the Wider Caribbean Region | March 24, 1983 |
| Convention for the Protection of the Natural Resources and Environment of the South Pacific Region (SPREP Convention) | November 25, 1986 |
| Convention for the Protection of the Ozone Layer | March 22, 1985 |
| Convention for the Regulation of Whaling | |
| Convention of the World Meteorological Organization (WMO) | |
| Convention on Assistance in the Case of a Nuclear Accident or Radiological Emergency | September 26, 1986 |
| Convention on Biological Diversity | June 4, 1993 |
| Convention on Conduct of Fishing Operations in the North Atlantic | November 25, 1967 |
| Convention on Early Notification of a Nuclear Accident | September 26, 1986 |
| Convention on Environmental Impact Assessment in a Transboundary Context | February 26, 1991 |
| Convention on Fishing and Conservation of the Living Resources of the High Seas | September 15, 1958 |

| Date Entered into Force | Description of the Treaty or Its Environmental Aspects |
|---|---|
| March 3, 1950 | Maintains populations of yellow fin and skipjack tuna in the eastern Pacific Ocean to permit maximum sustained catches. |
| April 18, 1973 | New constitution for the International Council for the Exploration of the Sea, originally established in Copenhagen in 1902. |
| February 28, 1992 | Prohibits nations and vessels documented under nations' laws from engaging in driftnet fishing activities within the Convention Area. |
| October 11, 1986 | Protects and manages the marine environment and coastal areas of the Caribbean region. |
| July 10, 1991 | Strengthens implementation of the general objective of the Action Plan for Managing the Natural Resources and Environment of the South Pacific. |
| September 22, 1988 | Encourages action to restrict substances believed to deplete the ozone layer. |
| January 16, 1935 | Protects all species of whales from overfishing and establishes a system of international regulation for the whale fisheries. |
| March 23, 1950 | The WMO coordinates global scientific activity of weather information and provides weather information for public, private, and commercial use, including international airline and shipping industries. WMO also focuses on environmental issues. |
| October 20, 1988 | Requires parties to provide prompt assistance to minimize the consequences of a nuclear accident or radiological emergency to protect life, property, and environment from the effects of radioactive releases. |
| | Requires countries to conserve biological diversity, restrict natural resources, and share all benefits arising from the use of genetic resources. |
| | Governs fishing practices in the North Atlantic. |
| October 20, 1988 | Establishes a notification system for nuclear accidents, which have the potential for international transboundary release that could be a safety issue. |
| | Promotes environmentally sound and sustainable economic development through environmental impact assessment, especially as a preventative measure against transboundary environmental degradation. |
| March 20, 1966 | Solves problems of conserving living resources of the high seas that are in danger of being overexploited. |

(appendix continues)

| U.S. Treaties in Force Containing Environmental Provisions | Date of Signature by the United States |
|---|---|
| Convention on Future Multilateral Cooperation in the Northwest Atlantic Fisheries (NAFO) | |
| Convention on International Civil Aviation Annex 16 Aircraft Noise (ICAO) | December 7, 1944 |
| Convention on International Liability for Damage Caused by Space Objects | March 29, 1972 |
| Convention on International Trade in Endangered Species of Wild Fauna and Flora | March 3, 1973 |
| Convention on Long-Range Transboundary Air Pollution | November 13, 1975 |
| Convention on Nature Protection and Wild Life Preservation in the Western Hemisphere | October 12, 1940 |
| Convention on Nuclear Safety | September 20, 1994 |
| Convention on Registration of Objects Launched into Outer Space | January 24, 1975 |
| Convention on Road Traffic | September 19, 1949 |
| Convention on the Carriage of Goods by Sea | April 30, 1979 |
| Convention on the Conservation of Antarctic Marine Living Resources | September 11, 1980 |
| Convention on the Continental Shelf | September 15, 1958 |
| Convention on the Control of Transboundary Movements of Hazardous Wastes and Their Disposal | March 22, 1990 |
| Convention on the High Seas | September 15, 1958 |
| Convention on the Inter-American Institute of Agricultural Sciences | January 15, 1944 |

| Date Entered into Force | Description of the Treaty or Its Environmental Aspects |
|---|---|
| November 29, 1995 | Promotes conservation of the fishery resources of the Northwest Atlantic area. |
| April 4, 1947 | ICAO develops, adopts, and amends international standards related to the operation of aircraft. Annex 16 deals with noise pollution. |
| October 9, 1973 | Defines which parties are accountable to make retribution in the event of a spacecraft accident. |
| July 1, 1975 | Protects certain endangered species from overexploitation through import/export permits and restrictions. |
| March 16, 1983 | Protects humans and their environment from air pollution and seeks to limit and eliminate air pollution, including long-range transboundary air pollution. |
| May 1, 1942 | Preserves all species and genera of native American fauna and flora from extinction, and preserves areas of extraordinary beauty, striking geological formations, or aesthetic, historic, or scientific value. |
| | Establishes legal obligations on parties to apply safety principles to the construction, operation, and regulation of land-based civilian nuclear power plants under their jurisdiction and to submit periodic reports on the implementation of those obligations. |
| September 19, 1976 | Mandatory registry of objects launched into outer space to assist identification. |
| March 26, 1952 | Develops, establishes, and promotes uniform international road traffic rules to increase safety. |
| | Establishes responsibilities and liabilities of owners and carriers of goods shipped by sea. |
| April 7, 1982 | Safeguards the environment and protects the integrity of the ecosystem of the seas surrounding Antarctica and conserves Antarctic living marine resources. |
| June 10, 1964 | Defines and limits the rights of States to explore and exploit the natural resources of the continental shelf. |
| | Obligates treaty parties to reduce transboundary movements of wastes, minimize amounts and toxicity of hazardous materials, and assist developing countries in environmentally sound management of hazardous and other wastes they generate. |
| September 30, 1962 | Codifies international law relating to the high seas. |
| November 30, 1944 | The purpose of the Inter-American Institute of Agricultural Sciences is to encourage, promote, and support agricultural and sustainable rural development. |

*(appendix continues)*

| *U.S. Treaties in Force Containing Environmental Provisions* | *Date of Signature by the United States* |
|---|---|
| Convention on the International Maritime Organization (IMO) | March 6, 1948 |
| Convention on the International Regulations for Preventing Collisions at Sea | October 20, 1972 |
| Convention on the Law of Treaties between States and International Organizations or between International Organizations | June 26, 1987 |
| Convention on the Organization for Economic Cooperation and Development (OECD) | |
| Convention on the Physical Protection of Nuclear Material | March 3, 1980 |
| Convention on the Prevention of Marine Pollution by Dumping of Wastes and Other Matter | December 29, 1972 |
| Convention on the Prohibition of Military or Any Other Hostile Use of Environmental Modification Techniques | May 18, 1977 |
| Convention on the Prohibition of the Development, Production and Stockpiling of Bacteriological (Biological) and Toxin Weapons and on Their Destruction | April 10, 1972 |
| Convention on the Prohibition of the Development, Production, Stockpiling and Use of Chemical Weapons and Their Destruction | January 13, 1993 |
| Convention on the Recognition and Enforcement of Foreign Arbitral Awards | |
| Convention on the Regulation of Antarctic Mineral Resource Activities | November 25, 1988 |
| Convention on the Territorial Sea and the Contiguous Zone | September 15, 1958 |
| Convention on Transboundary Effects of Industrial Accidents | March 18, 1992 |
| Convention on Wetlands of International Importance Especially as Waterfowl Habitat | September 13, 1985 |

| Date Entered into Force | Description of the Treaty or Its Environmental Aspects |
|---|---|
| March 17, 1954 | The IMO encourages maritime safety standards, including environmental safety and navigation efficiency. |
| July 15, 1977 | Maintains a high level of safety at sea. |
| | Prohibits, with exceptions, dumping wastes or other matter. |
| September 30, 1961 | The OECD is a cooperative body focused on promoting sustainable economic growth in member countries. |
| February 8, 1987 | Averts unlawful taking and use of nuclear material and establishes effective measures for protecting nuclear material used for military purposes. |
| August 30, 1975 | Seeks to control pollution dumping at sea and to encourage similar regional agreements. |
| January 17, 1980 | Each party to the convention agrees not to engage in any hostile use of environmental modification techniques that have widespread, long-lasting, or severe effects as the means of destruction, damage, or injury to any other party nor assist, encourage, or induce any state, group of states, or international organization to engage in those activities. |
| March 26, 1975 | Prohibition and elimination of all types of weapons of mass destruction and effective international control. |
| | Prohibits production and use of chemical weapons and requires parties to destroy all chemical weapons. |
| December 29, 1970 | Recognition and enforcement of arbitral awards made in the territory of a state other than the state where the recognition and enforcement of such awards are sought. |
| | Creates principles and rules to govern institutions to assess the possible effect on the environment of Antarctic mineral resource activities. |
| September 10, 1964 | Establishes the sovereignty of a state on the territorial sea and the contiguous zone. |
| | Promotes, coordinates, and enhances policies and action to prevent, prepare for, or respond to the transboundary effects of industrial accidents. |
| April 18, 1987 | Seeks to stem encroachment on and loss of wetlands now and in the future due to the fundamental ecological, economic, cultural, scientific, and recreational value. |

*(appendix continues)*

| *U.S. Treaties in Force Containing Environmental Provisions* | *Date of Signature by the United States* |
| --- | --- |
| Convention placing the International Poplar Commission within the Framework of the Food and Agriculture Organization of the United Nations | |
| Framework Convention on Climate Change | June 12, 1992 |
| General Agreement on Tariffs and Trade (GATT) | |
| Indus Basin Development Fund Agreement | |
| Indus Basin Development Fund (Supplemental) Agreement | |
| International Agreement for the Creation of an International Office for Dealing with Contagious Diseases of Animals at Paris | |
| International Covenant on Economic, Social and Cultural Rights | October 5, 1977 |
| International Convention for Safe Container (CSS) | December 2, 1972 |
| International Convention for the Conservation of Atlantic Tunas | May 14, 1966 |
| International Convention for the Prevention of Pollution from Ships (MARPOL) | March 7, 1974 |
| International Convention for the Prevention of Pollution from Ships (MARPOL) Annex V | |
| International Convention for the Prevention of Pollution from Ships as modified by the Protocol of 1978 | June 27, 1978 |
| International Convention for the Prevention of Pollution from Ships, 1973 (MARPOL) Annex III (Optional) | |
| International Convention for the Prevention of Pollution of the Sea Oil, 1954, as amended in 1962 and 1969 | |

| Date Entered into Force | Description of the Treaty or Its Environmental Aspects |
|---|---|
| August 13, 1970 | Places the commission in FAO to study the scientific, technical, social, and economic aspects of poplar and willow cultivation. |
| March 21, 1994 | Regulates levels of greenhouse gas concentration in the atmosphere, so as to avoid the occurrence of climate change. |
| January 1, 1948 | GATT is a fundamental agreement in liberalizing trade. GATT rulings can override environmental regulation if it is a prejudicial barrier to trade. |
| April 1, 1960 | India agrees to pay the costs of replacing irrigation canals in Pakistan through the Indus Basin Development Fund to be established and administered by the World Bank. |
| April 1, 1964 | Supplements the Indus Basin Development Fund Agreement. |
| July 29, 1975 | Establishes an international office to study and deal with animal-borne contagious disease. |
| | Establishes the right of self-determination (meaning a people may freely determine their political status and freely pursue their economic, social, and cultural development) and requires treaty parties to respect and promote that right. |
| January 3, 1979 | Formalizes structural requirements to ensure safety in the handling, stacking, and transporting of containers. |
| March 21, 1969 | Maintains populations of tuna and tuna-like fish in the Atlantic Ocean at levels permitting the maximum sustainable catch for food and other purposes. |
| | Eliminates intentional marine pollution by oil and other harmful substances and minimizes accidental discharge of such substances. |
| December 31, 1988 | MARPOL establishes rules pertaining to the discharge of shipboard solid waste from vessels operating in designated "special areas" of the world. Annex V establishes guidelines on disposal of garbage from ships. |
| October 2, 1983 | Modifies various provisions of the International Convention for the Prevention of Pollution from Ships, particularly Annex I. |
| July 1, 1992 | Optional annex to the International Convention for the Prevention of Pollution from Ships. |
| December 8, 1961 | Agreement to prevent pollution of the sea by oil discharged from ships. |

*(appendix continues)*

| U.S. Treaties in Force Containing Environmental Provisions | Date of Signature by the United States |
|---|---|
| International Convention for the Protection of New Varieties of Plants (consolidated version) | October 25, 1991 |
| International Convention for the Protection of New Varieties of Plants as amended | October 23, 1978 |
| International Convention for the Regulation of Whaling | December 2, 1946 |
| International Convention for the Safety of Life at Sea | |
| International Convention for the Safety of Life at Sea (SOLAS) | November 1, 1974 |
| International Convention on Civil Liability for Oil Pollution Damage | November 29, 1969 |
| International Convention on Oil Pollution Preparedness, Response and Cooperation | November 30, 1990 |
| International Convention on Salvage | April 28, 1989 |
| International Convention on Standards of Training, Certification and Watchkeeping for Seafarers | July 7, 1978 |
| International Convention on the Establishment of an International Fund for Compensation for Oil Pollution Damage | December 18, 1971 |
| International Convention relating to Intervention on the High Seas in Cases of Oil Pollution Casualties | November 29, 1969 |
| International Convention to Combat Desertification in Those Countries Experiencing Serious Drought and/or Desertification, particularly in Africa | October 14, 1994 |
| International Covenant on Civil and Political Rights | October 5, 1977 |
| International Plant Protection Convention | December 6, 1951 |

| Date Entered into Force | Description of the Treaty or Its Environmental Aspects |
| --- | --- |
|  | Signatories agree to recognize and protect the rights of breeders of new varieties of plants and their successors in title. |
| November 8, 1981 | Recognizes and protects the rights of breeders of new varieties of plants and their successors in title. |
| November 10, 1948 | Convention for the proper conservation of whale stocks and orderly development of the whaling industry. |
| May 26, 1968 | Regulates packing and carriage of dangerous goods in ships. |
| May 25, 1980 | Applies to carriage of dangerous materials at sea. Requires notification of accidents that may affect the environment. |
|  | Standardizes international rules and procedures for determining questions of liability and adequate compensation and ensures that adequate compensation is available to persons who suffer damage caused by discharge of oil from ships. |
| May 13, 1995 | Strengthens the legal framework governing environmental pollution by oil, particularly marine pollution, and increases preparedness and capability to deal with incidents of oil pollution in the marine environment. |
| July 14, 1996 | Establishes uniform international rules regarding salvage operations in light of the need for timely operations and to protect the environment. |
| October 1, 1991 | Promotes safety of life and property at sea and the protection of the marine environment by establishing in common agreement international standards of training, certification, and watchkeeping for seafarers. |
|  | Provides a regime for compensation for the costs of measures, wherever taken, to prevent or minimize pollution damage. |
| May 6, 1975 | Enables countries to take action on the high seas to address oil pollution at sea and along coastlines without violating the principle of freedom of the high seas. |
| December 26, 1996 | Seeks to address the economic and environmental problems of desertification, particularly in Africa. |
| September 8, 1992 | Promotes universal respect for, and observance of, human rights and freedoms. |
| August 18, 1972 | Maintains and increases international cooperation in controlling and preventing the spread of plant pests and diseases or those in plant products. |

*(appendix continues)*

| *U.S. Treaties in Force Containing Environmental Provisions* | *Date of Signature by the United States* |
|---|---|
| International Plant Protection Convention (Revised Text) | |
| International Tropical Timber Agreement | April 26, 1985 |
| International Tropical Timber Agreement | July 1, 1994 |
| North American Agreement on Environmental Cooperation | September 13, 1993 |
| North American Free Trade Agreement (NAFTA) | December 17, 1992 |
| North Atlantic Treaty | April 4, 1949 |
| Optional Protocol of Signature concerning the Compulsory Settlement of Disputes | September 15, 1958 |
| Protocol Additional to the Geneva Conventions of 12 August 1949 and relating to the Protection of Victims of International Armed Conflicts (Protocol I) | December 12, 1977 |
| Protocol Additional to the Geneva Conventions relating to the Protection of Victims of Noninternational Armed Conflicts (Protocol II) | December 12, 1977 |
| Protocol amending the International Convention for the High Seas Fisheries of the North Pacific Ocean | |
| Protocol concerning Cooperation in Combating Oil Spills in the Wider Caribbean Region | March 24, 1983 |
| Protocol concerning Cooperation in Combating Pollution Emergencies in the South Pacific Region | November 25, 1986 |

| Date Entered into Force | Description of the Treaty or Its Environmental Aspects |
|---|---|
| April 4, 1991 | Seeks to prevent the spread and introduction of pests of plants and plant products and to promote measures for their control. |
| May 25, 1990 | Facilitates cooperation and consultation between countries producing and consuming tropical timber. |
| January 1, 1997 | Provides framework for cooperation and consultation between countries producing and consuming tropical timber in order to promote expansion and diversification of international trade in tropical timber, improve the structural condition in the tropical timber market, and promote sustainable use of resources. |
| January 1, 1994 | Fosters the protection and improvement of the environment in the territories of the parties; promotes sustainable development; increases cooperation between the parties to better conserve, protect, and enhance the environment; and supports the environmental objectives of NAFTA.

NAFTA became one of the first trade agreements in history to link environmental protection to foreign trade. |
| August 24, 1949 | The North Atlantic Treaty created an alliance of twelve independent nations committed to each other's defense. Four more European nations later acceded to the treaty between 1952 and 1982. Identifies several environmental concerns as security issues.

Establishes the compulsory jurisdiction of the International Court of Justice, unless some other form of settlement is provided in the Convention or has been agreed upon by the parties within a reasonable period.

Reaffirms and develops provisions protecting the people from armed conflicts or their consequences.

Supplements the Geneva Conventions of 12 August 1949 without modifying its existing conditions of application. |
| February 15, 1979 | Ensures sustained productivity of the fishery resources of the north Pacific Ocean and coordinates research and conservation measures to that end. |
| October 11, 1986 | Protects and manages the marine environment and coastal areas of the wider Caribbean region. |
| July 10, 1991 | Protects and manages the natural resources and environment of the South Pacific region. |

*(appendix continues)*

| *U.S. Treaties in Force Containing Environmental Provisions* | *Date of Signature by the United States* |
|---|---|
| Protocol Concerning Specially Protected Areas and Wildlife to the Convention for the Protection and Development of the Marine Environment of the Wider Caribbean Region | January 18, 1990 |
| Protocol for the Prevention of Pollution of the South Pacific Region by Dumping | November 25, 1986 |
| Protocol for the Prohibition of the Use in War of Asphyxiating, Poisonous or Other Gases, and of Bacteriological Methods of Warfare | |
| Protocol I to the Convention for the Prohibition of Fishing with Long Driftnets in the South Pacific | February 27, 1991 |
| Protocol on Substances that Deplete the Ozone Layer | September 16, 1987 |
| Protocol relating to Intervention on the High Seas in Cases of Pollution by Substances Other than Oil | March 7, 1974 |
| Protocol relating to modification of the International Convention for the Conservation of Atlantic Tunas (amendment) | September 10, 1984 |
| Protocol relating to the International Convention for the Safety of Life at Sea (SOLAS Protocol) | June 26, 1978 |
| Protocol relating to the International Convention for the Safety of Life at Sea (SOLAS Protocol 1988) | November 11, 1988 |
| Protocol to amend Paragraph 2 of Article X of the International Convention for the Conservation of Atlantic Tunas (ICCAT) | October 22, 1992 |
| Protocol to amend the Convention on Wetlands of International Importance especially as Waterfowl Habitat | September 13, 1985 |
| Protocol to amend the International Convention on Civil Liability for Oil Pollution Damage | May 25, 1984 |
| Protocol to amend the International Convention on the Establishment of an International Fund for Compensation for Oil Pollution Damage | May 25, 1984 |

| Date Entered into Force | Description of the Treaty or Its Environmental Aspects |
| --- | --- |
| | Protects coastal and marine areas of the wider Caribbean region and ensures the protection of endangered species of wild fauna and flora in the region. |
| July 10, 1991 | Controls and reduces pollution through dumping wastes and other matter in the South Pacific with the aim of total prevention. |
| April 10, 1975 | Bans the use of chemical and biological weapons during war. |
| February 28, 1992 | Signatories agree to restrict and prohibit the use of drift nets in the South Pacific region in order to conserve marine living resources. |
| January 1, 1989 | Protects the ozone layer by taking precautionary measures to control and ban manufacture of and trade in substances believed to deplete it. |
| March 30, 1983 | Enables countries to take action on the high seas under circumstances of grave and imminent danger of pollution to their coastline or related interests by substances other than oil. |
| | Maintains tuna and tuna-like fish populations in the Atlantic Ocean at levels permitting the maximum sustainable catch for food and other purposes. |
| May 1, 1981 | Extends and clarifies the International Convention for the Safety of Life at Sea. |
| | Includes requirements for ship masters to report incidents or accidents that may cause environmental damage. |
| | Amends the ICCAT to codify annual contributions to the budget of the Commission in accordance with the "total round weight of catch and net weight of canned products of Atlantic tuna and tuna-like fishes and the degree of economic development of the Contracting Parties." |
| December 18, 1986 | Stems encroachment on and loss of wetlands due to the fundamental ecological functions of wetlands and their economic, cultural, scientific, and recreational value. |
| | Amends International Convention on Civil Liability for Oil Pollution Damage. |
| | Extends the scope and compensation outlined in the International Convention on the Establishment of an International Fund for Compensation for Oil Pollution Damage. |

(appendix continues)

| U.S. Treaties in Force Containing Environmental Provisions | Date of Signature by the United States |
| --- | --- |
| Protocol to the 1979 Convention on Long-Range Transboundary Air Pollution concerning the Control of Emissions of Volatile Organic Compounds or Their Transboundary Fluxes | November 19, 1991 |
| Protocol to the Antarctic Treaty on Environmental Protection | October 4, 1991 |
| Protocol to the Convention for the International Council for the Exploration of the Sea | August 13, 1970 |
| Protocol to the Convention on Long-Range Transboundary Air Pollution concerning the Control of Emissions of Nitrogen Oxides or Their Transboundary Fluxes | November 1, 1988 |
| Protocol to the Convention on Long-Range Transboundary Air Pollution on Long-Term Financing of Cooperative Programme for Monitoring and Evaluation of the Long-Range Transmission of Air Pollutants in Europe (EMEP) | September 28, 1984 |
| Protocol to the International Convention for the Regulation of Whaling | November 19, 1956 |
| Provisional Understanding Regarding Deep Seabed Matters | August 2, 1984 |
| South Pacific Fisheries Treaty | April 2, 1987 |
| Statute of the Hague Conference on Private International Law | |
| Statute of the International Atomic Energy Agency | |
| Statute of the International Institute for the Unification of Private Law | |
| Statutes of the International Center for the Study of the Preservation and Restoration of Cultural Property | |
| Tarbela Development Fund Agreement | |

| Date Entered into Force | Description of the Treaty or Its Environmental Aspects |
|---|---|
| | Enhances control of long-range transboundary air pollution. |
| | Reaffirms the status of Antarctica as a special conservation area and enhances protection of the Antarctic environment and dependent or associated ecosystems. |
| November 12, 1975 | Amends the Convention for the International Council for the Exploration of the Sea. |
| February 14, 1991 | Controls or reduces nitrogen oxides and their transboundary fluxes. |
| January 28, 1988 | Establishes cost-sharing for the Convention on Long-Range Transboundary Air Pollution—specifically for collecting emission data for $SO_2$, $NO_x$, VOCs, and other air pollutants; measuring air and precipitation quality; and modeling atmospheric dispersion. |
| May 4, 1959 | Protects all species of whales from overfishing and safeguards whale stocks through a system of international regulation. |
| September 2, 1984 | Agreement on use of deep seabed resources. |
| | Explores, assesses, and improves harvesting techniques, biological resource monitoring, and economic evaluation of fisheries in the South Pacific. |
| October 15, 1964 | Establishes the Hague Conference on Private International Law "to work for the progressive unification of the rules of private international law." |
| July 29, 1957 | The International Atomic Energy Agency is the intergovernmental inspectorate for the application of nuclear safeguards and verification measures covering civilian nuclear programs. |
| March 13, 1964 | Creates the International Institute for the Unification of Private Law to examine ways of harmonizing and coordinating the private law between states and prepare for the adoption of uniform rules of private law. |
| January 20, 1971 | Gives advice and recommendations to protect, collect, and study cultural property. |
| May 2, 1968 | Provides funds for environmentally sound development in Tarbela, Pakistan. |

(appendix continues)

112

| U.S. Treaties in Force Containing Environmental Provisions | Date of Signature by the United States |
|---|---|
| Treaty Banning Nuclear Weapon Tests in the Atmosphere, in Outer Space and Under Water | August 5, 1963 |
| Treaty on Principles Governing the Activities of States in the Exploration and Use of Outer Space, Including the Moon and Other Celestial Bodies | January 27, 1967 |
| Treaty on the Non-Proliferation of Nuclear Weapons | July 1, 1968 |
| Treaty on the Prohibition of the Emplacement of Nuclear Weapons and Other Weapons of Mass Destruction on the Sea Bed and the Ocean Floor and in the Subsoil thereof | February 11, 1971 |
| Treaty regulating the Status of Spitsbergen and conferring the Sovereignty on Norway | |
| Vienna Convention on the Law of Treaties | April 24, 1970 |

SOURCE for treaty charts: Environmental Treaties and Resource Indicators (ENTRI) at <http://sedac.ciesin.org/entri>, based on data provided by The World Conservation Union (IUCN); the United Nations Environment Program (UNEP); Freedom House; the Fletcher School of Law and Diplomacy; the World Resources Institute; the British Columbia Ministry of Environment, Land, & Parks; and the Cooperative Research Centre for Antarctica and the Southern Ocean (ACRC). ENTRI is jointly funded by the Center for International Earth Science Information Network (CIESIN) and Socioeconomic Data and Applications Center (SEDAC) within the Columbia Earth Institute at Columbia University and the National Aeronautics and Space Administration (NASA).

| Date Entered into Force | Description of the Treaty or Its Environmental Aspects |
| --- | --- |
| October 10, 1963 | Bans all testing of nuclear weapons in an effort to end the contamination of the environment by radioactive substances. |
| October 10, 1967 | Ensures that exploration and use of outer space, including the moon and other celestial bodies, shall be carried out for the benefit and in the interests of all countries. Specifically, outer space should be free for exploration, scientific investigation, and use by all States without discrimination of any kind and not subject to national appropriation by any means. |
| March 5, 1970 | Aims to end the nuclear arms race and to undertake nuclear disarmament. |
| May 18, 1972 | Bans the placement or use of nuclear arms on or within sea beds, ocean floors, and the subsoil. |
| August 14, 1925 | Grants Norway sovereignty over the arctic archipelago of Svalbard, the largest island being Spitsbergen. |
| | Codifies status of treaties between States. |

# CHAPTER 4

# U.S. International Interests, Sustainable Development, and the Precautionary Principle

*John J. Cohrssen*

## INTRODUCTION

The interest of the United States in global environmental issues is not new. It has, however, grown dramatically since President Theodore Roosevelt spurred American interest in conservation of African wildlife (CEQ 1985, 492) and since early twentieth-century efforts addressed species loss.[1] The changes have occurred in three overall directions:

1. Deferring U.S. sovereignty to the will of international organizations

2. Expanding the scope of environmental concerns to include economic and social issues

3. Expanding regulation of hypothecated concerns

These changes resulted from demands for action to anticipate an expanding range of environmental impacts. These demands have come from international organizations, governments, businesses, and nongovernmental organizations (NGOs). The goals of the NGOs are to improve the global environment and human health and, to varying degrees, to enlarge the role of international government, control aspects of industrial production and competition, redistribute wealth, and manage the growth and conditions of humanity.

The shift has been most pronounced over the past three decades. During the Nixon administration, new levels of U.S. and international governmental environmental programs were launched. The White House Council on Environmental Quality (CEQ) and the U.S. Environmental Protection Agency (EPA) were established, and the international environmental interest coalesced at the UN-sponsored Stockholm Conference in 1972. Since then, environmental international activities have grown significantly in all U.S. agencies with environmental responsibilities. In the late 1980s and 1990s, efforts increased dramatically in favor of international environmental regulation.

The Stockholm Conference fostered the concept of "Only One Earth," in which interdependent species share the same environment, and it set a broad framework of environmental direction for the international community. Some 133 nations agreed upon 109 action recommendations and issued a Declaration on the Human Environment (CEQ 1990, 265).[2] The recommendations fell into five broad areas: human settlements, natural resources management, pollutants, education, and development. As a result of the conference, the United Nations Environment Program (UNEP) was established and became the first UN body based in the developing world.

Today, in addition to UNEP, other UN agencies (the Food and Agriculture Organization [FAO], the UN Development Program [UNDP], the World Meteorological Organization [WMO], and the UN Commission on Sustainable Development [UNCSD]) and smaller, more specialized secretariats develop and implement a broad range of environmental policies at the global level. Moreover, other international organizations, such as the Organization for Economic Cooperation and Development (OECD), have programs concerned with environmental protection. Typically, the United States has paid for 25 percent of the budgets of these organizations. Approximately two-thirds of existing international environmental agreements have been signed since the early 1970s. In addition, a number of U.S. regional and bilateral agreements have been signed that are directly or indirectly related to such environmental issues as science and technology.

International environmental agencies, including those of the United Nations, have mushroomed because of political support for a vast array of international economic, developmental, and environmental programs, the rising political strength of NGOs, and the bureaucratic skills of the involved international agencies. International organizations generally favor government solutions that correspond to the interests of national governments and NGOs.

United Nations agencies are under pressure from governments in the developing world for increased resources. Therefore, the agencies' proposals for international action often seek to transfer resources from industrialized nations to developing ones. The United States supports such transfers because of a combination of pressures from UN agencies, other governments, and NGOs and of favorable environmental and business interests in the United States. Sometimes, to promote a particular domestic U.S. issue, U.S. officials and NGO representatives encourage international organizations to become involved in the issue and argue the need for concerted international action. Officials and other beneficiaries of the policy in the United States, in turn, use the international organization's position as the reason for taking U.S. government action. An example of this practice is U.S. climate change activity.

Deference to and cooperation with international organizations, treaty obligations, and bilateral agreements can be antithetical to U.S. interests or lack rational bases. This is why President Bush alone refused to sign the Convention on

Biological Diversity at the 1992 UN Conference on Environment and Development in Rio. Bush explained that the "proposed agreement threatens to retard biotechnology and undermine the protection of ideas" (Bush 1992).[3] The U.S. view changed under President Clinton, who signed the treaty in 1993, shortly after assuming office. The Senate, however, has refused to ratify the treaty.

Loss of sovereignty by participating in international agreements means less accountability to American citizens for actions taken by international organizations and the U.S. government. Accountability appears to diminish progressively as one examines government agencies from the local level, through state, national, and international levels. David Schoenbrod, former Senior Counsel for the Natural Resources Defense Council, wrote that it is time for the U.S. government to return the control of environmental issues to state and local governments because of the lack of public accountability of the EPA (Schoenbrod 1998). Schoenbrod's reasoning is even more applicable to the ceding of environmental control to multinational organizations. To whom are the nameless, faceless, unelected bureaucrats of multinational organizations responsible? Certainly not to U.S. voters. International organizations can take credit for efforts with little accountability for failure or untoward effects. Similarly, the burgeoning NGO community, increasingly relied upon by UN agencies for expert advice and assistance, lacks public accountability.

## THE DEPARTMENT
## OF STATE

Secretary of State Warren Christopher's pre-Earth Day "green speech" in April 1996 at Stanford University announced a new role for the United States and the U.S. State Department—

to "safeguard the global environment" (Christopher 1996).[4] Since then, Vice President Gore and Christopher's successor, Secretary Madeleine K. Albright, have also asserted environmentalism as the central theme of U.S. foreign policy. This assertion may be exaggerated inasmuch as few, if any, genuinely new initiatives immediately appeared, although some ongoing activities may have been renamed or repackaged to fit the concept. However, the array of existing international environmental activities conducted by U.S. agencies and the aggressive efforts of the administration for climate change and related international agreements confirm the realization of this new role.

Secretary Albright (1997) has said that environmental issues are part of the "mainstream of American Policy" because of three premises: environmental problems transcend national borders, environmental problems are "at the heart" of political and economic challenges, and environmental problems caused by man can be solved by man. Albright asserts that we would not be good democracy builders if we were not good stewards of the environment and that these problems can be solved if America works in partnership with governments, NGOs, and businesses that share our commitment to a cleaner, healthier world.

Albright's modifications for the State Department included appointment of an Under Secretary for Global Affairs; requests to embassies and bureaus to develop regional environmental activities; "new" regional environmental hubs at five embassies, making environmental cooperation with other countries important; the pursuit of environmental priorities for climate change, toxic chemicals, species extinction, deforestation, and marine degradation; and advances in several treaty areas. Although these modifications represent a growth in emphasis, they were not necessarily new programs. Secretary Albright ends this list of efforts with the confident statement that "environmental diplomacy is a work in progress" and then identifies a need to work with "Congress and the American people to obtain the resources to support our diplomacy in this area, as in all others" (Albright 1997). A look at the secretary's published remarks before the appropriations committees and at the president's FY 99 Budget for the State Department, however, fails to reveal a significant environmental diplomacy initiative.

In her Earth Day speech, "Global Problems and Global Solutions," Albright (1998) again stressed that the "health of families will be affected by the health of the global environment"—whether other nations develop in sustainable ways and whether the world cuts back on the use of toxic chemicals. "Diplomacy can do much to achieve these goals," Albright (1998). This time her examples include promoting efficient management of the Nile River Basin, supporting better forestry practices in Southeast Asia, and striving to negotiate a worldwide ban on the release of pollutants such as DDT and PCBs. Her view of diplomacy clearly involves expanded U.S. assistance. She spoke of "the need for funds for USAID [U.S. Agency for International Development] to help other countries grow in ways that balance economic progress, social development and environmental concerns and support for the Global Environment Facility (GEF), which embodies the partnerships for sustainable development that were forged in Rio" (Albright 1998).

The State Department's goal is to "secure a sustainable global environment in order to protect the United States and its citizens from the effects of international environmental degradation." A list of strategies includes "conclude key multilateral negotiations, giving priority to climate change, toxic chemicals, sustainable forestry, and biosafety." The strategy contains indicators or measures of success, including "status of multilateral environmental treaties and other agreements, rate of increase in atmospheric greenhouse gas concentrations in the atmosphere, status of the ozone layer, bilateral, multilateral and NGO environmental cooperation, levels of fish stacks and forests, public opinions about global environmental issues."

## THE DEPARTMENT
## OF DEFENSE

The Department of Defense's (DoD) international environmental initiatives of the late 1990s extend well beyond good environmental practices related to military operations. The Defense Department's Environmental Security program is charged with implementing preventive defense and supporting the military mission. Sherri W. Goodman (1997), Deputy Under Secretary of Defense, in a speech to the Army War College, explained that environmental issues may contribute to international conflict, and thus, their solutions may fall within the purview of the military. According to Goodman (1997), the DoD "must determine where defense environmental cooperation with other nations can contribute significantly to building democracy, trust and understanding" (all contained in http://www.denix.osd.mil/denix/public/ES-programs/speeches/speeches-25.html).

## SUSTAINABLE DEVELOPMENT

Sustainable development provides a conceptual basis for making the environment the overarching organizing principle for governments domestically and multinationally. Sustainable development includes consideration of broadly defined aspects of economic and social development as components of environmental policy. A ubiquitous definition permits interpretations ranging from prohibiting development and innovation to "balancing" environmental, economic, and other social goals. Environmental activists tend to favor stringent restrictions on economic development and to invoke environmental considerations during the formulation of policies concerning individual rights, property rights, and the role and power of government.

## Sustainable Development in the United States and OECD

A decade after the 1972 UN Stockholm Conference, the 1982 follow-up UN Nairobi Conference advanced the concept of "environmentally sound and sustainable socioeconomic development" (CEQ 1982, 223). In 1983, the UN General Assembly passed a resolution that led to establishment of the World Commission on Environment and Development (WCED) and urgently called for formation of long-term environmental strategies to achieve sustainable development by the year 2000 and beyond. Gro Harlem Brundtland, then Prime Minister of Norway, was named its chair.

In 1987, the Brundtland Commission published its report, *Our Common Future*, which argues that the environmental consequences of population increases and economic development have become intertwined. The report states that the development of the global economy and the protection of the global ecology may appear to be separate issues, but they are, in fact, different facets of the same problem:

> Until recently, the planet was a large world in which human activities and their effects were neatly compartmentalized within nations, within sectors (energy, agriculture, trade), and within broad areas of concern (environmental, economic, social). These compartments have begun to dissolve. This applies in particular to the various global "crises" that have seized public concern, particularly over the last decade. These are not separate crises: an environmental crisis, a development crisis, an energy crisis. They are one.[5] (WCED 1987, 356–357)

*Our Common Future* defines the concept of sustainable development in very simple terms. Humanity has the ability to make development sustainable—to ensure that development meets the needs of the present without compromising the ability of future generations to meet their own needs (WCED 1987, 4). According to the report, the sustainable development concept is not rigid. It can be interpreted flexibly, depending on scientific, social, economic, and political circumstances. Moreover, such circumstances help to define how the costs of sustainable development are to be characterized and, ultimately, how the costs are to be borne. The report also stresses that international efforts to protect the environment in the 1990s must include various domestic issues:

• Population and its effect on natural resources and economic development, including (1) food security—making food available where needed; (2) species and ecosystems—maintaining biological diversity; and (3) energy—energy efficiency and conservation of energy sources

• Industry—use of less environmentally invasive technologies

• Urban challenge—proper planning and development of cities and establishment of settlement practices

In 1992, the United Nations convened the Conference on Environment and Development (UNCED) in Rio. A major purpose of the conference was to commit governments to the sustainable development concept. The concept of sustainable development appears in the various products of the conference, which included [Agenda 21] a compilation of principles for the twenty-first century. By agreeing to Agenda 21, the United States committed itself to sustainable development. Goklany and Sprague (1992), U.S. government officials writing in their private capacity after the UNCED meeting, explained that sustainable development means different things to different people. Its definition is intentionally vague in order to have wide appeal and to increase the possibility of compromise on thorny issues on which reasonable people may differ. Goklany and Sprague believe that "development" implies balancing economic and environmental goals, and "sustainable" implies a full consideration of environmental factors. It is abundantly clear, however, that to others the term implies the absence of additional economic development. The latter position is based on the argument—made with great emotion but insufficient facts and analysis—that the current path of development is clearly unsustainable because the planet is about to suffocate on humanity's wastes and there is insufficient land to meet everyone's demands. Even though that faction, inherently suspicious of technological change and economic growth, has not obtained all that it wanted, it is much closer to its goal as laid out explicitly in the early drafts of the Agenda 21 documents.

Jerry Taylor (1997), Director of Natural Resources at the Cato Institute, points outs the illogic in making sustainable development a single overriding criterion for public policy.

> While sustainability can certainly be an important consideration for certain economic or social arrangements, it does not necessarily follow that it should be elevated to the status of some overriding criterion for public policy. . . . We must make a distinction between sustainability as a purely technical concept, and optimality, which is a normative concept. Many economic activities that are unsustainable may be perfectly optimal, and many that are sustainable may not be desirable, let alone optimal. (Section 2. "Technical Definition")

Taylor goes on to point out that a "hard" definition of sustainable development is circular and irrational. For example, no generation would ever be permitted to draw down stocks of natural resources, no matter how great the need, because other generations would always follow. Thus, sustainable development cannot be thought of as maximizing the options for future generations because all generations are denied the right to exercise these options. Because of the impracticality of this definition, a "weak" definition is used, allowing for some natural resources to be depleted as long as adequate compensation is provided by increases in other resources. The question then arises, What is adequate compensation? Taylor's answer is that what society is actually aiming for is not sustainability but the maximization of welfare. And, thus, the concept of sustainable development is not a sustainable idea.

In agreeing to UNCED's Agenda 21 (UNCED chapters 8, 38), the United States supported not only the sustainable development concept but also the establishment of a U.S. National Council for Sustainable Development (NCSD) to implement sustainable development strategies and policies. UNCED's Agenda 21 recommended the establishment of NCSDs in each nation to effect the implementation of sustainable development strategies and policies by governments. These worldwide efforts are directed by the Earth Council and its chair, Maurice Strong, who also chaired the 1972 UN Stockholm Conference and the 1992 UNCED. Strong was also the first UNEP director. NCSDs are viewed as key mechanisms for phasing in and implementing worldwide sustainable development policy and practice. Strong's Earth Council (1998) sees these national councils as the means of realizing the potential of the Rio agreements and of sustainable development on a national and local level.

President Clinton (1993) established the President's Council on Sustainable Development to formalize his sustainable development effort in 1993. By executive order, Clinton defined sustainable development "as economic growth that will benefit present and future generations without detrimentally affecting the resources or biological systems of the planet" (Clinton 1993, Section 2).

The Council on Sustainable Development (1996) envisions a "life-sustaining Earth."

We are committed to achievement of a dignified, peaceful, and equitable existence. A sustainable United States will have a growing

economy that provides equitable opportunities for satisfying liveli-
hoods and a safe, healthy, high quality of life for current and future
generations. Our nation will protect its environment, its natural resource base, and the functions and viability of natural systems on
which all life depends. (iv)

The council's mandate goes well beyond simply advising the president. By clever lawyering, the council's revised charter gets
around the federal restriction that advisory bodies should only
provide advice. The charter states that the council "will carry out
its mission to advise the President on matters involving sustainable development by carrying out four essential objectives"
(Council on Sustainable Development 1997, 3):

1. Forging consensus on policy by bringing together diverse
interests to identify and develop innovative economic, environmental, and social policies and strategies that advance sustainable
development

2. Demonstrating the implementation of sustainable development in real-world settings

3. Getting the word out about sustainable development

4. Recommending national-, community-, and enterprise-
level frameworks for tracking sustainable development. (Council
on Sustainable Development 1997, 5)

The council's activities have extraordinary breadth. The council is to develop a vision of innovative environmental management that fosters sustainable development relying on the triad of
environment, economy, and equity.

The council is mandated not only to aid the proliferation of
national sustainable development councils, but also to recommend an international consensus on sustainable development
activities, including foreign investment.[6] Moreover, the council
is instructed to "ensure that social equity issues are fully inte-

grated into all of the Council's efforts" (Section 4, "Scope of Activities," subsection (e)). The council's mandate shows convincingly that sustainable development embraces all aspects of foreign and domestic social, economic, welfare, judicial, and education policy.[7]

Reacting to the March 1996 report of the President's Council, Fred Smith (1996) of the Competitiveness Enterprise Institute noted that the report serves two primary purposes. First, it gives credence to a whole array of discredited and failed welfare state programs, such as an adequate minimum wage, more federal job training, greater federal involvement in education, and more foreign aid. Second, the report recommends new environmental programs that would further exacerbate the anticompetitive and antigrowth features of environmental laws. Particularly objectionable is the recommendation for extended product responsibility.

## THE ORGANIZATION FOR ECONOMIC COOPERATION AND DEVELOPMENT

The Clinton administration's efforts on sustainable development, and those of Maurice Strong's Earth Council, reverberated in the recent major initiative of the Organization for Economic Cooperation and Development (OECD) in Paris. The OECD is the successor organization to the Marshall Plan.[8] Its twenty-nine member governments include the industrial nations and several emerging nations. The United States has been the largest financial contributor of the OECD, providing some 25 percent of its operating budget. The 1961 OECD convention charges the organization to promote policies that achieve the highest sustainable economic growth and employment and a rising standard of living in member countries, while maintaining financial stability, and thus contributing to the development of the world economy. These policies should also contribute to sound economic expansion in member as well as nonmember countries and contribute to the expansion of world trade on a multilateral, nondiscriminatory basis in accordance with international obligations.

The OECD has had an environment program since the early 1970s. The program reached agreement on various environmental issues in its report *Guiding Principles Concerning the International Aspects of Environment Policies,* which recommended that there be more stringent standards and that governments should harmonize their standards. The OECD has pursued international safety standards for chemicals and has pushed sustainable development as one aspect of its other environment programs.

In 1996 the new secretary general of the OECD established a special High-Level Advisory Group on Environment. Jonathan Lash, the co-chair of the group, was then co-chair of President Clinton's Council on Sustainable Development and president of the environmentally activist World Resources Institute. Thus, it was no surprise when the High-Level Advisory Group's 1997 report recommended that sustainable development should become an overarching theme for OECD activities.

The High-Level Advisory Group on the Environment (1997) reported that government policies addressing the economy, the environment, and equity remain badly disconnected. The group recommended that the OECD itself should, "as a matter of urgency, develop into the key intergovernmental organization providing the industrialized nations with the analytical and comparative framework of policy necessary for their economies to make the transition to sustainable development" (General Mandate 1.A.). The report proposed a new strategic direction for OECD.

> In harmonizing market systems and ecosystems, the OECD's main role should be to promote policies designed to make eco-efficiency profitable and eco-inefficiency unprofitable. It must become impossible for a company, a farm, a fishery, or any human enterprise to be financially successful while seriously degrading the value of

ecological goods and services. In the past OECD tested sectoral policies against economic and financial needs. Henceforth, it must test policies against economic, environmental, and social needs. (High-Level Advisory Group on the Environment, "Strategic Directions" 1997)

The High-Level Advisory Group (1997) also advocated that "OECD should work with governments further to develop systems of environmental governance to enable more effective coordination of necessary environmental, social, economic, and sectoral policies within and among nations"(11). To do this, the authors propose "nothing less than a new interpretation of the mission given the OECD in its original convention" ("Strategic Directions").

The OECD secretary general crafted the report into his own plan and presented it to the OECD governing council. His sustainable development objective was to "maximize human welfare, and provide a sound economic, social and environmental base for future generations" (www.oeco.org as of 10/12/98; no longer available). His major sustainable development projects included climate change; effect of support measures, taxes, and resource pricing; technology and sustainable development; and developing indicators of sustainable development.

The OECD, at its governing council meeting in April 1998, not only agreed that the achievement of sustainable development is a key priority for OECD countries,[9] but also agreed to newly interpret the term *sustainable economic growth* in its underlying OECD convention to add "social and environmental" to economic considerations. Thus, the U.S. government, represented by the executive branch, unilaterally concurred in an OECD agreement to redefine the organization's own mandate, presently defined in a treaty ratified by the U.S. Senate with a significantly different meaning.

The OECD Council also concurred in the elaboration of the organization's strategy for wide-ranging sustainable development efforts over the next three years in the areas of climate change, technological development, sustainability indicators, and the environmental impact of subsidies. The United States and the other OECD countries that form the OECD Council agreed to play their part in combating climate change by implementing national strategies, including measures such as clear targets and effective regulatory and economic measures, as well as through international cooperation. This commitment was made contrary to Congressional opposition to the United States implementing these measures absent ratification.

## THE PRECAUTIONARY PRINCIPLE

In 1990 the UN Economic Commission for Europe convened a conference in Bergen, Norway, for the implementation of the Brundtland Commission report, with ministerial representatives from European countries (as well as the United States and Canada). The Bergen declaration linked sustainable development to the precautionary principle.

> In order to achieve sustainable development, policies must be based on the precautionary principle. Environmental measures must anticipate, prevent and attack the causes of environmental degradation. Where there are threats of serious or irreversible damage, lack of full scientific certainty should not be used as a reason for postponing measures to prevent environmental regulation. (Danish EPA, The Precautionary Principle, Appendix http://www.mst.dk/199902pubs/87-7909-203-9/bil01_eng.htm)

The U.S. EPA (1998) has defined the precautionary principle as

> When information about potential risks is incomplete, basing decisions about the best ways to manage or reduce risks on a preference for avoiding unnecessary health risks instead of on unnecessary economic expenditures.

The precautionary principle has the following elements in its applications, according to Elizabeth Wilson (1997) and Tim O'Riordan and James Cameron (1994):

- Duty of care—shifting the burden of proof from a showing of risk to a showing of safety

- Preventive anticipation—willingness to take regulatory action in advance of scientific proof where inaction may be socially or environmentally costly

- Safeguarding ecological space—leaving wide margins of tolerance in environmental capacities

- The intrinsic value of the environment—"nature" is better in its "natural" state

- Proportionality of response—cost-effectiveness must broadly safeguard the environment

- Promoting the cause of intrinsic natural rights

- Paying for past ecological debt

- "Futuricity"—the future is uncertain, but needs to be given due weight

The precautionary principle could significantly change the guiding environmental impact assessment process that since 1970 has controlled government actions "significantly affecting the human environment."[10] Completion of an environmental impact statement (EIS) is a procedural requirement intended to bring transparency and thoughtfulness to government decisions. The EIS neither presumes an environmental impact, nor does it impose a particular environmental response regarding a proposed action. In contrast, the precautionary principle takes a proactive prescriptive approach toward environmental decision making. This alliteratively attractive concept shifts the burden of proof concerning safety toward environmental pessimism in those situations where a degree of uncertainty exists—a "chicken little" approach. By adopting the deceptively reasonable-sounding cautionary concept, the precautionary principle dictates taking government action to prevent a hypothecated harm whenever uncertainty exists over whether the harm might happen. Popular applications of the precautionary principle are actions proposed for climate change, the Biodiversity Convention's biosafety protocol, or the control of hormonally active agents in the biosphere.

As the free market–oriented Competitive Enterprise Institute views it, the precautionary principle—the proposition that new technologies or products should not be permitted until we know they will not endanger health, safety, or biodiversity—is central to the environmentalist's vision and underlies most nanny-state regulation.

Dr. Elizabeth M. Whelan, of the America Council on Science and Health, objects to the precautionary principle:

> First, it always assumes worst-case scenarios. Second, it distracts consumers and policy makers alike from the known and proven threats to human health. And third, it assumes no health detriment from the proposed regulations and restrictions. By that I mean that the Precautionary Principle overlooks the possibility that real public health risks can be associated with eliminating minuscule, hypothetical risks. As an ancient philosopher said, "It is a serious disease to worry over what has not occurred." (Whelan 1996)

In the mid-1980s, the Reagan White House had eliminated from EIS requirements in the United States the mischievous worst-case approach because of the trouble it caused by relying on dubious scientific information. The worst-case analysis is an open-ended opportunity to claim the possible nth degree result of a terrible consequence whenever there is incomplete or unavailable information regarding a particular environmental action. The revised CEQ regulation[11] deals with missing or unavailable information in a scientifically sound manner without presuming a worst case.

Christopher Douglass (1998), of the Center for the Study of American Business, has characterized an algorithm for the application of the precautionary principle. A series of domestic and international processes take place to learn more about a supposed environmental problem, with the twin goals of strengthening the "scientific support" and reaching an international agreement. Governments, UN agencies, and NGOs work together to develop a consensus on an international agreement through five steps:

1. Scientific or interest-group concern

2. Agenda-setting at unofficial conferences

3. Intergovernmental (usually ministerial level) meetings

4. Creation of a voluntary, or "soft," multilateral agreement

5. Development of a binding, or "hard," agreement

Douglass points out that this process approach has potential pitfalls. First, the problem can create political momentum that pushes policy beyond the mandate of science. Second, it can confer too much power on international agencies, thereby becoming a vehicle for agency self-aggrandizement. Lastly, the final product of the process, a binding agreement, can have serious repercussions on economies around the globe through the use of enforcement mechanisms such as trade sanctions. Douglass reviewed the U.S. climate change negotiations and concluded that, based upon this process approach, the United States is backing into a basic change in its global warming policy without the national debate that an issue of this magnitude warrants.

The precautionary principle has permeated a number of multilateral treaties, including the 1987 Montreal Protocol on Substances that Deplete the Ozone Layer, the 1992 Convention on Biological Diversity, the 1992 Climate Change Convention, the 1992 Treaty on European Union, the 1992 Convention for the

Protection of the Marine Environment of the North-East Atlantic, and the 1992 Helsinki Convention on protection of the Baltic marine environment. International declarations containing the precautionary principle include the 1990 Bergen Declaration, issued by ministerial representatives from European countries (as well as Canada and the United States), and the 1992 Rio Declaration on Environment and Development.


## CONCLUSION

On environmental matters, as well as other matters of vital human interest, warm and fuzzy rhetoric can give rise to pleasing feelings and bad public policy. Green foreign policy, sustainable development, and the precautionary principle can all be Trojan horses—using the cover of environmental concerns to drive broad social and political agendas.

For most of the twentieth century, the United States engaged in international environmental activities. For the past three decades, the intensity and scope of these activities have greatly increased at various government agencies. The newly announced State Department initiative to coalesce foreign policy around the environment appears designed more to raise the profile of the numerous aggressive environment initiatives than to establish a set of new activities. The State Department's spotlight on international environmental efforts, however, offers a good opportunity to look more closely at U.S. environmental activities. Likewise, focus on the environmental activities of international organizations offers a welcome opportunity for scrutiny of their activities by the public, public interest groups, and Congress.

We should be cautious when looking at the world through the concept of sustainable development when it is used for political purposes rather than for effective problem solving. A clear example of the political utility of sustainable development is the Clinton administration's Council on Sustainable Development, which advocates a government-centered perspective, primarily fueled with the fear of global warming. Not surprisingly, others, such as the OECD, have found the concept attractive for their own sustainable development. The OECD sustainable development initiative has a parallel to the Christopher/Albright foreign policy initiative. Both seek increased attention to and a new organizational focus on environmental issues that have obvious rhetorical and political traction. They both use existing resources by repackaging them, and they may use this increased attention as a means of gaining additional resources. In a sense, sustainable development is as much for the institutions themselves as for the environment they seek to protect.

Finally, the precautionary principle should be approached with extreme caution. The world does not need, nor could it benefit from, a policy that requires an a priori regulatory safety determination for the vast range of all human endeavors. Life is not risk free, nor is risk-free life a viable option.

## ENDNOTES

1. Concerns about loss of species led to the Fur Seal Convention of 1911; the Conventions, Protocols and Agreements regulating whaling initiated in 1931; the Antarctic Treaty (1959) and the related Polar Bear Conservation Agreement of 1973; and various fishery conventions and Conventions on Protection of Migratory Birds with Mexico (1936), Japan (1972), and the Soviet Union (1976).

2. The Declaration included the following:

> The protection and improvement of the human environment is a major issue which affects the well-being of peoples and economic development throughout the world; it is the urgent desire of the peoples of the whole world and the duty of all Governments.
>
> Man has a special responsibility to safeguard and wisely manage the heritage of wildlife and its habitat, which are now gravely imperilled by a combination of adverse factors.
>
> States have, in accordance with the Charter of the United Nations and the principles of international law, the sovereign right to exploit their own resources pursuant to their own environmental policies, and the responsibility to ensure that activities within their jurisdiction or control do not cause damage to the environment of other States or of areas beyond the limits of national jurisdiction.

States shall cooperate to develop further the international law regarding liability and compensation for the victims of pollution and other environmental damage caused by activities within the jurisdiction or control of such States to areas beyond their jurisdiction. (*Report of the United Nations Conference on the Human Environment,* Stockholm, June 5–16, United Nations, New York, 1972 pages 3–5)

3. The reference to the Convention on Biological Diversity contained the following text:

We come to Rio prepared to continue America's unparalleled efforts to preserve species and habitat. And let me be clear. Our efforts to protect biodiversity itself will exceed, will exceed, the requirements of the treaty. But that proposed agreement threatens to retard biotechnology and undermine the protection of ideas. Unlike the climate agreement, its financing scheme will not work. And it is never easy, it is never easy to stand alone on principle, but sometimes leadership requires that you do. And now is such a time. (President Bush, address to UNCED, June 12, 1992, The George Bush Presidential Library Presidential Papers. http://www.csdl.tamu.edu/bush-lib/papers/1992/92061200.html)

4. Secretary Christopher said the following:

The United States is providing the leadership to promote global peace and prosperity. We must also lead in safeguarding the global environment on which that prosperity and peace ultimately depend. . . . As the flagship institution of American foreign policy, the State Department must spearhead a government-wide effort to meet these environmental challenges. Together with other government agencies, we are pursuing our environmental priorities—globally, regionally, bilaterally, and in partnership with business and nongovernmental organizations. Each of these four dimensions is essential to the success of our overall strategy. (Christopher 1996)

5. The World Commission on Environment and Development selected eight issues for analysis during the course of its work: (1) Perspective on Population, Environment, and Sustainable Development; (2) Energy; (3) Industry; (4) Food, Security, Agriculture, and Forestry; (5) Human Settlements; (6) International Economic Relations; (7) Decision Support Systems for Environmental Management; and (8) International Cooperation.

6. Specifically, the council shall promote the creation and continuation of national sustainable development councils around the world, advise the president on the promotion of sustainable development in international fora, and gather and disseminate information about U.S. and international sustainable development policies. In addition, given the increasing flow of financial capital from developed to developing countries, the council shall recommend policies that encourage foreign

investment by the U.S. government, businesses, investors, and, as appropriate, multilateral institutions that are consistent with the principles of sustainable development.

7.  Goal 1 (goals are from the President's Council on Sustainable Development): Health and the Environment—Ensure that every person enjoys the benefits of clean air, clean water, and a healthy environment at home, at work, and at play.

Goal 2: Economic Prosperity—Sustain a healthy U.S. economy that grows sufficiently to create meaningful jobs, reduce poverty, and provide the opportunity for a high quality of life for all in an increasingly competitive world.

Goal 3: Equity—Ensure that all Americans are afforded justice and have the opportunity to achieve economic, environmental, and social well being.

Goal 4: Conservation of Nature—Use, conserve, protect, and restore natural resources—land, air, water, and biodiversity—in ways that help ensure long-term social, economic, and environmental benefits for ourselves and future generations.

Goal 5: Stewardship—Create a widely held ethic of stewardship that strongly encourages individuals, institutions, and corporations to take full responsibility for the economic, environmental, and social consequences of their actions.

Goal 6: Sustainable Communities—Encourage people to work together to create healthy communities where natural and historic resources are preserved, jobs are available, sprawl is contained, neighborhoods are secure, education is lifelong, transportation and health care are accessible, and all citizens have opportunities to improve the quality of their lives.

Goal 7: Civic Engagement—Create full opportunity for citizens, businesses, and communities to participate in and influence the natural resource, environmental, and economic decisions that affect them.

Goal 8: Population—Move toward stabilization of U.S. population.

Goal 9: International Responsibility—Take a leadership role in the development and implementation of global sustainable development policies, standards of conduct, and trade and foreign policies that further the achievement of sustainability.

Goal 10: Education—Ensure that all Americans have equal access to education and lifelong learning opportunities that will prepare them for meaningful work, a high quality of life, and an understanding of the concepts involved in sustainable development.

8. The OECD is successor to the Organization for European Economic Cooperation (OEEC), the post–World War II coalition of

European countries grouped to rebuild war-ravaged economies using U.S. aid under the Marshall Plan. In 1961, OEEC was transformed into OECD by the United States, Canada, and the European countries to continue to assist the newly rebuilt economies. Within the next dozen years, Japan, Australia, New Zealand, and Finland joined, and within the past several years, Mexico, the Czech Republic, Hungary, Poland, and South Korea joined. Based in Paris, the OECD now consists of twenty-nine member governments. OECD maintains contact with the rest of the world through dialogue and cooperation programs in the countries of the former Soviet bloc, Asia, and Latin America.

The OECD convention charges the organization to promote policies designed to:

- Achieve the highest sustainable economic growth and employment and a rising standard of living in member countries, while maintaining financial stability, and thus contribute to the development of the world economy;

- Contribute to sound economic expansion in member as well as non-member countries in the process of economic development; and contribute to the expansion of world trade on a multilateral, non-discriminatory basis in accordance with international obligations.

OECD member countries are Australia (1971), Austria (1961), Belgium (1961), Canada (1961), the Czech Republic (1995), Denmark (1961), Finland (1969), France (1961), Germany (1961), Greece (1961), Hungary (1996), Iceland (1961), Ireland (1961), Italy (1961), Japan (1964), South Korea (1996), Luxemburg (1961), Mexico (1994), The Netherlands (1961), New Zealand (1973), Norway (1961), Poland (1996), Portugal (1961), Spain (1961), Sweden (1961), Switzerland (1961), Turkey (1961), the United Kingdom (1961), and the United States (1961).

9. The communiqué of the April 1998 Ministerial Meeting stated the following:

Ministers agreed that the achievement of sustainable development is a key priority for OECD countries. They encouraged the elaboration of the Organization's strategy for wide-ranging efforts over the next three years in the areas of climate change, technological development, sustainability indicators, and the environmental impact of subsidies. . . . Further, Ministers asked the OECD to enhance its dialogue with non-member countries in these areas and to engage them more actively, including through shared analyses and development of strategies for implementing sustainable development. (OECD News Release, Paris, April 28, 1998, http://www.oecd.org/daf/clp/Recommendations/nw98-51a.htm)

10. The U.S.-initiated concept is found in the *National Environmental Policy Act of 1969* (Public Law 91-190, 4321–4347), as amended by Public Law 94-52 (July 3, 1975) and Public Law 94-83 (August 9, 1975). Section 102.(C) of the act requires agencies of the federal government to:

Include in every recommendation or report on proposals for legislation and other major Federal actions significantly affecting the quality of the human environment, a detailed statement by the responsible official on—

1. The environmental impact of the proposed action,

2. Any adverse environmental effects which cannot be avoided should the proposal be implemented,

3. Alternatives to the proposed action,

4. The relationship between local short-term uses of man's environment and the maintenance and enhancement of long-term productivity, and

5. Any irreversible and irretrievable commitments of resources which would be involved in the proposed action should it be implemented. (P.L. 91–190, Sec. 102(c)(i)–(v))

11. Council on Environmental Quality, Executive Office of the President, Regulations for Implementing the Procedural Provisions of the National Environmental Policy Act, 40 CFR 1502.22. (b) If the information relevant to reasonably foreseeable significant adverse impacts cannot be obtained because the overall costs of obtaining it are exorbitant or the means to obtain it are not known, the agency shall include within the environmental impact statement:

1.    a statement that such information is incomplete or unavailable;

2.    a statement of the relevance of the incomplete or unavailable information to evaluating reasonably foreseeable significant adverse impacts on the human environment;

3.    a summary of existing credible scientific evidence which is relevant to evaluating the reasonably foreseeable significant adverse impacts on the human environment; and

4.    the agency's evaluation of such impacts based upon theoretical approaches or research methods generally accepted in the scientific community. For the purposes of this section, "reasonably foreseeable" includes impacts which have catastrophic consequences, even if their probability of occurrence is low, provided that the analysis of the impacts is supported by credible scientific evidence, is not based on pure conjecture, and is within the rule of reason.

## REFERENCES

Albright, Madeleine K. 1997. Environmental Diplomacy: The Environment and U.S. Foreign Policy. 22 April at Washington, D.C.

———. 1998. Earth Day 1998: Global Problems and Global Solutions. 21 April at Washington, D.C.

Baker, James A. 1992. Remarks to the Intergovernmental Panel on Climate Change. 30 January at Washington, D.C.

Bush, George H. W. 1992. Address to the United Nations Conference on Environment and Development. 12 June at Rio de Janeiro, Brazil.

Christopher, Warren. 1996. American Diplomacy and the Global Environmental Challenges of the 21st Century. 9 April at Stanford University, Palo Alto, California.

Clinton, William J. 1993. Executive Order No. 12852, June 29.

Council on Environmental Quality (CEQ). 1982. *Environmental Quality: 12th Annual Report*. Washington, D.C.: GPO.

———. 1985. *Environmental Quality: 15th Annual Report*. Washington, D.C.: GPO.

———. 1990. *Environmental Quality: 20th Annual Report*. Washington, D.C.: GPO.

Council on Sustainable Development. 1996. *Sustainable America* (March). Washington, D.C.

———. 1997. *Revised Charter*. Washington, D.C. April 25.

Douglass, Christopher. 1998. Environmental Crossing Guards: International Environmental Treaties and U.S. Foreign Policy, Working Paper #168. Center for the Study of American Business. May.

Douma, Wybe Th. 1996. The Precautionary Principle. Icelandic Legal Journal *Úlfljótur* (vol. 49, nrs. 3/4, p. 417–430). Updated and amended at <http://eel.nl/virtue/precprin.htm>.

Earth Council. 1998. National Councils for Sustainable Development. *Mechanisms for Civil-Society Participation in Decision-Making and for Localizing Sustainable Development*. At <http://www.ncsdnetwork.org/global/reports/background.htm> (9/17/98).

Goklany, Indur M., and Sprague, Merritt W. 1992. *Sustaining Development and Biodiversity: Productivity, Efficiency, and Conservation*. Policy Analysis No. 175. August 6.

Goodman, Sherri W. 1997. Speech to Army War College on 10 February. www.denix.osd.mil/denix/PUBLIC/ES-Programs/speeches/speech/speech-25.html. Viewed 10/7/98. At <http://denix.cecer.army.mil/denix/Public/ES-Programs/Speeches/speech-25.html>.

High-Level Advisory Group on the Environment. 1997. *Guiding the Transition to Sustainable Development: A Critical Role for the OECD*. Paris: OECD. http://www.oecd.org/subject/sustdev/hlage.htm.

Lewis, Marlo. 1997. *Precautionary Petard*. The Competitiveness Enterprise Institute. At <http://jupiter.cei.org/update/0697-ml.html>.

O'Riordan, Tim, and Cameron, James (eds.). 1994. *Interpreting the Precautionary Principle*. Earthscan Publicans. At <http://www.aloha.net/~jhanson/page31.htm>.

Schoenbrod, David. 1998. *Time for the Federal Environmental Aristocracy to Give Up Power*. Policy Study 144. St. Louis: Center for the Study of American Business.

Taylor, Jerry. 1997. Cato Institute Conference on China as a Global Economic Power. *Sustainable Development in China: An Agenda in Search of a Problem* (June 18). At <http://www.cato.org/events/china/papers/taylor.html>. Viewed 9/20/98.

United Nations Conference on Environment and Development (UNCED). 1992. *Agenda 21*. (June 14). At <gopher://unephq.unep.org:70/11/un/unced/agenda21>.

———. 1992. *Rio Declaration on Environment and Development*. At <http://www.unep.org/unep/rio.htm>.

U.S. Department of State. 1997. Strategic Plan. At <http://www.state.gov/www/global/general_foreign_policy/dosglobal_1.html>. Viewed 9/10/98.

U.S. Environmental Protection Agency (EPA). 1998. Terms of Environment, Revised Edition, 13 May. At <http://www.epa.gov/OCEPAterms/>. Viewed 9/20/98.

U.S. Public Law 91-190. 4321–4347, 1 January, 1970. *National Environmental Policy Act of 1969*.

Wilson, Elizabeth. 1997. ISOCARP-JAPA World Planning Congress. Ogaki, Japan, 17–20 September. At <http://www.soc.titech.ac.jp/uem/governance/precaution.html>.

World Commission on Environment and Development (WCED). 1987. *Our Common Future*. New York: Oxford University Press.

# CHAPTER 5

# Sustainable Development:
# The Green Road to Serfdom?

## *James M. Sheehan*

## INTRODUCTION

The unifying theme of sustainable development has become enshrined in a growing number of environmental treaties and international summits. Norwegian Prime Minister Gro Harlem Brundtland coined the term in 1987, when she chaired the World Commission on Environment and Development and published what has become the bible of the global environmental movement, *Our Common Future.*

On its face, sustainable development sounds innocuous, suggesting a moderate approach to the global environment in which resources are managed prudently as the economy grows. In this respect, the idea appears less alarmist than previous generations of environmentalism, which demanded an immediate halt to industrial activity to avert an imminent eco-catastrophe. Having failed to convince the world to renounce economic growth, environmentalists have adopted a more congenial, less threatening message. However, sustainable development is still based on the earlier premise that current consumption levels are not ecologically sustainable, and therefore, it reaches the virtually identical conclusion that consumption must be politically controlled throughout the world.

Sustainable development is not only an international repackaging of the powerful environmentalist cause, but also an overarching political philosophy merging the twin goals of conservation and controlled economic development. *Our Common Future* defines sustainable development as "a framework for the integration of environment policies and development strategies" on a global basis such that all trade, capital, and technology flows are "better synchronized to environmental imperatives" (WCED 1987, 40–41). It puts forth sustainable development as the central organizing principle for a world of economically and ecologically interdependent nations. A 1995 sequel, entitled *Our Global Neighborhood*, compiled by the Commission on Global Governance,[1] reiterates the point that "environmental sustainability requires restraint on consumption at the global level" (Commission on Global Governance 1995, 145). The latter volume weaves sustainable development into a broad agenda for world economic planning to be coordinated internationally through the UN system. Sustainable development is a recipe for the creation of a vast array of economic regulations and an expansion of global political institutions that pose a unique threat to individual liberty and economic progress.

## GLOBALIZING ENVIRONMENTAL POLICY

A potent mixture of economic, environmental, and security imperatives is driving the movement toward global planning for sustainable development. The need to protect the global environment is seen by many internationalists as the last best hope of resurrecting the dormant Keynesian schemes for world economic planning conceived after World War II. Council on Foreign Relations senior fellow Jessica Tuchman Mathews illustrates the parallel by declaring that the early Earth Summit negotiations may someday be seen "in the same light we now see Bretton Woods, as one of the places where the rules of a new order were born" (Mathews 1991, C7).

The premise of the new "green" multilateralism is that environmental concerns are interconnected with all human activities—that all environmental problems are essentially global. Environmental problems are becoming more global as economies are increasingly integrated. Technological innovations in telecom-

munications, transportation, trade, and finance have facilitated
the instantaneous movement of capital around the globe. This
globalization of world markets is seen as inherently threatening to
the environment: "Growing economic interdependence brings in
its wake freer trade in 'bads' as well as goods," warns the
Commission on Global Governance (1995, 135–151). National
governments are powerless to protect the environment. Economic
integration has allowed private capital to evade government regulation by relocating to more favorable jurisdictions. Multilateral
cooperation, which curtails regulatory competition between national governments, is the only way to restore top-down planning
and control of the market. An international framework of restrictions on individual and economic freedoms—on trade, on economic and technological progress, on the use of energy, on agriculture—must be enacted to ensure the survival of the planet.
"The United Nations charter may still forbid outside interference
in the domestic affairs of member states, but unequivocally 'domestic' concerns are becoming an endangered species," writes
Mathews (1991, C7).

If environmental and economic problems transcend national
boundaries, then, so the argument goes, political authority must
also transcend national boundaries. National sovereignty is seen as
an obsolete and antiquated relic of an older order. The political infrastructure must be updated for sustainable development, and
when the metamorphosis is complete, a new world order of shared
sovereignty must emerge. "In dealing with global environmental
problems, it is only by surrendering a bit of national sovereignty
and by participating in an international regime that we can ensure
our freedom from environmental harms and protection of our own
natural resources," explains Daniel C. Esty (1994, 93), Senior
Fellow of the Institute for International Economics.

Characterizing all environmental threats as global converts the
environment into a national security concern not unlike organized
crime, drug trafficking, or terrorism. "The fears of nuclear conflict
that once exercised enormous power over people's minds and
translated into political support for today's massive defense estab-
lishments are declining. But certain environmental threats could

come to have the same power over people's minds" (MacNeill, Winsemius, and Yakushiji 1991, 69).

Because protection of the "global" environment can only be achieved collectively, sustainable development as currently understood is the basis for large-scale ecological central planning and the accumulation of power and resources in the state. Like the doctrine of collective security, which gives war-making powers to international institutions such as NATO and the United Nations, sustainable development is a justification for amassing increasingly potent regulatory and police powers in the United Nations and associated organizations. To carry out its responsibilities, the United Nations must be given detection and monitoring capabilities to counter global environmental threats, similar to the authority it now has to spy on missile sites and chemical weapons plants. According to Mathews (1991), "Intelligence collection, risk assessment, contingency planning, budget projection, and all the other elements of a national response to a traditional [security] threat will be far more complex" (C7) in a global environmental regime.

Although the movement to transfer sovereignty to a global regime has not yet produced a powerful global superagency, it has effectively centralized international law, with profound implications for traditional political relationships. In a global sustainable development regime, nation-states are relegated to internally enforcing internationally negotiated standards. Thus, nation-states have no real independence; they function as administrative units of a global regime. Likewise, individuals have almost no role, except perhaps to lobby for more powers for the state (Mathews 1989; MacNeill, Winsemius, and Yakushiji 1991; Sand 1990).

## LAUNCHING SUSTAINABLE DEVELOPMENT: THE EARTH SUMMIT

A coordinated effort to institute sustainable development was launched officially at the UN Conference on Environment and Development, or the Earth Summit, held in Rio de Janeiro in June 1992. This effort set in motion a flurry of activity to implement the global transition to sustainability and to save the planet from supposed imminent ecological danger. The conference's Secretary General, Maurice Strong (1992), described the transition to sustainability as a profound change in the political, social, and economic order:

> The change will have an effect on the structure of industry and relationships between industry and society, as profound as anything that has taken place since the industrial revolution; indeed, it adds up to a veritable "eco-industrial revolution" in which environmental considerations will more and more drive economic policy and industrial transformation. (1)

If the United Nations is to preside over an eco-industrial revolution, the presumption is that economic expansion cannot be sustained without planning and direction from government. The revolutionary terminology also implies that current modes of production and consumption are fundamentally unstable. As Strong, a Canadian multimillionaire himself, lamented: "Lifestyles of the rich . . . are the source of the primary risks to our common future. They are simply not sustainable" (Strong 1992, 1).

The transition to sustainability will no doubt require a period of painful adjustment and restructuring in many areas of the U.S. economy and culture. Strong's Earth Summit called for placing restrictions on virtually every sector of industry, including energy, forestry, mining, chemical, and automotive—indeed on every part of the economy that requires transportation, packaging, or the use of fossil fuels. Participating governments, including the United States, signed Agenda 21, an 800-page blueprint for sustainable development planning through the twenty-first century. The agreement details international coordination of numerous trade, technology, social, demographic, health, and land use policies. The similar *Rio Declaration on Environment and Development* outlined twenty-seven broad sustainable development principles. As the overindulgent "rich" in industrial societies are converted to a life of "sophisticated modesty," their wealth will be redistributed to the developing countries to pay for the changes sustainable development will bring to the Third World (Strong 1992; United Nations 1992a; United Nations 1992b).

Two important framework conventions were negotiated in preparation for Rio:

1.  **The Global Climate Convention.** The preeminent threat to
the planet is said to be global warming—the fear that a buildup of
carbon dioxide and other greenhouse gases in the atmosphere will
cause the earth's temperature to rise dramatically. Signed at the
Earth Summit, the Framework Convention on Climate Change
entered into force in 1994 with the goal of stabilizing emissions of
carbon dioxide—a greenhouse gas—at 1990 levels by the year
2000. All signatories are required to take inventories of their emissions and to submit action plans detailing how emissions will be
reduced. Although most nations are expected to fall short of their
present commitments, signatories from more than 160 nations
pledged at a Berlin conference to complete by 1997 a legally binding convention protocol to target greenhouse gas emission levels
after the year 2000 (Kinzer 1995).

2.  **The Convention on Biological Diversity.** As with the climate convention, the Convention on Biological Diversity sets up
an international framework for environmental protection. The
convention calls for national plans and strategies to maintain genetic diversity, as well as a national biological survey to inventory
existing species. Implicit in the protection plan is the concept of
ecosystem management, which stresses the interconnectedness of
all life. National governments are expected to pass legislation
regulating access to genetic resources within their borders. The
convention also contains controversial provisions regarding intellectual property rights and technology transfer, both of which
protect patents on biotechnologies and facilitate the equitable
sharing of those technologies derived from biodiversity.[2]

The many post–Earth Summit international initiatives are
aimed at progressively strengthening government coordination of
the world's economy and environment. After the Earth Summit,
the United Nations formed a Commission on Sustainable Development to follow up the Rio process and to monitor the implementation of Agenda 21. Conferences of the parties for two major
treaties have met to press for action on climate change and biodiversity. In September 1994, Cairo hosted the International
Conference on Population and Development, which was convened

to step up global population control measures to restrict the world's human population to a target level of 9.8 billion by 2050. The March 1995 Conference on Social Development gathered world leaders in Copenhagen to focus attention on world poverty, unemployment, and sustainable development. The Commission on Global Governance has taken the dramatic step of proposing an Economic Security Council, similar to the UN Security Council, to promote sustainable development. Perhaps reflecting the immense costs of such an endeavor, the council would be funded through a variety of global taxes on corporations, foreign exchange transactions, air and sea transportation, ocean fishing, or use of orbital satellites and the electromagnetic spectrum. Global commons resources would be placed under the UN Trusteeship Council, as would the administrative functions for environmental treaties. The Commission on Global Governance defines *commons* in exceedingly broad terms: the atmosphere, the oceans, outer space, and "related environment and life-support systems that contribute to the support of human life" (Commission on Global Governance 1995, 251–252).

Despite considerably well-orchestrated international activity, the apparent lack of interest among peoples and governments of the world has slowed earlier momentum. In part, this slowing is due to the enormous economic costs implied by the energy restrictions, taxation schemes, and foreign aid transfers that comprise the global environmental program. Sustainable development is a very expensive proposition. Agenda 21, if implemented in its entirety, would cost in excess of $600 billion, including $125 billion in new foreign aid transfers. The current international focus on environmental governance represents an attempt to jump-start the process, begun in Rio, of forging a consensus for international cooperation on a range of environmental issues.

## ENVIRONMENTAL TREATIES AND THE DEVELOPMENT OF INTERNATIONAL LAW

The sustainable development concept has become embedded in a variety of multilateral environment agreements and international institutions. The first wave of environmental treaties began in 1972, spurred by the UN Conference on the Human Environment in Stockholm. The Earth Summit accelerated this process. More than 180 environmental agreements are in force today (WTO 1994, 1).

The sustainable development principles in the Rio Declaration form a sort of global ecological charter. The declaration urges governments to cooperate "in the further development of international law in the field of sustainable development." International law generally obligates nations not to permit degradation of the global commons and to prevent transboundary pollution. Thus, the global environment is effectively placed within international jurisdiction, to be safeguarded by multilateral agreement. The Rio Declaration states that governments are obligated, under the UN charter, to "ensure that activities within their jurisdiction or control do not cause damage to the environment of other States or of areas beyond the limits of national jurisdiction."[3] The all-encompassing Rio charter also requires governments to enact legislation to eliminate the "unsustainable patterns of production and consumption" (United Nations 1992b) that are responsible for pollution.[4]

To carry out this objective, Agenda 21 obligates each government, in cooperation with international organizations, "to adopt a national strategy for sustainable development." If a national sustainable development strategy sounds like an attenuated variant of the communist five-year-plan, it is because the two have common ideological roots. Although most First World countries have had difficulty formulating a sustainable development plan, communist China adapted one almost effortlessly. Beijing's State Planning Commission unveiled its national Agenda 21 plan for agricultural, energy, and population control policies in April 1994 (United Nations 1992a; Reuters 1994).

No treaty was as pathbreaking in extending the reach of international law as the 1987 Montreal Protocol, an agreement for the protection of the ozone layer. This treaty, which produced an unprecedented system of international regulation, is considered a landmark multilateral achievement and a model for future agreements. Through the nonbinding 1985 Vienna Convention, the world community pledged to protect the stratospheric ozone layer.

The Vienna Convention did not contain many binding commitments, but it set in motion a momentum-building process that would lead to a subsequent binding protocol—the 1987 Montreal Protocol. The Montreal Protocol mandated the phaseout of all chemical compounds thought to pose a threat to the stratospheric ozone layer. All production of chloroflourocarbon refrigerants (CFCs), for example, must have ceased by 1996 under this agreement.

More important than its policy implications was the Montreal Protocol's institutional impact. It became the prototype for the incremental evolution of nonbinding conventions into formally binding protocols, a phenomenon described as "the hardening of soft law." Through customary use, nonbinding instruments and practices gradually accrue legal status and are used to lay the groundwork for binding commitments. The interaction of UN-organized scientific assessment bodies, ideological activist groups, and national environmental officials provides the catalyst for increasingly stringent government regulations. The convention-protocol model effectively draws many nations into an international regulatory regime. It was employed in global climate change and biodiversity negotiations at the Earth Summit. When the climate convention was signed in Rio, Jessica Tuchman Mathews (1992b) noted its importance in terms of institutional momentum: "This is going to start a process that isn't going to be walked backwards."

The quick triumphs of the ozone layer and climate change conventions contrast sharply with the languishing Law of the Sea convention, which was spurned by the United States in 1982. After fifteen years of negotiation, the Law of the Sea withstood a twelve-year hiatus before finally entering into force in 1994. Although the United States still has not ratified this convention, many of the convention's provisions have come to be recognized as international law. The Law of the Sea forms a global environmental protection regime for the oceans, placing marine resources under international jurisdiction. The oceans are declared the "common heritage of mankind" that must be shared through a "just and equitable economic order" (French 1992, 158–159).

The treaty is extremely wide-ranging, incorporating numerous agreements that regulate ocean dumping, mining and oil exploration, maritime shipping, and fisheries harvesting. Disputes are arbitrated by an international tribunal, and the International Seabed Authority oversees deep-sea mining and the transfer of mining technology to developing countries. Nations are given a specific responsibility to prevent marine pollution (from cities, for example) within a two hundred–mile zone from the coastline. The Earth Summit, through the Agenda 21 agreement, provided the impetus for the negotiation of more extensive treaties on fisheries and land-based sources of marine pollution, which may lead to international standards in these areas (Weber 1994).

The Law of the Sea effort faltered, in part, because it was overly ambitious; its seemingly limitless scope made the treaty too contentious for rapid conclusion. Industrialized nations were reluctant to cede so much power to developing countries within the ocean's regime. Frustration with the Law of the Sea's cumbersome pace caused negotiators to abandon a proposed Law of the Atmosphere, which would have been a similar umbrella-style convention. Instead, smaller initiatives on the ozone layer and global warming were pursued (Sand 1990, 19).

The various multilateral treaties have one thing in common—their effect on national sovereignty is quickly becoming distinctive. Expansion of the Law of the Sea through multilateral fisheries agreements, for instance, causes countries to cede sovereignty over coastal waters. Mathews (1992a) praised the climate convention "because it is so potentially invasive of domestic sovereignty," noting that it has the potential of "forcing governments to change domestic policies to a much greater degree than any other international treaty . . . with the possible exception of the Helsinki Accords as they affected Eastern Europe, which led quite unexpectedly to the collapse of the Warsaw Pact."

## THE GREENING OF TRADE

The growth of globalist environmental restrictions is having a discernible effect on international trade. In the case of the Montreal Protocol, trade in CFC products with nonparties to the convention is banned during the phaseout period. This trade provision is intended as an inducement for participation in the agreement and to prevent countries from gaining trade advantages by remaining outside the agreement. Differential regulations of this sort, though integral to the agreement's purpose, impose significant barriers to trade. Indeed, a primary reason U.S. CFC producers supported the treaty was because they feared compliance with federal regulations would leave them at a trade disadvantage against competitors abroad. Global regulation seemed like the lesser of two evils (Benedick 1991; McInnis 1992).

Green trade barriers were developed further in the 1989 Basel Convention on the Control and Transboundary Movement of Hazardous Wastes and Their Disposal, which regulates trade in a variety of waste, scrap, and recyclable materials. The agreement establishes burdensome international standards for the production, transport, and disposal of a long list of "environmentally sensitive" materials. The various regulated items consist of wastes containing trace amounts of lead, copper, zinc, and other metals and their related compounds. Pharmaceutical wastes, hydrocarbons, solvents, and other chemical residues are included in the treaty's extensive list of controlled substances. Although Basel's trade restrictions thwart specialization under free trade, they are quite counterproductive environmentally. By increasing transportation and compliance costs, developing countries are excluded from world waste disposal and recycling markets and are thereby cut off from significant economic opportunities. By limiting the availability of waste disposal and recycling services, Basel markedly raises the environmental costs associated with these activities (Evans 1995).

Basel imposes an outright ban on commerce in listed products between industrialized OECD nations and developing countries (non-OECD) and between signatories and nonsignatories. It also creates complex export notification and consent requirements for trade in these materials. The Basel Convention does not furnish the United Nations with regulatory enforcement powers, so it does not displace national governments altogether. Instead, the agreement facilitates reciprocal recognition of national trade licenses in which national bureaucracies mutually enforce each other's standards. Thus, the power to authorize or restrict trade is left to national licensing bodies collaborating internationally to promote the global compatibility or harmonization of environmental regulations (Sand 1990, 40).

The antimarket bias is likewise prevalent in the 1973 Convention on Trade in Endangered Species (CITES), which regulates the $8 billion trade in wildlife and wildlife products. CITES prohibits commerce in certain categories of endangered and threatened species, even with nonsignatories. For example, trade in elephant ivory has been banned under the convention, even though commerce would protect elephants more effectively by imparting economic value to conservation of the species. As with Basel, CITES's global regime of trade permits and controls is enforced by signatory governments acting in tandem (Sand 1990, 40).

The sustainable development concept is slowly permeating a number of reciprocal trade pacts and regional economic entities, establishing a growing linkage between trade and the environment. Regional integration of trade and environmental policies was pioneered in the European Community, where Basel-style collaborative standards are applied across the board. To minimize trade disputes between European states, a broad range of environmental standards is harmonized at a minimum level that member countries may exceed. Policy convergence is also facilitated by the reciprocal recognition of other members' environmental standards (Esty 1994, 174–176; French 1993, 56–57).

The North American Free Trade Agreement (NAFTA) between the United States, Mexico, and Canada has several environmental components that complement its reciprocal trade provisions. The main treaty incorporates the trade barriers of the Montreal Protocol, the Basel Convention, and CITES. It also prevents the relaxation of environmental standards within the trade bloc to attract investment. An environmental side agreement moves further toward collaborative environmental policy making by establishing a trilateral review process to promote environmental enforcement and to harmonize environmental policies over time. A North American Commission on Environmental Cooperation oversees the effective enforcement of national environmental laws and serves as a mechanism to settle disputes through a lengthy arbitration process, which can result in trade sanctions for noncompliance.

With the lowest standards in the trade bloc, Mexico will be affected most by harmonization under NAFTA. Mexico has taken advantage of NAFTA by upgrading its hazardous waste requirements, emission standards, food inspection rules, and many other regulations. Meanwhile, the treaty's environmental bureaucracy has provided environmental activist groups the opportunity to encumber commercial activity through legal appeals for stricter enforcement of bureaucratic regulations—a process that began in earnest when environmentalist organizations petitioned the North American Commission on Environmental Cooperation to block legislative modifications of the endangered species act in the United States (AP 1995a; AP 1995b).

Harmonization of trade and environmental policies is beginning to take place on the global level in the General Agreement on Tariffs and Trade (GATT). Because GATT was designed to open export markets through reciprocal trade concessions, it has been harshly criticized by environmentalists. The WCED's *Our Common Future,* for instance, highlighted the need to incorporate environmental concerns into GATT's operations. Although GATT makes several gestures toward the environment in agreements for the partial harmonization of technical regulations, sanitary standards, and other nontariff trade barriers, institutional checks designed to prevent GATT's amendment frustrated a fuller embrace of sustainable development policies. Consequently, Agenda 21 calls on governments to "clarify the role of GATT . . . in dealing with trade and environment-related issues, including, where relevant, conciliation procedure and dispute settlement" (United Nations 1992a, 2.21[b]; cf. Arden-Clarke 1991; Jackson 1992; Esty 1994; UN Secretariat 1992).

As a result of the Uruguay Round of multilateral negotiations, the World Trade Organization (WTO) succeeded the GATT in 1995. The WTO enforces global rules on dispute settlement, conducts national trade policy reviews, and coordinates global economic policies with the International Monetary Fund (IMF) and World Bank. An underlying objective of the WTO is to promote

sustainable development and higher global environmental standards. With broader participation from nongovernmental organizations, the WTO Committee on Trade and the Environment explores
ways to "green" world trade rules in the context of a growing body
of international environmental law. By facilitating greater economic
interdependence, the WTO fosters international cooperation on a
range of nontariff barriers. The WTO encourages the international
harmonization of import restraints through bureaucracies, such as
the International Standards Organization and the Codex
Alimentarius commission (Commission on Global Governance
1995, 167–172; WTO 1995). These technical bodies have the
power to develop and revise global standards independently—
bypassing the normal ratification procedures for international
agreements. Although international standards often start out as
nonbinding "soft" law, they can evolve into formally binding
"hard" law obligations at a later date.

Most significant for the integration of global environmental standards and trade law is the WTO's enhanced stature in international
affairs. Heeding Agenda 21's call for a strengthened international
trade policies system, the WTO represents a substantial upgrade of
GATT's institutional powers, which makes possible more rapid revision of trade and environment rules. According to Mathews
(1994), "The change is already beginning in the new committee on
trade and environment in the WTO, and because the WTO is the
standing organization, it finally, finally gives us the institutional setting to address the social and environmental issues" (cf. Esty 1994;
von Moltke 1992).[5]

The aim of the WTO is to reconcile world trade rules and the burgeoning environmental trade restrictions within multilateral agreements. One possibility for strengthening the trade–environment
linkage is GATT Article XX, which lays down exceptions to general
trade obligations. Article XX has already been used to uphold the
GATT-legality of U.S. fuel efficiency standards, despite the fact that
these standards protect U.S. manufacturers from European competition. More radical proposals would allow WTO member countries to counteract objectionable environmental practices in other
countries by means of trade sanctions, much as GATT permits

antidumping or antisubsidy measures. The effect of these changes will be to institutionalize "green" protectionism, thus cloaking trade restrictions behind environmental policies (Charnovitz 1993; United Nations 1994).

## THE CASE AGAINST GLOBALISM

### RENT-SEEKING

One of the most serious disadvantages of transferring authority to collectivist, supranational bodies is the heightened potential for rent-seeking. International bodies have vested special interests, with much influence in international decision making. Through mastery of the news media, nongovernmental organizations (NGOs) have been able to mold public opinion by generating public debate and focusing attention on issues of their choosing. In turn, they have also been effective at translating public debate into legislative victories. NGOs have become adept at activist lobbying and have acquired a vast amount of technical knowledge that they bring to bear on legislative matters (French 1995, 187).

In many cases, NGOs have specialized knowledge of the political process and how it functions and can use this knowledge to push an ideological agenda more effectively than other interest groups can. NGOs typically exert pressure within the political system for compliance with international standards and treaties. Citizen suits, in which private interest groups have legal standing to compel environmental law enforcement, are valuable tools in this regard. NGOs are the energized ideological force that provides the intellectual foundations for the exercise of state power. In the international arena, groups like the World Conservation Union–IUCN, the World Resources Institute, and the World Wide Fund for Nature have been the motivating forces behind a number of international environmental treaties. Acting through the courts, NGOs have catalyzed the incursion of international law into domestic legal systems (Commission on Global Governance 1995, 325).

NGOs have made environmental policies much more polarized and have driven public policy largely to the exclusion of sound science. At the Earth Summit, countries endorsed the precautionary principle (Commission on Global Governance 1995, 83), which encourages governments to proceed with regulatory remedies whether or not the environmental problem's scientific validity has been established. This principle does great violence to the scientific basis of policy debate. Remedial action is called for in all cases of theoretical harm and despite scientific uncertainty about the remedy's effectiveness. The precautionary principle signifies a more politicized role for scientists, who must become more intimately involved with policy formulation (Baliunas 1994).

Because of the precautionary principle, costly climate convention policies and protocol negotiations are proceeding apace. Policies to restrict emissions of carbon dioxide potentially include carbon or gasoline taxes, fuel economy standards, and alternative fuel subsidies. The Clinton administration's Climate Change Action Plan calls for $1.9 billion in federal spending and imposes more than $60 billion in costs on the energy manufacturing, transportation, and housing sectors of the economy. Some economists estimate that enforcement of climate convention commitments will result in a 1.5 percent to 2 percent reduction in GNP in the United States and potential job losses of 500,000 to 1 million. Despite these costs, UN policy proposals will have no appreciable effect on global warming. Should UN predictions of climate warming prove correct, even the UN's suggested mitigation policies "do not stop global warming at all," writes Arizona State climatologist Robert C. Balling, Jr. (1995). "Indeed they barely even slow it" (102).[6]

The precautionary principle is also precipitating hasty action to enforce the Montreal Protocol. The chief danger of stratospheric ozone layer thinning throughout the twenty-first century is an increase of roughly 10 percent in exposure to ultraviolet (UV) radiation. However, that estimated rise is roughly equivalent to the increased UV exposure associated with moving sixty miles closer to the equator, according to climatologist Fred Singer (1994). Because the ozone layer is naturally thinner toward the equator, moving from San Francisco to Los Angeles reduces the ozone layer by 25 percent. In addition, there are valid scientific questions about whether human activities are harming the ozone layer at all.

According to Baliunas (1994), "our most precise measurements of ozone have systematic errors much larger than the fraction of a percent annual change that is alleged to be the manmade ozone destruction" (5). Regardless, the benefits of ozone preservation appear all out of proportion with the economic costs of the CFC phaseout. In the United States alone, the cost of conversion to non-CFC refrigerants and coolants will total approximately $100 billion annually—the remedy will be more costly than the problem itself (Singer 1994; Lieberman 1994).

The CFC phaseout amply demonstrates how susceptible the business community is to politicization. American CFC manufacturers supported the Montreal Protocol (once their CFC patents had expired), hoping to benefit from the phaseout-induced price increase and from the increased demand for their expertise in manufacturing CFC alternatives. Corporate interests tend to benefit from the harmonization of international standards at a level that larger, established businesses can manage better than their smaller or overseas competition. This dynamic has prompted other efforts to enlist members of the business community in the environmental regulatory effort. At Rio, the Business Council on Sustainable Development produced *Changing Course: A Global Business Perspective on Development and the Environment,* a report on corporate environmental standards that is very supportive of government intervention in the market. A related group, the President's Council on Sustainable Development, brought together business leaders and the environmental lobby to devise national sustainable development policies and legislation (Schmidheiny 1992).

## THE KNOWLEDGE PROBLEM

In dealing with environmental problems, globalist environmental policies attempt to address "market failures," assuming that governments will do better. To manage global sustainable development, international institutions would have to assimilate vast amounts of scientific, economic, and technological data. The quantity and complexity of such an information-gathering task make central planning an exercise in futility.

The enormous knowledge problem is seen in the deficiency of information regarding greenhouse warming. Many climate scientists acknowledge that computer simulation models for climate change are too crude and primitive to be used as the basis for policy implementation. Although such models are the basis for the climate convention, they are unable to represent the role in climate change of complex factors such as cloud cover, oceans, sea ice, snow cover, localized storms, and biological systems (Balling 1995).

Sufficient knowledge is also lacking with regard to the Convention on Biological Diversity, which undertakes to protect all ecosystems. At present, the term *ecosystem* has not yet been precisely defined or scientifically classified in terms of its attributes. The ecological relationship between wildlife and its nonliving surroundings is not fully understood. Of the estimated 8 to 10 million different species on the planet, only 1.5 million have even been named (Edwards 1995).

Nation-states have not done an adequate job of protecting the environment thus far, and they cannot expect to do better by acting together in a coordinated fashion. Globalism does nothing to alter the dynamics of environmental mismanagement, which is primarily a function of mismanagement of the "commons," or the unowned portions of nature. Most environmental damage results from central governments exploiting and mismanaging the commons—diminishing freshwater resources, depleting renewables, cutting down forests, subsidizing overproduction in agriculture, and promoting excessive use of fertilizers and pesticides. Ecological mismanagement of the oceans, for example, is presently the fault of government planners. The UN Food and Agriculture Organization estimates that $124 billion is spent annually to catch only $70 billion worth of fish. The overspending can be attributed to government subsidies to fishing industries. The enhancement of government control of the environment in the Law of the Sea and other treaties will only perpetuate the mismanagement of the commons.

## GREEN REDISTRIBUTIONISM

A fundamental flaw of global environmentalism is that developing countries are asked to forego development, meaning that the world's poor must be held in conditions of grinding poverty. The impoverished Third World is uniquely threatened by sustainable development policies in terms of human and economic costs. International environmental policies tend to reflect the priorities of the wealthy, industrialized world, a phenomenon known as *eco-imperialism.* Developing countries recognize this as a means of keeping them underdeveloped while maintaining the status of richer countries.

## AN ALTERNATIVE: PRIVATE PROPERTY

Contrary to apocalyptic environmentalist warnings, overwhelming evidence suggests that the long-term effects of humankind upon the earth are positive. Despite very rapid population growth, humankind has achieved a vast increase in food supplies and has improved the nutritional level of the majority of the population. Currently, the most important resources are not growing scarce, but rather are becoming more abundant. Technological innovation has dramatically reduced the economy's stresses on the environment (Bailey 1995).

In agriculture, the use of high-yield farming techniques is instructive. According to Hudson Institute agricultural expert Dennis Avery, advances in pesticides, herbicides, fertilizers, and other technologies have increased food production while improving environmental quality. These technologies have saved ten million square miles of wildlife habitat since the 1950s. Similar private sector forestry management innovations are responsible for substantial timber growth in the United States (Bailey 1995, 50).

Thus, the global environment is not threatened by the market economy. Rather, it is most threatened by a lack of clearly defined property rights and market-based arrangements. Property rights truly reflect the sound "polluter pays" principle, which literally means that the polluter should pay for any damage caused to someone else's property. As Elizabeth Brubaker (1995), of the Toronto-based Environment Probe, explains, private ownership of resources is the best defense against pollution (cf. Adams 1992).

Proponents of sustainable development seek improved management of open-access commons—which is badly needed. By reducing economic freedom, however, global sustainable development policies will only exacerbate the problem. By focusing on the control of economic and political activity, current multilateral treaty-making violates the "polluter pays" principle by forcing taxpayers to pay for cleaning the mess of polluters. What is needed is a means to privatize the open-access commons—a process virtually impossible under global political management but feasible under a decentralized system.

Common law property rights, once predominant in the United States and Canada, have been emasculated by special interest manipulation. As government grew larger, its power was used to put collective goals, such as economic expansion, ahead of the protection of property. If environmental resources are to be better protected, political institutions must be closer to the people, and government must return to its basic function of protecting property. On an international level, where transboundary pollution occurs, international liability treaties could allow private parties to bring legal action addressing harms committed by polluters in other national jurisdictions (Smith 1990).

International institutions and multilateral regimes typically lack democratic accountability. A system of shared or pooled sovereignty over environmental matters puts great distance between the government and the governed. The Worldwatch Institute, a staunch advocate of globalism, acknowledges the contradiction of centralizing power in international institutions when "achieving sustainable development requires protecting the rights of local people to control their own resources—whether it be forests, fish, or minerals" (French 1995, 179).

Localized control better reflects the environmental credo: "Think globally, act locally." Development is truly sustainable not through global planning, but through competitive sovereignty—the devolution of power to national, local, and ultimately private levels. Several countries in west Africa are successfully decentralizing decision-making authority over land and wild species use to regional committees and villages. People are given rights to use and benefit from natural resources, and thus have built-in incentives to conserve those resources. Instead of empowering a watchful police force to determine the resource needs of the citizenry, localized control allows the people with the greatest stake in sustainability to plan their own resource use (Edwards 1995).

## ENDNOTES

1. The Commission on Global Governance, a successor to the World Commission on Environment and Development, was co-chaired by Ingvar Carlsson, former Prime Minister and head of the social democratic party of Sweden, and Shridath Ramphal, former Secretary-General of Guyana and former president of the World Conservation Union-IUCN.

2. The Convention on Biological Diversity is modeled on the 1992 Global Biodiversity Strategy proposal by the World Resources Institute, the World Conservation Union-IUCN, and the UN Environment Programme (UNEP). The proposal sets forth basic principles of sustainable use of biological resources, as well as a blueprint for biodiversity planning and wealth transfers at the local, national, and international levels. (World Resources Institute 1994.)

3. This Rio Declaration principle updates a nearly identical provision incorporated in the Stockholm Declaration of 1972.

4. Other legal authority derives from the UN Convention on the Law of the Sea; the Vienna Convention for the Protection of the Ozone Layer; the Convention for the Prevention of Marine Pollution from Land-Based Sources; the American Law Institute's *The Restatement (Third) of the Foreign Relations Law of the United States* (1988; as cited in Esty 1994).

5. Social standards refers to labor standards in trade policy.

6. UN policies would slow predicted warming by 0.07 to 0.3 degrees Centigrade by the year 2050.

## REFERENCES

Adams, Patricia. 1992. Property Rights and Bioregionalism: Lessons from the World. Address to the Conference on Ecological Renewal in the Greater Toronto Bioregion, on 3 April.

Arden-Clarke, Charles. 1991. The General Agreement on Tariffs and Trade, Environmental Protection, and Sustainable Development. *World Wildlife Fund Discussion Paper* (June).

Associated Press (AP). 1995a. Environmentalists Seek to Use NAFTA in Endangered Species Fight. 4 July. Lexis-Nexis.

———. 1995b. Environmentalists Asking International Panel to Help Block Logging Law. *The Washington Post*, 29 August.

Bailey, Ronald, ed. 1995. *The True State of the Planet*. Washington, D.C.: Free Press.

Baliunas, Sallie. 1994. Ozone and Global Warming: Are the Problems Real? Presented at the West Coast Roundtable on Science and Public Policy, at the George C. Marshall Institute and Claremont Institute, California, on 13 December.

Balling, Robert C., Jr. 1995. Global Warming: Messy Models, Decent Data, Pointless Policy. In *The True State of the Planet*, edited by Ronald Bailey. Washington, D.C.: Free Press.

Benedick, Richard Elliot. 1991. *Ozone Diplomacy*. Cambridge: Harvard University Press.

Brubaker, Elizabeth. 1995. *Property Rights in Defence of Nature*. Toronto: Environment Probe and Earthscan Publications.

Charnovitz, Steve. 1993. The Environment vs. Trade Rules: Defogging the Debate. *Environmental Law* 23, no. 2: 475–517.

Commission on Global Governance. 1995. *Our Global Neighborhood*. New York: Oxford University Press.

Edwards, Stephen R. 1995. Conserving Biodiversity. In *The True State of the Planet*, edited by Ronald Bailey. Washington, D.C.: Free Press.

Esty, Daniel C. 1994. *Greening the GATT: Trade, Environment, and the Future*. Washington, D.C.: Institute for International Economics.

Evans, Ray. 1995. The Basel Convention: Internationalism's Greatest Folly. Monograph, Competitive Enterprise Institute.

French, Hilary. 1992. Strengthening Global Environmental Governance. *State of the World*. New York: W. W. Norton, pp. 158–159.

———. 1993. Costly Tradeoffs: Reconciling Trade and the Environment. *Worldwatch* 113 (Worldwatch Institute), March 1993, p. 29.

———. 1995. Forging a New Global Partnership. *State of the World*. New York: Norton.

GATT Secretariat. 1992. Geneva: General Agreement on Tariffs and Trade. *Trade and the Environment*.

Jackson, John H. 1992. Changing GATT Rules. In *The Greening of World Trade*. Washington, D.C.: U.S. Environmental Protection Agency.

Kinzer, Stephen. 1995. Nations Pledge to Set Limits by 1997 on Warming Gases. *The New York Times*, 8 April, p. A4.

Lieberman, Ben. 1994. The High Cost of Cool: The Economic Impact of the CFC Phaseout in the United States. Monograph, Competitive Enterprise Institute.

MacNeill, Jim, Pieter Winsemius, and Taizo Yakushiji. 1991. *Beyond Interdependence: The Meshing of the World's Economy and the Earth's Ecology*. New York: Oxford University Press.

Mathews, Jessica Tuchman. 1989. Redefining Security. *Foreign Affairs* (Spring): 162.

———. 1991. Chantilly Crossroads. *The Washington Post*, 10 February, p. C7.

———. 1992a. Speech to the Atlantic Forum, Federal News Service, on 18 May. Lexis-Nexis.

———. 1992b. Weekend Edition. National Public Radio, 30 May.

———. 1994. Trading Points. *McNeil-Lehrer News Hour*, 29 November.

McInnis, Daniel F. 1992. Ozone Layers and Oligopoly Profits. In *Environmental Politics: Public Costs, Private Rewards*, edited by Michael S. Greve and Fred L. Smith, Jr. New York: Praeger.

Reuters. 1994. China Unveils Ambitious Plan for Sustainable Development. *Journal of Commerce* (18 April): 6.

Sand, Peter H. 1990. Innovations in International Environmental Governance. *Environment* (November): 40.

Schmidheiny, Stephan. 1992. *Changing Course: A Global Business Perspective on Development and the Environment.* Cambridge: MIT Press.

Sedjo, Roger. 1995. Forests: Conflicting Signals. In *The True State of the Planet,* edited by Ronald Bailey. Washington, D.C.: Free Press.

Singer, Fred. 1994. (N)O$_3$ Problem. *The National Interest* (Summer): 73.

Smith, Fred L., Jr. 1990. A Free-Market Environmental Program for the Soviet Union. Monograph, Competitive Enterprise Institute.

Strong, Maurice. 1992. *A Matter of People.* Earth Summit Publication No. 3. UN Conference on Environment and Development.

United Nations. 1992a. Agenda 21: Program of Action for Sustainable Development. Agreements negotiated by Governments at the Conference on Environment and Development, 3–14 June, in Rio de Janeiro, Brazil.

———. 1992b. Rio Declaration on Environment and Development. Conference on Environment and Development, 3–14 June, in Rio de Janeiro, Brazil.

———. 1994. Panel. United States—Taxes on Automobiles. DS31/R General Agreement on Tariffs and Trade, 29 September.

von Moltke, Konrad. 1992. Dispute Resolution and Transparency. In *The Greening of World Trade.* Washington, D.C.: U.S. Environmental Protection Agency.

Weber, Peter. 1994. Safeguarding Oceans. *State of the World 1994.* New York: Norton.

World Commission on Environment and Development (WCED). 1987. *Our Common Future.* New York: Oxford University Press.

World Resources Institute. 1994. Biodiversity. In *World Resources 1994–95.* New York: Oxford University Press.

World Trade Organization (WTO). 1994. Trade Measures for Environmental Purposes Taken Pursuant to Multilateral Agreements: Recent Developments. *International Trade 1990–91* (13 October).

———. 1995. Trade and the Environment. Press Release, 22 May.

# CHAPTER 6

# The War Against Warming: Climate Change, Kyoto, and American National Security*

*Jeffrey Salmon*

The environment is not a modest concept, it embraces . . . the universe and all that surrounds it. (Quoted in Rubin 1993, 8)

## A COMPREHENSIVE AGENDA

Environmentalism has catholic concerns and objectives. Popular environmentalist Paul Ehrlich once noted that "All too many people think in terms of national parks and trout streams when they say 'environment'" (Paul R. Ehrlich and John P. Holdren, "Impact of Population Growth," *Science* 171 (March 1971): 1215). However, such a narrow vision distorts the true meaning of the term. "Slums, cockroaches, and rats are ecological problems too. The correction of ghetto conditions in Detroit is neither more nor less important than saving the Great Lakes—both are imperatives." Ehrlich argues that the "'environment' must be broadly construed to include such things as the physical environment of urban ghettos, the human behavioral environment, and the epidemiological environment" (Ehrlich and Holdren 1971, 1212). In other words, virtually everything.

In his popular book, *Earth in the Balance,* Vice President Al Gore echoes Ehrlich's belief that environmentalism touches every corner of human and nonhuman existence. Gore's core concern is human

---

*This is a revised and expanded version of a paper prepared for the Committee to Preserve American Security and Sovereignty.

alienation from nature, which causes, he contends, a spiritual crisis evident in society's disrespect for the environment. One cure for this alienation is to see nature as a homogeneous rather than a hetero-geneous entity. "In order to recognize the pattern of [ecological] de-struction," Gore argues, "we have to see it from a distance, both in time and space. Since the pattern is truly global, we have to see the entire world in our mind's eye" (Gore 1992, 45–46). Indeed, "much of our success in rescuing the global ecological system will depend upon whether we can find a new reverence for the environment as a whole—not just its parts" (Gore 1992, 204).

No longer content to solve local difficulties, such as polluted lakes or polluting factories, today's environmentalism takes on global ecological devastation and even the crisis of the modern alienated soul. In fact, local environmental threats are generally seen as mere reflections of deeper, more profound problems with civilization. And let there be no mistake about the consequences of ignoring the global scope and interconnectedness of environ-mental degradation. "We now face the prospect," Gore writes, "of a kind of global civil war between those who refuse to con-sider the consequences of civilization's relentless advance and those who refuse to be silent partners in the destruction" (Gore 1992, 269). To avoid this catastrophe, Gore contends that "we must take bold and unequivocal action: we must make the rescue of the environment the central organizing principle of civilization" (Gore 1992, 274). When there is a threat to nature itself, it seems at the very least irresponsible to waste time worrying about some narrow regional or even national environmental problem, espe-cially when that problem is just a hint of a comprehensive ecolog-ical menace.

What problem today is not embraced by the professional envi-ronmental class? Consider the scope of some of the issues environ-mentalists consider to be within their portfolio: climate, population stabilization, elimination of poverty, improvement of living stan-dards (if done in a sustainable manner), gender and racial equity, de-crease in military spending, and allocation of energy resources. Environmentalism has virtually unlimited concerns and is willing to call upon unlimited political means (after all, saving the environment should be the "central organizing principle of civilization") to meet those concerns. And of all the real or imagined catastrophes that appear on the environmentalist's to-do list, climate change is the one most likely to cause global ruin and the one that will require the greatest degree of intervention if a solution is to be found.

## THE CENTRAL IMPORTANCE
## OF CLIMATE CHANGE

It is not surprising that the vice president called global warming "the most serious threat we have ever faced" (Gore 1992, 140). Not only does greenhouse warming know no borders, but its effects are potentially quite severe. What's more, and politically of greatest interest, is the fact that a commitment to taming climate change is a commitment to fundamental change in modern industrial civilization. If environmentalism has become "everythingism," then global warming is the policy issue that offers the environmentalists an opening to everything that is most important to modern society.

Consider the far-from-modest steps that will need to be taken to ameliorate human-induced global climate change.

Virtually all anthropogenic sources of carbon dioxide, methane, and other greenhouse gases will have to be controlled and managed. In fact, atmospheric concentrations of greenhouse gases will have to be stabilized at levels that would prevent serious human-made climate change. To do so might require cuts in global carbon dioxide emissions of at least 50 percent by 2030 (Houghton et al. 1990, 338–339).

What is more, to control worldwide energy production and use, international regimes with considerable authority will have to be established and traditional notions of national sovereignty will have to be modified.

The world's economy runs on fossil fuel. The economic consequences of global restrictions on the use of fossil fuel would clearly be enormous. Jet engines produce nitrogen oxide, a powerful greenhouse gas. Cows emit—from both ends—enormous amounts of methane. It appears that virtually everywhere you look, something is generating a greenhouse gas.

The sweeping consequences of tackling the global warming problem have helped make climate change the defining issue for environmental groups. This paper considers one aspect of global warming policy—the adverse effect of international agreements to curb greenhouse gas emissions, particularly the Kyoto Protocol, on American national security and the U.S. armed forces. To understand how climate change policy can harm military preparedness and readiness, it is necessary to provide some perspective on the climate change debate in general and then to assess the claim that human activity is causing, or will cause, serious global warming.

## THE GREENHOUSE DEBATE

Global warming anxiety arises largely from the coincidence of a 1 degree Fahrenheit rise in global temperature over the past one hundred years and an increase in atmospheric carbon dioxide largely from the burning of such fossil fuels as coal and oil. According to global warming theory, carbon dioxide ($CO_2$)—in addition to other humanmade gases such as methane—has already enhanced the earth's natural greenhouse effect and will continue to do so until the planet experiences an uncontrollable temperature rise. Preventing serious climate change, so the theory goes, means reducing the amount of humanmade greenhouse gases entering the atmosphere—in effect, globally reducing the use of energy.

Prior to the late 1980s, global warming was of little concern to scientists or environmentalists. Climate modelers ran computer simulations of how the atmosphere would react to increasing levels of $CO_2$ and found a substantial warming, but no one paid much attention. Indeed, during the 1970s, global cooling was a fashionable fear just at a time when the earth's temperature had experienced a thirty-year cooling trend (Ponte 1976). At that time Stephen Schneider, who is now one of the most vocal scientific proponents of the catastrophic global warming thesis, called the odds against global cooling "Russian roulette odds" (Ponte 1976, 4).

By the late 1980s, however, global temperatures had risen to about the levels that they had been before the previous cooling

trend. Fears of a new ice age were replaced (in the minds of politically sensitive scientists at least) by fears of warming.

In the summer of 1988, the greenhouse effect moved from the
scientific journals to the nightly news. On June 23, with the ther-
mometer hitting 98 degrees Fahrenheit in Washington, D.C.,
James Hansen, chief of NASA's Goddard Institute and a
well-known climate expert, told a Senate Committee that he was
"about 99 percent confident that the current temperatures represent a real warming trend rather than a chance fluctuation"
(Hansen 1988, 2). The news value of Hansen's statement was enhanced by the fact that he testified on one of the hottest days of
the summer during one of the hottest years in decades. Environmental groups quickly adopted climate change as one of their
major agenda items and then-Senator Al Gore became a tireless
promoter of climate change disaster scenarios.

To believe these scenarios, however, one must have faith in the
computer models that generate them. These general circulation
models (GCM) attempt to mimic our climate system by using
mathematical simulation of the earth, its oceans, and its atmosphere. Unfortunately, the mechanism of our climate is so complex
that reliable simulations are as yet impossible to achieve. Clouds,
for example, have a greater effect on climate than humanmade
$CO_2$, and yet the models come nowhere near being able to predict
what type of clouds will form under what circumstance, or even
whether these clouds would enhance or diminish global warming.
Indeed, even Hansen now doubts the ability of the GCMs to fore-
cast future climate (Hansen et al. 1998). The models do a poor job
of predicting the climate changes we have already experienced. If
they are incapable of accounting for the past, how confident can
we be about their ability to predict the future?

There are other reasons to question the basis of global warming
fears. First, perhaps the most persistent myth of the entire global
warming debate is the idea that there is a scientific consensus on
the cause of the 1 degree Fahrenheit temperature rise over the past
one hundred years. The summary for policymakers of the 1995 report of the UN Intergovernmental Panel on Climate Change
(IPCC) contained the statement that "the balance of evidence

suggests a discernible human influence on global climate" (Houghton et al. 1996, 4). It is routinely claimed that more than 2,000 scientists support this statement, allegedly defining a true consensus on the issue of the effect of humans on climate. But it is not true that 2,000 scientists endorsed this statement or indeed any part of the IPCC report. The number of scientists involved in the primary technical chapter of the IPCC report totals thirty-four (four lead authors and thirty contributors). Some five hundred "reviewers" are listed for the entire first volume of the report, but there is no reason to believe they agreed with the "balance of evidence" statement. There is considerable reason to believe that many of them would not. Upon examination, 2,000 adherents quickly becomes 34.

What consensus does emerge from the IPCC report, in fact, undermines concerns about serious human-caused climate change, or at least introduces a considerable level of uncertainty about what science can tell us about climate change. The report observes that human-caused global warming one hundred years from now might be as high as 3.5 degrees Celsius—a significant increase—or as low as 1 degree Celsius—an insignificant temperature rise (Houghton et al. 1996, 6). Although this range represents a measure of agreement within the scientific community, it is entirely irrelevant for policy makers, because the range of predicted global warming is between important and unimportant.

Another reason to doubt that global warming is a serious threat is the ever-dwindling predictions of doom generated by the GCMs. For example, the IPCC estimates have dropped rather significantly in just five years—from a midrange of 3.3 degrees Celsius in 1990 to just 1 to 2 degrees Celsius in 1995 (Houghton et al. 1996, 6). As the models improve, predictions of serious global warming become less, not more, worrisome.

Additional skepticism derives from temperature measurements taken by NASA satellites from 1978 to date, which show no global temperature increase at all. (The GCMs predicted a rise of about 0.5 degrees Celsius over this same period.[1])

Finally, when put in perspective, global warming quickly loses its claim as a timely public policy issue. The predicted warming that is fueling today's debate will not take place until early in the twenty-second century. No one really expects that energy production, transportation, and other energy-intensive activities will remain tied to fossil fuel technology for the next one hundred years.

Nevertheless, in late 1997 in Kyoto, Japan, the Clinton Administration committed the United States to a reduction in greenhouse gas emissions to 7 percent below 1990 levels, a goal that would put the United States back to 1979 emission levels. This commitment went considerably beyond the administration's original objective—reductions to, but not below, 1990 levels. Equally important, Kyoto went beyond the Rio Earth Summit agreement, signed by President Bush in 1992. (The Kyoto agreement called for binding commitments to greenhouse gas reductions, whereas Rio looked for voluntary efforts to curb emissions.) Rio and Kyoto are both part of the UN Framework Convention on Climate Change (FCCC), which seeks to prevent the accumulation of "dangerous levels of heat trapping gases" in the atmosphere. By 1995, however, it had become clear that voluntary measures were not working and so, as a result of the so-called "Berlin Mandate" agreed to by the Clinton administration in April 1995, the industrialized nations determined to move toward legally binding commitments.

The developing nations (e.g., China and Brazil) are exempt from any commitments to greenhouse gas reductions and indeed have never been a party to FCCC agreements, a fact that has raised a fundamental problem for the Framework Convention. Without the participation of the developing world in a climate change treaty, emissions reductions made by developed nations will be quickly offset by increases in energy use in the developing world. For example, a 50 percent reduction in current U.S. emissions would reduce the world's total emissions by about 600 million tons of carbon per year, but that reduction would be more than counterbalanced by China, which is expected to increase its emissions by some 600 million tons by 2025. For this reason, in the Byrd-Hagel Resolution, the Senate made approval of the Kyoto Treaty contingent on full participation by the developing world.

Not surprisingly, the Kyoto Protocol has generated considerable debate. Its cost to the American and global economies, its lack of equity in terms of which nations are included in the emissions reduction plan, its implications for U.S. sovereignty, and its scientific grounding have all been raised as potential problems.

One aspect of the Clinton administration's commitment under Kyoto that has received scant attention is the treaty's national security implications, which are addressed in the remainder of this chapter.

## NATIONAL SECURITY ISSUES ARISING OUT OF THE KYOTO PROTOCOL

As noted earlier, the seemingly limitless scope of issues included in the term *environmental* lends itself to infusing environmental concerns in novel areas. Environmental diplomacy is an explicit part of the U.S. State Department's mission, and environmental security is now an important mission of the Department of Defense (DOD). In a 1997 DOD conference, Principal Deputy Undersecretary of Defense (Environmental Security) Gary Vest set out the department's broad role in environmental protection.

> In the words of Secretary of Defense William Cohen, ". . . environmental protection is critical to the Defense Department's mission, and environmental considerations shall be integrated into all defense activities." The U.S. military is no longer a negative impact on the environment and is now having a positive impact. The U.S. military views environmental protection as important. (Vest 1997, II-9–II-10)

Mr. Vest then shared a vision: "What if the militaries of the world went through similar transformations like the U.S. military and became neutral or even positive in terms of the environment? What if the militaries of the world became examples of environmental leadership (Vest 1997, II-9–II-10)?[2] He stated that he believed that the militaries of the world could be a positive thrust for the environment throughout the world.

For the military to become a positive force in the climate change question means a potential conflict with its requirement for access to energy. As one military analyst noted recently,

> Global climate change will affect the ability of the U.S. military to train and operate. National and international responses to greenhouse gas emissions will directly impact the type and quantity of training

conducted. U.S. forces may, at best, have to modify training regime to maintain readiness. At worst, the military may be less combat ready. (Bidlack 1998, 34)

Will the national security establishment of the United States accede to a less well trained and less prepared armed forces based on fear of a potential change in global climate of some 3 degrees Celsius over the next one hundred years? The answer to that question is more open than one might at first imagine.

Let us consider this issue in some detail.

The United States emits about 20 percent of the world's total carbon dioxide. Of those nations currently involved in the FCCC, the United States is attributed with more than 36 percent of the world's total $CO_2$ emissions. The Russian Federation is second, with about 17 percent of the world's total carbon emissions. Most of these emissions result from America's dependence on fossil fuels for energy, such as coal and oil. The federal government is the single largest energy user within the United States (about 2 percent of the national total), and the Department of Defense is the largest energy user within the federal government, accounting for about 70 percent of the government's total (Defense Environmental Alert 1997, 4).

Therefore, it is not surprising that the Clinton administration would include the military in any plans for meeting greenhouse gas reduction commitments agreed to under the Framework Convention. To exclude the nation's largest single energy user from the sacrifices asked of all other Americans would make reaching its overall emissions goals more difficult and would open the administration up to criticism for showing favoritism and not taking the problem of global warming seriously enough. What is more, the Pentagon has reduced its energy use (and so its $CO_2$ emissions) since the baseline year of 1990, making its inclusion in the nation's overall emissions total advantageous to the prospects for meeting U.S. commitments made in Kyoto.

Deputy Undersecretary of Defense for Environmental Security Sherri Goodman noted that the military had "reduced its emissions, when measured by energy consumption, by more than 20 percent since 1990" (Goodman 1998a, 3). Overall energy use, she noted, was down at DOD facilities by about 15 percent between 1985 and 1996.

Recognizing the contributions the Pentagon might be asked to make in the war against warming, the Defense Department made its case in a position paper subsequently leaked to the press. According to this position paper:

> America's national security requires that its military forces remain ready. While global climate change may be a serious threat to the nation's long-term interests, there are other threats we must not forget. We must not sacrifice our national security or our ability to offer humanitarian assistance to those in need to achieve reductions in greenhouse gas emissions. We must not see this as an issue of being able to achieve either national security or protection of the global climate. The United States must pursue both objectives. (Defense Environmental Alert 1997, 6)

To accomplish this, DOD strongly recommends that the United States insist on a national security provision in the climate change protocol now being negotiated (Defense Environmental Alert 1997, 6).

The Department's vague reference to a "national security provision" was made concrete in its proposal for a broad exemption from emissions reductions. The draft noted that

> Each Annex A and B Party shall exclude from its measurement of anthropogenic emissions by sources any emissions attributable to military tactical or strategic systems used for military operations in support of national or collective security, humanitarian activities, peacekeeping, peace enforcement, or United Nations, NATO, and other multinational actions and any such emissions attributable to military tactical or strategic systems used in training to maintain readiness for conducting military operations. (Defense Environmental Alert 1997, 4)

There is no telling to what extent this draft provision reflected a consensus in the Pentagon with respect to its need to be excluded from $CO_2$ emissions restrictions. The draft does set out, however, what appears to be a complete exemption from greenhouse gas limits for military operations. The draft includes multilateral operations such as NATO- and UN-sanctioned activities, but it also includes actions related very broadly to national security, which would appear to encompass all forms of unilateral military actions and training for such actions. The proposed exemption would not cover DOD facilities and nontactical vehicles—areas, as noted above, in which the Pentagon has already made significant cuts in energy use amounting to slightly more than 40 percent of DOD emissions.

A background paper from the Pentagon's environmental office, made public in the trade press and apparently intended to bolster the claim for this blanket exemption, looks at the impact on readiness of a 10 percent reduction in fuel, which, the analysis notes, is equivalent to a 10 percent cut in greenhouse gas emissions. As published, the paper does not include a detailed justification for the selection of the 10 percent figure. Still, as a benchmark for reductions that might be required of the military, the analysis is instructive.

- For the army, a 10 percent reduction in fuel use "would reduce [the amount of operations and training] . . . to a level that would downgrade unit readiness and require up to six additional weeks to prepare and deploy. Strategic deployment schedules would be missed, placing operations at risk" (Defense Environmental Alert 1997, 4–6).

- For the navy, this 10 percent reduction would cut some 2,000 steaming days per year from training and operations for deployed ships, causing cancellation of both bilateral and multilateral exercises. And because reductions would not be taken from ships and aircraft deployed in trouble spots, other units would be required to take proportionately greater cuts, meaning less training and "a potentially significant threat to crew safety" (Defense Environmental Alert 1997, 4–6).

- In the air force, a 10 percent reduction in fuel use "would result in the loss of over 210,000 flying hours per year." Readiness would be reduced "to the point [that the air force] would be incapable of meeting all the requirements of the national Military Strategy" (Defense Environmental Alert 1997, 4–6).

One can always fault such analysis as worst-case overstatement and special pleading. Nevertheless, as the report itself points out, because this is a static analysis, the true impact of energy-use reductions on national security is difficult to gauge. Future threats, unforeseen contingencies, chance, fluctuations in fuel prices, interservice rivalries, and dozens of other unknowns complicate any calculation of how mandated greenhouse gas reductions will influence military readiness in the years to come. It would be difficult to conclude, however, that cuts in the range discussed by this DOD report would be anything but destructive to preparedness and morale. The analysis concludes that a 10 percent reduction in fuel use would "represent a serious threat to national security" (Defense Environmental Alert 1997, 6).

How did the military fare in the Kyoto agreement? Here are the relevant provisions:

> Decision 2/CP.3
> The Conference of the Parties
> *Recalls that*, under the Revised 1996 Guidelines for National Greenhouse Gas Inventories of the IPCC, emissions based upon fuel sold to ships or aircraft engaged in international transport should not be included in the national totals, but reported separately; and *urges* the Subsidiary Body for Technological and Scientific Advice to further elaborate on the inclusion of these emissions into the overall greenhouse gas inventories by the Parties.
>
> *Decides that* emissions resulting from multilateral operations pursuant to the United Nations Charter shall not be included in national totals but reported separately; other emissions related to operations shall be included in the national emissions totals of one or more parties involved. (Kyoto Protocol 1997, 31)

We are told by the State Department that the above provisions represent "everything" the Pentagon "outlined as necessary to protect military operations and our national security" (Eizenstat 1998a, 9). The uniformed military has issued no protest and the DOD Office of Environmental Security supports the Kyoto language.

Three broad exemptions or areas of flexibility for the military from the Kyoto Protocol greenhouse gas limits were at first discussed by the administration and presented as comprehensive in terms of what DOD requested. Later statements by administration officials, however, served to confuse the exemption question. According to Undersecretary Stuart Eizenstat, who headed the

U.S. delegation in Kyoto, "every requirement the Defense Department and uniformed military who were at Kyoto by my side said they wanted, they got. This is self-defense, peacekeeping, humanitarian relief" (Eizenstat 1998a, 9).

Despite the abundant disorder (outlined in full below) that now surrounds administration policy with respect to the Pentagon's role in future greenhouse gas reduction efforts, it is best to begin with a review of the administration's understanding of precisely what kinds of military operations would be exempt from Kyoto-agreed-upon limits.

## THE ADMINISTRATION'S POSITION ON KYOTO AND NATIONAL SECURITY

The most important exemption for the military, from the administration's point of view, is that concerning multilateral operations pursuant to or consistent with the UN Charter. For example, according to Undersecretary Eizenstat, Desert Storm, Bosnia, and Somalia—all UN-sanctioned operations—would clearly not be counted against U.S. greenhouse gas limits. He also claimed that operations such as the invasion of Grenada and Panama, which we deemed to be consistent with the charter, would be exempt from the Kyoto limits as well. This exemption is critical because the administration has difficulty conceiving of any military operation that would not be considered multilateral. Deputy Secretary Goodman argues that strictly unilateral military operations are "quite rare" in "today's day and age" (Goodman 1998a, 10), and in February 11 testimony, Undersecretary Eizenstat does not even seem to consider such engagements as a reasonable option, inasmuch as they are never mentioned. Indeed, he contends that everything the military needs to "protect military operations and our national security" was achieved at Kyoto, apparently not regarding an exemption for unilateral operations important or relevant (Eizenstat 1998b, 6).

The second area subject to exemption is emissions from fuel sold for international maritime or aviation, so-called bunker fuels. According to Deputy Secretary Goodman, this exemption covers fuel used by the U.S. Air Force and Navy when operating in international waters, meaning our allies who sell fuel to our forces will not have the fuel counted against their national greenhouse gas limits (Goodman 1998a, 3).

The third area is not an exemption. Rather it allows flexibility in determining whether emissions associated with overseas training of U.S. forces are charged against the host country's account or that of the nation using the fuel. This flexibility is really quite favorable to the host country because American force structure has shrunk since the baseline year, 1990, and host countries can take advantage of the lower emission levels that have resulted.

In her prepared statement for a March 1998 hearing before Senator Inhofe's readiness subcommittee, Deputy Secretary Goodman emphasized that the Pentagon does not "seek special treatment" and "can and should reduce its greenhouse gas emissions . . . in the same way the rest of the nation will be called on to do" (Goodman 1998b, 6). Congressional leaders had a variety of problems with the global warming accord agreed to in Kyoto, however, and worried that inclusion of the military in efforts to limit greenhouse gases could encumber the nation's ability to execute national strategy. The core of Congress' problem with the national security implications of the climate change accord appears, at this writing, to be the administration's lack of clarity or candor over the military's specific obligations under Kyoto.

Implementation of Kyoto without Senate ratification of the treaty tops the list of concerns in Congress, especially in the minds of Republican members. In turn, the Senate has made it clear that until developing nations, especially China, Brazil, and India, are included in the binding limits on greenhouse gas emissions the treaty would not be ratified. Senator Biden told Undersecretary Eizenstat "the truth of the matter is absent dealing with [this and other] issues . . . , there will be no ratification of this treaty" (Eizenstat 1998a, 15).

At this point in the political struggle over Kyoto, at least as far as Congress is concerned, national security appears to be outweighed by the fundamental concern over the accord's equity and by suspicions that the Clinton administration will attempt to implement the treaty through regulatory or other means before, or even instead of, submitting it to the Senate for formal ratification. Still, it is likely that the ambiguities over how defense-related matters are treated in the overall effort to meet Kyoto's steep energy reduction goals will become a major stumbling block to treaty ratification.

Initial confusion arose over the precise scope of the exemption that military leadership requested prior to Kyoto. As noted above, Undersecretary Eizenstat argued that the military was granted "everything" they need to "protect national security." Senator Hagel, apparently assuming that a blanket exemption from Kyoto's energy limits would in fact be the only thing that could satisfy the military, asked the Undersecretary to explain how an exemption for only multilateral operations could meet all military requirements to protect national security. The exchange between Hagel and Eizenstat raises questions about the Pentagon's full participation in Kyoto decision making on military matters.

**Sen. Hagel:** So, in essence, there is a blanket exemption for the United States military here?

**Mr. Eizenstat:** There is the kind of exemption that they wanted, yes, sir.

**Sen. Hagel:** Does that mean a blanket exemption? Did they ask for a blanket exemption?

**Mr. Eizenstat:** They asked for what we gave them. That's what they asked for. I'm not trying—

**Sen. Hagel:** They asked for what you gave them?

**Mr. Eizenstat:** —to be coy. We asked them, What do you need?, and this is what they told us, and this is what we—

**Sen. Hagel:** So if I would ask any of our commanders, they would give me the same answer?

**Mr. Eizenstat:** Well, if they were the same ones that were with me they certainly would, and I hope that that is the case. But—

**Sen. Hagel:** You hope that's the case—

**Mr. Eizenstat:** Yes, sir, because—

**Sen. Hagel:** I want a little more precise answer than that, Mr. Secretary. (Eizenstat 1998a, 29)

There is strong evidence that at least some in the military were worried about Kyoto because prior to Kyoto, they had draft language in hand for what amounted to a blanket military exemption from greenhouse gas limits for military operations.

Interestingly, the exemption issue was not at first raised by Republicans, but rather by Senator John Kerry (D-MA), who raised the question when he asked Mr. Eizenstat to comment on the claim made in a letter developed by the Committee to Preserve American Sovereignty and Security (COMPASS) and signed by a number of former senior national security officials, including Richard Burt and Dick Cheney. The letter argued that because Kyoto did not exempt unilateral actions, it would complicate military operations politically and diplomatically. Eizenstat emphasized that any action that the United States takes that is pursuant to the right of self-defense under the UN charter is exempt, and he explicitly included the Grenada operation within this category.

Still, the distinction between multilateral and unilateral, while perhaps helpful in limiting the military's exposure to treaty restrictions, still leaves open huge areas of uncertainty regarding which military activities will or will not be counted against the national emissions total, including domestic operations and training.

This already murky issue was further complicated when Deputy Secretary Goodman claimed that, from the administration's point of view, domestic military operations would be exempt from the Kyoto limits.

According to Ms. Goodman, "the administration has decided that it will oppose efforts to impose emissions limits or constraints on domestic military operations and training" (Goodman 1998a, 9). Senator Inhofe requested clarification, and Ms. Goodman said that this was "new news" and that she "did not have that information at the time I submitted my written statement"(Goodman 1998a, 9).

This opposition was not only "new news" to the Senator, but also "good news." Nonetheless, Inhofe requested authoritative documentation of the policy and was promised a memo from the National Security Council (NSC). The memo was released less than a week later, on March 27, 1998. It fell short, however, of what Ms. Goodman suggested the administration's reassurance would be. The relevant passage notes that

> it has been determined that measures intended to promote reductions in emissions of greenhouse gases shall not impair or adversely affect military operations and training (including tactical aircraft, ships, weapons systems, combat training and border security) or the ability to reallocate to the Defense Department emissions resulting from overseas activities and bases pursuant to the agreement at Kyoto. (NSC Memorandum on Climate Change)

Nowhere in the NSC memorandum is there mention of the central issue Goodman said would be addressed by the NSC— domestic implementation. Rather it contains, at most, a tepid pledge that military operations and training will not be "impaired or adversely" affected by climate change policy. The NSC document, in fact, represents a step back from the position articulated at virtually the same time by the secretaries of state and defense. In a letter to the signers of the COMPASS document, the secretaries reveal that "the President recently determined that, to ensure defense readiness, he will propose that military operations and training be 'held harmless' from any national emissions limits that might be adopted" (Cohen and Albright 1998, 1). The secretaries then went on to repeat word for word that part of the NSC document reproduced above. But "held harmless" implies much more than what is set out in the official NSC document, for the phrase suggests that emissions from operations and training simply will not be counted against the military. The NSC document offers no such assurance and allows maximum room for interpretation by this and future administrations.

According to the Kyoto agreement, nations have a right to allocate emissions in any way they please. Consequently, it is completely within the administration's authority simply to state that emissions from domestic military training and operations will not count against the U.S. national total. That it was unwilling to do so indicates that the White House is interested in reserving the option to count these emissions.

If the administration's explanation of how it intends to treat emissions from domestic military training and operations seems opaque, it is a model of clarity when compared with the administration's interpretation of the key Kyoto provision regarding how emissions from multilateral and unilateral operations are to be counted. In the same March 11 hearing discussed above, Senator Inhofe read Ms. Goodman the protocol's language on military operations and asked if there is "an interpretation of this that would lead you to feel comfortable that that applies to not just multi-national operations, but also just us, if we should get involved? Let's just say, for example, if we had to go into Iraq by ourselves or we were training for such a thing." Ms. Goodman offers the following response:

> Yes, Mr. Chairman, our view on—if you're asking what about if we undertake unilateral operations, which is—actually, in today's day and age, is quite rare. Even, as I said, we consider Panama and Grenada to be a multilateral operation conducted pursuant to the UN Charter. Our view is that if we were to undertake, for some reason, a completely unilateral operation, we do not need an international treaty to tell the United States how to operate unilaterally. This is a matter of United States sovereignty. (Goodman 1998a, 10)

The deputy secretary's statement is perhaps true, but irrelevant since the question is not whether the treaty would directly dictate how the United States managed a unilateral operation or training for that operation, but rather whether the greenhouse gas emissions expended in that operation would count against the U.S. national total and so be subject to Kyoto-agreed-upon limits. But the very idea of an actual U.S. military operation being undertaken without some kind of international cooperation or approval is so foreign to Deputy Secretary Goodman that she seems simply to miss the senator's point. In a follow-up answer, Ms. Goodman says, "I'm hard-pressed to even think of a case of a military operation that has been conducted that would be defined in such a narrow way as to be unilateral" (Goodman 1998a, 10).

But many people have regarded past U.S. military operations as unilateral. The Panama operation, for example, was denounced by the chair of the Senate Foreign Relations Committee as a "unilateral" and "go-it-alone" action (Dewar and Kenworth 1989, A35). Foreign reaction was even harsher. Former Secretary of Defense Carlucci made this precise point in a newspaper article that was broadly critical of the administration's treatment of the military in the climate change negotiations (Carlucci 1998, A21). In response, Ms. Goodman set out for the first time a detailed description of what constitutes a unilateral versus a multilateral operation. In essence, she defines unilateral operations out of existence. Without any reference to supporting language in the protocol (because none exists) Ms. Goodman states, "Under the Kyoto agreement, a multilateral operation is broadly defined to include those undertaken by U.S. forces with *any* support from another country (including, for example, the permission of a country to pass through its airspace or to use U.S. forces based in its territory) so virtually all current military operations are multilateral in nature" (Goodman 1998c, C12).

There is no formal paper on this definition, there is no formal agreement from Annex I countries on this definition, and there is no recognition of this definition—formal or otherwise—from the NSC, State, or Defense. When asked about this lack of formal agreement on this interpretation of the Kyoto Protocol, a responsible Pentagon official said that the government has decided to act as if this definition were accepted and to have it affirmed over time by the parties to the protocol (Salomon 1998a). In other words, according to Ms. Goodman, the Pentagon intends to treat all emissions from any operation as exempt from Kyoto.

But there are no grounds for her interpretation. There is nothing in the treaty language itself to support this broad definition of *multilateral,* and it would seem too easy to challenge on the grounds of common sense. Lacking further high-level clarification of the national security aspects of the protocol, we are left with an entirely open-ended treaty whose meaning seems flexible to a dangerous degree.

In May 1998, in the face of the administration's handling of the national security aspects of the Kyoto agreement, the House passed, by a vote of 420 to 0, an amendment to the Defense Authorization Bill stating that "no provision of the Kyoto Protocol . . . shall restrict the procurement, training, or operation and maintenance of the United States Armed Forces."[3] The amendment was approved by Congress.

Although useful for the military, the amendment begs the question: What is the definition of *restriction*? One can imagine a heated debate between the military and global warming enthusiasts over this issue.

## EMISSIONS TRADING AND
## NATIONAL SECURITY

The administration argues that the use of "flexible market mechanisms" will lessen the cost of compliance with the protocol. The concept of emissions trading is popular with the administration and others and has been used by the President's Council of Economic Advisors to demonstrate that the costs of Kyoto will be modest. At this point, however, it is impossible to determine how this system will function or what it will cost. Nevertheless, the idea itself may have significant national security implications.

The source of concern stems from the fact that the primary market for emissions credits will be Russia, which could have anywhere from 200 to 800 million metric tons of carbon to market (EIA 1998; IIASA 1998). Depending on the size of the carbon bubble and the permit price, this could mean an unrestricted transfer to Russia of between $30 and $160 billion (EIA 1998; IIASA 1998). These estimates assume that Russia will be willing to sell its permits in a nondiscriminatory fashion. However, as one of the few net sellers of emissions permits, it is likely that Russia would restrict sales in order to increase prices.

Determining how many dollars Russia might be able to gain from a Kyoto permit-trading scheme is impossible. It is clear, however, that permit trading can raise national security issues when it implies the unrestricted transfer of billions of dollars to an unstable regime, such as Russia.

## A BRIEF NOTE ON THE
## SOVEREIGNTY QUESTION

Among the arguments that have been raised against the Kyoto Protocol, not the least concerns the issue of American sovereignty. If not clarified, the sovereignty issue threatens to become a distraction from the subtle, but real, dangers to American national security contained in the Kyoto accord. Clarity on this issue is essential if genuine security concerns are to be separated from both real and exaggerated concerns about American sovereignty.

As discussed above, national security issues arise in the context of the Kyoto Protocol because the protocol itself exempts emissions arising from multilateral military operations "pursuant to the United Nations Charter" but requires that "other operations shall be included in the national emissions totals" (Kyoto Protocol 1997, 31). Now, it is certainly the case that international bodies set up to administer the treaty would have a role in decisions about which missions fell within the Kyoto limits. But those bodies clearly would not have a veto over these operations, although there would inescapably be new diplomatic and political pressures that would play a role in decision making on U.S. military deployments. There is no direct challenge to sovereignty, however, because the United States could engage in whatever actions it chose, so long as it was willing to accept the greenhouse penalty that would be charged against the national emissions total. The issue is not sovereignty so much as it is whether the United States wishes to agree to a treaty that imposes novel political and diplomatic restraint on military action and training and opens the possibility of wealth transfers to Russia.

Focusing on the potential mischief that international bureaucrats might exert on the execution of U.S. national security strategy is useful, but misses two important points. First, international bureaucrats would have no direct authority to prevent American action, unilateral or multilateral. And second, the real restraint on military action and training will more likely come from domestic pressure groups, perhaps supported by the international greenhouse bureaucracy, arguing that some planned military action or other would be unjust, immoral, and illegal because it would threaten to expend so much energy that it would jeopardize the ability of the United States to meet its commitment to the Kyoto greenhouse gas limits. In addition to the War Powers Act, the ghosts of Vietnam, the fears of loss of life, calls for giving diplomacy one more chance, international pressures, and other impediments to the use of military power or even to the credible threat of force, one might now add the "greenhouse restraint."

## HOW KYOTO CAN COMPROMISE AMERICA'S NATIONAL SECURITY

Apparently, the potential for harm to American defense policy, and to our ability to project power around the globe, was not taken seriously enough by the administration during its negotiations in Kyoto. A brief summary of the ways in which national security may be impaired by the Kyoto treaty demonstrates the need for fundamental and prompt action by the administration and Congress to correct this flawed agreement.

1. The very ambiguity that now surrounds the meaning of this protocol with respect to the military's use of energy is an open invitation to mischief. Hostile nations will read this treaty in ways most likely to inhibit American military power. It is conceivable that every movement our army, navy, air force, marines, and coast guard—including training exercises within the United States—will become the subject of debate and controversy about whether greenhouse gas use was properly accounted for, or was properly reported, or was reported in a timely fashion, or was reported at all, or should have been counted against the nation's national total, or should be counted against another nation's total and not ours, and on and on. Unless we have a clear picture of our obligations under this treaty, we could be subject to endless negotiation, discussion, and debate over every tank maneuver and ship deployment. The treaty presents a potential world of nightmares to the U.S. military.

2. The exact procedures the military will use to account for its emissions has yet to be worked out. According to one Pentagon official, whether or not reporting requirements are reasonable will depend on how zealous the regulators choose to be (Salomon 1998b). For example, the military uses many chemicals—for coolant and other functions—that are powerful greenhouse gases. Small amounts of these chemicals are released into the atmosphere every

year as a matter of course, just as Freon slowly leaks from home air-conditioning systems. How is the military to account for the release of these chemicals into the atmosphere? Regulators could allow relatively simple accounting procedures, such as reporting the amount of these specific chemicals replaced each year. Or they could require an exact account for every piece of equipment. In other words, by becoming involved in the Kyoto process, the military has handed regulators considerable power over its future operations.

3. Political and regulatory pressures, however, are not the only kinds of interference the military needs to fear if it becomes entangled in the Kyoto environmental net. It is worth contemplating the possibility that direct legal action could be taken against our armed forces by foreign governments, corporations, or nongovernmental organizations. Whether through the international courts of justice or through a foreign government's legal system, the military could potentially be sued for violating Kyoto greenhouse gas limits if it somehow tripped up in the way it reported its emissions, or in some other way failed to comply with the treaty. Since the protocol is itself so ambiguous, the options for falling into some arguable violation are almost endless. Because it operates globally, the military is particularly vulnerable to hostile legal action of the sort discussed.

4. The administration's belief that the exemptions in the treaty for multilateral operations pursuant to the UN Charter are sufficient to cover virtually all conceivable cases, including controversial engagements such as Panama and Grenada, is at best naive. Does the administration really believe that there would not have been demands for imposition of greenhouse gas restraints on these operations had Kyoto been in effect at the time? What is more, greenhouse restraints would surely have come into play in the Panama case long before the first shots were fired. Planners would have had to calculate how fuel use connected to the operation would figure into the nation's overall greenhouse gas budget and to contend with domestic and international pressure to hold fire else they further contribute to greenhouse warming.

5. Unless the administration or Congress acts quickly to correct the pernicious aspects of this greenhouse protocol and to

clarify precisely the conditions under which $CO_2$ emissions during military operations might be counted against the U.S. national greenhouse gas limit, it is likely that we will be compelled to adhere to the protocol despite the fact that it has not been ratified by the Senate. It is almost inevitable that a bureaucracy will be established within the Pentagon to monitor compliance with the accord, regardless of the Senate's explicit failure to ratify the agreement. Indeed, it is likely that an entirely new national security bureaucracy similar in reach to that established to monitor arms control agreements will set limits and establish procedures that will offer new constraints to the legitimate exercise of American power.

6. The complete lack of verification procedures in the treaty ignores the lessons learned during decades of arms control negotiations. There are legitimate concerns over exactly how one might verify such a pact and questions about the feasibility of verifying the treaty under any circumstances. But the question of how one verifies such a treaty cannot be answered until the idea of verification itself is taken seriously.

7. The protocol undermines international stability by creating mechanisms that, in effect, penalize the United States for being a global military power. As the only nation in the world capable of maintaining an environment that allows free governments to prosper and that creates the kind of stability necessary for growth in international commerce, the United States is compelled to sustain a global military presence. Kyoto imposes a greenhouse tax on that military presence, which can only serve to weaken the military's influence.

8. The protocol presents the possibility that to meet its reduction obligations, the United States will be forced to purchase emission credits from Russia, in the process transferring billions of dollars to an unstable regime. Unrestricted cash transfers are not wise policy when dealing with allies, let alone former foes.

Each of these eight impediments to the effective functioning of American national security policy is compounded by a troubling fact—the administration sees Kyoto as only the beginning of a sustained effort to reduce carbon dioxide emissions. Secretary Eizenstat has noted correctly that Kyoto is "only one step in a long process," and one enthusiast for global warming regulations noted "it might take another thirty Kyotos over the next century" to control human-induced climate change (Malakoff 1997, 2048).

Combined with the many incentives to use the military as a primary source for achieving greenhouse gas reductions, the first-step character of Kyoto suggests interminable problems for U.S. national security and that the problems reviewed in this chapter are likely to get worse, not better.

It could be argued that because the military has downsized so profoundly over the last decade, and because it contributes such a relatively small amount to total U.S. greenhouse gas emissions, it will be left alone by the environmentalists and by any administration seeking to meet internationally agreed-upon limits. There is reason to believe this is the Pentagon's hope (Salomon 1998a), but the Pentagon is best advised not to count on environmentalists' goodwill. One of the primary targets for additional regulation because of its global warming potential is the sports utility vehicle (SUV), which taken as a fleet emits a fraction of the $CO_2$ that the military emits. But the SUV is a symbol of American excess, and so it has come under a level of scrutiny and attack that outweighs its actual importance as an environmental threat. If the SUV can be taken seriously as a contributor to climate change, the military can expect that its own much greater contribution to greenhouse warming will not be ignored.

## CONCLUSION

The threat of serious humanmade climate change is too tentative and uncertain to claim equal status with existing and future threats to America's national security. Inclusion of military operations in a climate change treaty is inconsistent with the international obligations of our military forces.

## ENDNOTES

1. See <http://www.science.nasa.gov/newhome/headlines/essd06oct 97_htm>.
2. I am grateful to Henry I. Miller for bringing this information to my attention.
3. Gilman Amendment to H.R. 3616.

## REFERENCES

Bidlack, Harlod. 1998. The Impact of Global Climate Change on National Security. Unpublished manuscript. Department of Political Science, U.S. Air Force Academy.

Carlucci, Frank. 1998. Making Military Sense Out of Kyoto. *The Washington Times*, 18 May, A21.

Cohen, William, and Albright, Madeleine. 1998. Letter to Signers of COMPASS Document. At <http://www.denix.osd.mil/denix/Public/News/OSD/Climate/ climate.html> on December 7, 1999.

Defense Environmental Alert. 1997. DOD Weighs National Security Exemption for Climate Change Treaty. *Inside Washington Publishers* (newsletter) 5:20, September 23.

Dewar, Helen, and Kenworth, Tom. 1989. Decision "Was Made Necessary by Reckless Actions of General Noriega." *The Washington Post*, 21 December, A35.

Eizenstat, Stuart. 1998a. *Kyoto Global Climate Change Agreement.* U.S. Senate Committee on Foreign Relations. 105th Cong., 1st sess., 11 February. Federal News Service Transcript.

———. 1998b. Prepared Statement.

Energy Information Agency (EIA). 1998. International Energy Annual. Washington, D.C. At <http://www.eia.doe.gov> on December 7, 1999.

Goodman, Sherri. 1998a. *Defense Environmental Programs and FY 1999 Military Construction and Housing.* U.S. Senate Armed Services Committee, Readiness Subcommittee. 105th Cong., 2d sess., 11 March. Federal News Service Transcript.

———. 1998b. Prepared Statement.

———. 1998c. Letter to the Editor. *The Washington Times*, 6 June, C12.

Gore, Albert. 1992. *Earth in the Balance: Ecology and the Human Spirit.* Boston: Houghton Mifflin.

Hansen, James. 1988. *Greenhouse Effect and Global Climate Change.* U.S. Senate Committee on Energy and Natural Resources. 100th Cong., 1st sess., 23 June.

Hansen, James, Makiko Sato, Andrew Lacis, Reto Ruedy, Ina Tegen, Elaine Matthews. 1998. Climate Forcing in the Industrial Era. *Perspective* 95(22): 12753–12768.

Houghton, J.T., G.J. Jenkins, J.J. Ephraums, eds. 1990. *Climate Change: The IPCC Scientific Assessment.* Cambridge: Cambridge University Press.

Houghton, J.T., L.G. Meira Filho, B.A. Callander, N. Harris, A. Kattenberg, K. Maskell. 1996. *Climate Change 1995: The Science of Climate Change.* Cambridge: Cambridge University Press.

International Institute for Applied Systems Analysis (IIASA). 1998. The Kyoto Protocol Carbon Bubble: Implications for Russia, Ukraine, and Emission Trading. At <http://www.iiasa.ac.at/Publications/Documents/IR-98-094.pdf> on December 7, 1999.

Kyoto Protocol. 1997. Report of the Conference of the Parties on Its Third Session, at Kyoto, Japan, December 1997.

Malakoff, David. 1997. Thirty Kyotos Needed to Control Warming. *Science* 278 (December 19): 2048.

Ponte, Lowell. 1976. *The Cooling.* Englewood Cliffs, N.J.: Prentice-Hall.

Rubin, Charles. 1993. That Obscure Object of Desire: The Environment and Contemporary Environmentalism. Paper presented at the American Political Science Association Convention, 2–5 September, at Washington, D.C.

Salomon, Roy. 1998a. Interview with author, 23 June.

———. 1998b. Interview with author, 29 September.

Vest, Gary. 1997. Environmental Change and Regional Security. Conference Report at the Center for Strategic Leadership, September 1997, at U.S. Army War College.

# CHAPTER 7

# Bootleggers, Baptists, and Global Warming

## Bruce Yandle

## INTRODUCTION

Since the conference on climate change in Kyoto, Japan, in December 1997, the world's industrialized nations have been grappling with the realities of a costly treaty. Passionate expressions of concern about global warming have given way to tough political bargaining over who bears the pain. The stakes are high. The decisions made in the near future—including the decision by the United States to ratify or not—will determine which countries, which industries, and which firms (if any) will bite the bullet of costly reductions in carbon emissions.

The Kyoto Protocol calls for thirty-eight countries in the developed world to cut greenhouse gases to roughly 95 percent of 1990 levels by 2008–2012. This cut will happen mostly by reducing the use of fossil fuels, which emit large quantities of carbon dioxide (UNFCCC 1997).

Total emissions of carbon dioxide and other greenhouse gases (primarily methane and nitrous oxide) are much larger than they were in 1990. Thus, the industrialized countries, and especially the United States, face a daunting and perhaps impossible challenge. The United States must reduce the emissions projected for the years 2008 to 2012 by some 40 percent to meet its goal of reducing 1990 level emissions by 7 percent.

Yet the developing world, which emits large quantities of green-house gases, faces no challenge at all. By the terms of Kyoto, developing countries can continue to expand their output of carbon. So, with major emitters cutting back and minor ones expanding, it is highly likely that total carbon emissions will be larger in the future, not smaller, in spite of Kyoto.

This situation suggests that more is going on as a result of Kyoto than a commitment to reduce carbon emissions. The Kyoto Protocol creates a new and enhanced stage upon which nations, groups, and companies can pursue their special interests. The treaty opens up opportunities for favor-seeking that were previously closed. This chapter looks at the activities of companies and national governments in the light of a "bootleggers and Baptists" theory of regulation. It is not a pleasing sight.

## THE KYOTO CHALLENGE

The Kyoto Protocol,[1] which evolved over the past decade, has as its fundamental premise the idea that developed countries, which are large energy users and greenhouse gas producers, should bear the brunt of reducing emissions to avoid climate change. By the years 2008 to 2012, developed countries aim to bring their total greenhouse gas emissions to 5 percent less than they were in 1990. Meanwhile, developing countries will be expanding emissions at roughly 3 percent per year.

To give the reader an idea of the relative emission magnitudes, in 1990 the industrialized world, with the United States leading the pack, produced roughly 64 percent of all greenhouse gases, which then totaled six billion tons annually.[2] The developing countries produced the remaining 36 percent, led by China with approximately 11 percent. If emissions are not controlled, emissions for the year 2015 are expected to be 8.45 billion tons, with the developing countries producing 52 percent of the total. By the year 2100, forecasts (again, assuming no controls) call for a total of 19.8 billion tons of greenhouse emissions, with the developing world producing 66 percent.

These forecasts are far from certain. However, because only the industrialized countries are expected to cut back, it is unlikely that the goal of limiting total emissions to 1990 levels will be met in the foreseeable future. Groups alarmed about global warming can still support the treaty on the grounds that carbon emissions may decline eventually. But others, including companies and countries who want bigger markets, appear to be paying more attention to the strategic here-and-now possibilities offered by regulation under the Kyoto Protocol. There will be winners and losers in the post-Kyoto struggle, and expectations about who will win and lose are guiding much of today's political jockeying.

## THE POST-KYOTO FUTURE

It is clear that if the Kyoto Protocol is fully implemented, the relative prices of major energy commodities will change. Economic studies show that the demand for natural gas will rise, as will the demand for oil, to a lesser extent. The demand for coal, however, will plummet. Many nations that now have comparative advantages based on large coal reserves and related technologies and manufacturing will lose those advantages. Certain ozone-depleting chemicals will be banned, expanding markets for their substitutes.

National governments will engage in trade with other governments, but the items to be traded will be such things as the still-undefined "marketable emission permits" and "offsetting" actions to reduce greenhouse gases. In addition, countries will make bilateral agreements to transfer clean technology and provide development assistance, possibly creating emission offsets for participating countries.

Marketable greenhouse gas emission permits are the centerpiece of the Kyoto Protocol, although the scope of the market and the trading process have not yet been defined. An emission permit is a right to consume carbon and emit carbon dioxide in the course of production or manufacturing. To carry out the protocol, governments are likely to define a fixed number of emission rights equal to their Kyoto goals and divide them up among present carbon emitters. Because the goal in most developed countries is less carbon than is now emitted, emitters will have to cut back their emissions or buy the rights to emit from someone else. Either action is equivalent to paying a tax on carbon emissions.

Under a permit system, firms or countries that face high costs in cutting back (or that want to increase their carbon output) would buy carbon-emission rights from firms or countries that could cut back at lower cost. An international permit-trading market is especially attractive to countries with high costs, such as the United States. Some countries with firms that have done little to control emissions could reduce their carbon output through relatively simple, low-cost changes. These credits could be purchased by countries facing high costs.

The concept of permit trading is so popular among influential economists that just starting a market in carbon permits sometimes seems to justify taking action on global warming, no matter what economics or science might say. A permit market offers the prospect of significantly reducing the control costs of achieving the protocol's goals—a fact that helped generate support for the protocol.

In this new international environment, however, trade becomes quite different from trade as we normally think of it. Actions that might be seen as attempts by industries to restrict output and raise rivals' costs (what might be called attempts at cartelization) are encouraged, in the name of global environmental protection, rather than frowned upon. National policies that might be seen as violations of GATT (the rules that guide international trade) are viewed benevolently. This change of attitude magnifies the ability of well-organized interest groups to obtain advantages by crafting the rules guiding these trades and agreements.

Other changes will also occur. When the Kyoto agreement was signed, it joined an estimated 180 other environmental treaties on deposit with the United Nations Secretary General.[3] These treaties are fundamentally different from national decisions to legislate in the interest of cleaner air or water. These treaties seek to impose a homogeneous rule—in this case, greenhouse gas reductions based on 1990 emissions—on a diverse set of global communities. Economists know that a "one-size-fits-all" rule applied to diverse situations leads to waste and inefficiency. Furthermore, such rules can compromise constitutional constraints and domestic rules of law and property that normally protect property rights and spur competition in domestic economies.

## BOOTLEGGERS AND BAPTISTS

To understand what is happening now in the implementation of the Kyoto Protocol, it is helpful to consider some theories that economists use to explain why regulation takes the form it does. Three basic theories of regulation will assist our analysis.[4]

The first, called the public interest theory, reflects traditional views of regulation that prevailed before it was studied carefully by economists and political scientists. The theory simply states that governments attempt to maximize the collective well-being of citizens. According to this theory, politicians weigh the benefits and costs of policies and attempt to maximize net benefits for the public. For example, if taxes are to be imposed to reduce the harms from global warming, politicians will carefully calibrate and impose taxes in ways that cause the least economic impact.

The capture theory is more realistic. It is based on the idea that politicians attempting to serve the public interest encounter persuasive special interests. The dedicated politician is "captured" by the special interest group and begins to serve the wishes of the group (perhaps unwittingly). One problem with this theory is that it does not help determine which of many special interest groups will succeed in winning the struggle.

The third and most developed theory, called the economic theory of regulation, asks us to consider the political arena as a marketplace where favors are bought and sold. Interest groups that have the most to gain or lose will bid the highest prices for favors. Politicians dedicated to preserving their jobs, and needing large amounts of campaign funds, auction off the favors. Under this theory, if carbon emissions are to be controlled, the politician will seek the group with the largest economic stake in the outcome (and therefore presumably the most generous with campaign funds) and favor that group. Competing groups will attempt to outbid the winner. Usually, the smaller the group, the more each member can gain by crafting regulatory rules. The larger the group, the less likely each individual member will have a strong reward or heavy burden as a result of the rules. So, small special interest groups usually are the most actively involved in the negotiations.

However, even this theory is incomplete. Being a small, well-organized special interest group is not enough. My theory of bootleggers and Baptists, a subset of the economic theory of regulation, further helps explain environmental regulation like that imposed by the Kyoto Protocol (Yandle 1983). Although powerful interest groups still matter, this theory tells us that there must be at least two quite different interest groups working in the same direction—"bootleggers" and "Baptists."

The term stems from the southern United States, where in the past and even today Sunday closing laws prevent the legal sale of alcoholic beverages. This is advantageous to bootleggers, who sell alcoholic beverages illegally; they get the market to themselves on Sundays. Baptists and other religious groups support the same laws, but for entirely different reasons. They are opposed to selling alcohol at all, but especially on Sunday. They take the moral high ground, while the bootleggers persuade politicians quietly or behind closed doors. Such a coalition makes it easier for politicians to favor both groups. In other words, the Baptists lower the costs of favor-seeking for the bootleggers.

The post-Kyoto period promises to be rich with bootlegger–Baptist coalitions. The Baptists are the active environmental groups pushing for ratification and enforcement of the treaty and working to prevent backsliding. They are passionate and persuasive to the public as they argue that cutting back on carbon emissions is a moral necessity. They are creating a groundswell for action on the Kyoto Protocol. Indeed, the protocol even enjoys a "Baptist" supporter that gets close to the name itself. It is the United Methodist Church. On December 17, just a few weeks after the Kyoto meetings, Jaydee R. Hanson, assistant general secretary of the United Methodist Board of Church and Society, pronounced his denomination's support for Kyoto (United Methodist News Service 1997). Hanson urged the U.S. Senate to "protect God's creation by ratifying" the agreement. Other denominations are doing the same.

To determine which groups are the bootleggers, we should search for special interest groups who are positioned to gain from regulatory enforcement and stringency or who must fend off losses that spring from proposed rules. In this role we see national governments, industries, and firms.

## THE EMERGING COALITION

National governments are strategically positioning themselves to benefit from the negotiations while operating under cover of the international environmental groups sounding the alarm about global warming. When we survey the participants, we find that some countries, such as the United Kingdom, are positioned to exploit carbon reductions they have made in the past by raising the cost to economies that still rely heavily on coal. Other countries, including developing countries and some European nations under one proposal, are allowed higher emissions. These countries see opportunities for payments from the developed countries for reducing carbon emissions or for offsetting actions such as planting trees. In addition, within countries, some industries are favored by the rules and, within industries, some firms will also be favored. Meanwhile, environmentalists are running interference and providing cover.

Some signs of an emerging bootlegger-and-Baptist coalition are beginning to emerge. For example, environmentalists provide the cover story on which media attention is focused, while companies, industries, or countries work quietly in the background to gain benefits.

### ALTERNATIVE-ENERGY BOOTLEGGERS

In January 1997, Enron Corporation, a major provider of low-carbon natural gas, announced the formation of Enron Renewable Energy Corporation. The company indicated that it was "preparing to take advantage of the growing interest in environmentally sound alternatives of power in the $250 billion U.S. electricity market" (Salisbury 1998). The new division faces the difficult challenge of producing solar and other nontraditional energy products at costs that can compete with conventional energy sources. Not surprisingly, Tom White, Enron Renewable Energy CEO, endorsed

President Clinton's $6.3 billion plan to fight global warming. This plan includes $3.6 billion in tax credits to spur the production and purchase of renewable energy and related technologies. Kyoto-justified taxpayer subsidies will make life easier for firms like Enron. Other producers who have long enjoyed federal subsidies now hope to justify those subsidies in the glow of global warming. The National Corn Growers Association (1998) has been trying to stall congressional efforts to end the 5.4 cents-per-gallon federal tax incentive provided to producers of corn-based ethanol. Originally enacted on the dubious basis of providing energy self-sufficiency, the large ethanol subsidies were on shaky ground in early 1998. In April, the Renewable Fuels Association (1998a) joined forces with ethanol producers to celebrate Earth Day by calling attention to ethanol's beneficial effects on global warming. Secretary of Agriculture Dan Glickman indicated his strong support for extending the ethanol subsidy, noting that "renewable fuels provide an important opportunity . . . to lower greenhouse gas emissions" (Renewable Fuels Association 1998b).

Mary Nichols, U.S. EPA Assistant Administrator for Air and Radiation, had spoken in January 1998 at the National Ethanol Conference, telling the audience: "One area where I think we can do more together is the area of climate change and global warming" (quoted in Stark 1998). No one mentioned that ethanol production is so costly that it might require more energy than it produces or that half of the federal government's $600 million annual ethanol subsidy goes to one ethanol producer, Archer-Daniels-Midland.[5] Nor did anyone mention a literal bootlegger–Baptist connection: The taxpayer subsidy assists the production of beverage as well as industrial alcohol (Bandow 1997).

All this concentrated effort came to a successful conclusion on May 6, 1998, when then-House Speaker Newt Gingrich salvaged the ethanol program, much to the dismay of Senator Bill Archer (R-TX), who wanted to end the program because ethanol blends reduce demand for Texas-produced gasoline products (Pianin 1998). But global warming helped save the day for the corn producers.

Following in their American cousins' footsteps, the Canadian Commercial Alcohol Association trumpeted ethanol's carbon-reducing virtues. They suggested that any $CO_2$ produced by burning ethanol would be recycled into corn plant tissue, thereby yielding a net reduction in atmospheric carbon dioxide levels (Commercial Alcohols Canada 1998).

Not to be outdone by corn growers, the National Biodiesel Board, representing U.S farmers who produce soybean and other vegetable oil products, testified before Secretary of Energy Federico Peña on February 19, 1998. The board pointed out the environmental benefits of blending farm-produced oil products with diesel fuel (National Biodiesel Board 1998) and lobbied the Department of Energy (DOE) to give official approval to biodiesel as an alternative fuel, thus ensuring a market through DOE programs. The trade association officials said that "biodiesel helps reduce the effects of global warming by directly displacing fossil hydrocarbons" (National Biodiesel Board 1998).

## NATURAL GAS AND OIL BOOTLEGGERS

While the ethanol and biodiesel bootleggers were joining with environmental Baptists, a coalition of major oil producers and other firms was having trouble keeping members opposed to Kyoto. The Global Climate Coalition, consisting of major oil firms and thousands of other firms, attempted to speak with one voice in debunking Kyoto's shaky scientific underpinnings and calling attention to the economic effects of the protocol. But in June 1998, Shell Oil announced it was leaving the coalition.

Claiming credit for Shell's green conversion, Friends of the Earth spokesperson Anna Stanford said, "We're delighted that our hard work has paid off, that Shell has bowed to public pressure and seen that the future lies in fighting climate change and investing in green energy. Now is the time to turn our attention to Exxon to make them follow Shell's lead" (Friends of the Earth 1998). Shell's response was that "there are enough indications that $CO_2$ emissions are having an effect on climate change" (Magada 1998). Being more specific about the firm's strategy, Mark Moody-Stuart, Chairman of Shell Transport and Trading, said that Shell is "promoting the development of the gas industry, particularly in countries with large coal reserves such as India and China" (Magada 1998). What may not be obvious to the public is that tough implementation of Kyoto implies growing demand for natural gas.

Shell's departure from the Global Climate Coalition was made easier by British Petroleum's earlier defection. John Browne, CEO of British Petroleum (BP), stated that industry must play a "positive and responsible part in identifying solutions" to the global warming problem (EDF 1997)—a statement that sounds both concerned and responsible, just the sort of thing that environmental activists praise. But BP also expects to see an increase in demand for oil, its chief product, because oil is a substitute for coal that produces fewer carbon emissions. BP also announced a significant investment increase in solar and alternative energy technology development.

To be sure, many major industries, or at least major firms, still oppose Kyoto. Not everyone is teaming up with the Baptists. Coal producers and related unions are among the most vocal in their opposition. Coal interests in West Virginia were successful enough to obtain state legislation prohibiting the state government from "proposing or implementing rules regulating greenhouse gas emissions from industrial sites," according to the press release issued by the office of Cecil Underwood, West Virginia's governor (April 2, 1998).

Yet even the coal-producing states are acting a bit like bootleggers. On signing the bill, Governor Cecil Underwood made his own overture to the Baptists. He indicated that although actions like the Kyoto Protocol must be opposed, we "should continue to encourage the development and implementation of technologies that allow the clean burning of coal." He supports research on clean-coal technologies (a term that in the past referred to production that emitted fewer pollutants but now includes production with fewer carbon dioxide emissions), if it is subsidized by the nation's taxpayers. The press release from the governor's office said that he and Governor Paul Patton of Kentucky, another coal-producing state, had persuaded the Southern Governors' Association to pass a resolution saying basically the same thing.

Although corn producers who supply the raw material for ethanol see a pot of gold in Kyoto, farmers who must operate in a globally competitive market generally oppose it. Dean Kleckner, president of the 4.8-million-member American Farm Bureau Federation, opposes the protocol "because of its potential harm to U.S. farmers," according to a Reuters report (March 6, 1998). Reinforcing his concern, Mary Novak, senior vice president of the consulting firm WEFA, Inc., predicted that food prices would go up 10 percent as a result of Kyoto. She also predicted higher fuel and fertilizer prices. There are winners and losers within the same economic sector.

## COUNTRIES AS BOOTLEGGERS

Even before ratification, some governments were taking steps to capitalize on the opportunities stemming from Kyoto. One country even found it possible to gain additional wealth for actions it was going to take anyway.

In April 1998, Costa Rica announced a new version of its program to save 1.25 million acres of rain forest. Costa Rican President Jose Maria Figueres said that environmental bonds, called certified tradable offsets (CTOs), will be sold to industrial firms. Each CTO corresponds to one ton of carbon that will be absorbed by trees. Under this arrangement, each CTO is backed by a specific number of trees left standing, which absorb one ton of carbon annually. By paying Costa Rica to protect its rain forest, polluters elsewhere can release more carbon emissions. The planned offsets will accommodate one million metric tons of carbon annually (Allen 1998). The program will be managed by the prestigious Swiss commercial inspection firm SGS. It will cost Costa Rica nothing, since it is something that the government is doing anyway, but it was expected to produce $20 million in revenues in 1998. Companies will pay $20 per ton of carbon emissions that are offset by the bonds. Costa Rica hopes to generate $300 million this way over the next twenty years.

At about the same time, Japan and Russia engaged in what is believed to be the world's first greenhouse gas emissions swap

(Takenaka 1998). The alliance illustrates Kyoto-inspired "offsetting" actions. Japan will send technicians to approximately twenty Russian power plants and factories to help Russia cut carbon emissions. In return, Japan can obtain credits to offset its required cutbacks. The agreement between Japan and Russia has other features, too. The two countries will share information on nuclear energy production. (Both have something to offer—Japan is a leading producer of nuclear energy technology, and Russia a leader in the development of breeder reactors.) And Japan will become a larger investor in the search for offshore gas and oil in Russian waters.

This arrangement is facilitated by the fact that Russia has no difficulty in meeting its Kyoto goal, a zero increase in carbon emissions above the 1990 baseline. With the Russian economy in shambles, production has fallen well below 1990 levels. However, Japan, which promised to cut baseline emissions by 6 percent, faces a real challenge. Reducing emissions of carbon there requires costly changes in fuel use.

## THE STAKES ARE HIGH

Political action by bootleggers occurs because there are big gains to be made by positioning oneself more favorably. Economic studies show that the implementation of Kyoto will create winners and losers. Long before Kyoto, academic economists were turning out studies on the effects of controlling greenhouse gases (Manne and Richels 1991; Nordhaus 1991; Pearce and Barbier 1991; Whaley and Wigle 1991; Jorgenson and Wilcoxen 1993; Kosobud, Daly, South, and Quinn 1994; Larsen and Shah 1994; Sinclair 1994; Holtz-Eakin and Selden 1995; Carrato, Galeotti, and Gallo 1996; Chen 1997).

Perhaps the most comprehensive study was the Jorgenson-Wilcoxen (1993) study, a large model of the U.S. economy that incorporates thirty-five industrial sectors as well as consumer behavior, investment, and trade. The authors studied what would happen if U.S. carbon emissions were held constant at 1990 levels[6] (a less ambitious goal than the cutbacks agreed on at Kyoto) and what fuel taxes would be required to achieve the goal. For example, one of the simulations indicated that coal should be taxed at $11.01 per ton, oil at $2.31 per barrel, and natural gas at $0.28 per thousand cubic feet. The resulting revenues, the authors estimated, would yield $26 billion annually to the federal government.

The authors concluded that the tax policies under consideration would cut annual GDP (gross domestic product) growth by between fractions of a percentage point and one percentage point. Although this may not seem dramatic, a change of one-half a percentage point in annual growth from 2.0 percent to 1.5 percent is a 25 percent reduction. It means that the time it will take for total GDP to double (a measure of increasing prosperity) will lengthen from 36 to 48 years. A one percent loss in GDP is not small potatoes, even for one year. If the loss continues for more than a decade in a growing economy, the cumulative loss can equal as much as half of what the GDP was when the cutbacks started. The cost in terms of human well-being could be large. More striking are the expected changes in energy prices. Jorgenson and Wilcoxen estimate that coal prices would go up by 40 percent and coal production would drop by 26 percent.

Manne and Richels (1991) took a global approach. They assumed that industrialized countries would seek to reduce carbon emissions by 20 percent by the year 2020 and that developing countries would limit their emissions to twice their 1990 levels. They found that the U.S. GDP would be 3 percent lower than its baseline by the year 2030 and would continue at a 3 percent lower level from that point to 2100. Mexico and oil-producing countries would sustain even larger losses, and China the largest of all, losing 10 percent of GDP in the last half of the twenty-first century. Losses for the Organization of Economic Cooperation and Development (OECD) countries other than the United States would be much smaller, however, reaching only 1 to 2 percent in 2030. In the most stringent set of circumstances, the price of coal would increase fourfold, and the demand for oil would increase, not decrease.

Other studies reported in professional journals follow the same lines. The academics agree that reducing carbon emissions to 1990 baseline levels places the brunt of the adjustment cost on the coal and coal-related sectors and that the GDP growth rates in the industrial world will be affected. Studies also indicate that the potential cost of the Kyoto Protocol to the United States is far greater in total and in relative terms than for other industrialized countries.

As Kyoto approached, these broad studies were supplemented by studies of the proposed protocol's impact on specific sectors. In most cases, these studies were performed by respected consulting firms for trade associations, organized labor, and government. These studies generally assumed that some permit trading—as opposed to taxation and regulation alone—would be used to implement the treaty. As we have seen, permit trading is attractive because the cost of reducing carbon emissions differs among and within countries. Much of the negotiation now taking place relates to the definition and regulation of permit trading.

The specialized industrial studies made a variety of assumptions about the role of permit trading, but generally assumed some trades would be allowed. DRI/McGraw-Hill (1997) prepared a major study for the United Mine Workers and Bituminous Coal Association. The study (reviewed by the Economic Policy Institute) assumes a government-issued marketable permit program. The study considers two scenarios: stabilizing greenhouse gas emissions at 1990 levels and reducing emissions by 10 percent below 1990 levels by the year 2010.

The study predicts a sevenfold price increase for coal by 2010. Electricity prices are expected to double and retail gasoline prices to increase 40 to 50 percent. Because of these price increases, coal, which now provides 24 percent of U.S. energy, will provide only 18 percent. Petroleum's share will increase, and natural gas will maintain its current market share.

The government's revenue from permit sales will rise to $776 billion in 2020 and yield a budget surplus of $388 billion by 2020. Annual losses in employment will reach 1.4 million for the years 2000–2020, and growth in GDP will be reduced by one percentage point (say, from 2.5 percent to 1.5 percent), as the economy adjusts to the constraints. Coal output is predicted to decline by 45 percent, rubber and plastics by 50 percent, and electricity production by 18 percent.

A study conducted by the economic consulting firm WEFA (1998) and sponsored by the American Petroleum Institute is even more pessimistic. It assumes that U.S. carbon emissions will stabilize at 1990 levels by the year 2010, but at a high cost. The analysts assume that emissions, if uncontrolled, would be 27 percent above 1990 levels by 2010 and 46 percent above the target by 2020. They also assume that trade in permits will occur only in the United States. To achieve the necessary reductions, carbon permit prices would have to rise across the control period from $100 per ton per year to $300 per ton per year of emissions. Companies that want the right to emit carbon dioxide may have to buy those rights from companies that can cut back.

The carbon reductions would lead to a 30 to 55 percent increase in overall consumer prices, with energy-intensive sectors sustaining shocks comparable to those associated with the Arab oil embargoes of the 1970s. Under WEFA's scenario, U.S. exports will become "relatively more expensive on the world market, while the prices of many imported products will fall" (WEFA 1998, 4–5). Exports will go down, and imports rise. The report noted that chemicals, paper, textiles and apparel, and computer and electronic parts production would be severely affected. By 2010, real GDP would be 2.4 percent lower than otherwise.

Ronald J. Sutherland (1998), senior economist for the American Petroleum Institute, prepared an interesting analysis of Kyoto policy options.[7] Using an elegantly simple econometric model for explaining carbon emissions, Sutherland showed that it is practically impossible for the United States to achieve Kyoto's goals, especially if nuclear energy production is ultimately replaced by gas-fired turbines, as is now expected.

Sutherland also contends that the price increases necessary for achieving Kyoto goals will not be accepted. Based on estimates of price elasticity of demand from ten large-scale studies, gasoline prices would need to rise from $1.25 per gallon now to $4.23 per gallon in 2010, just to achieve Kyoto levels. The target date for achieving the goal comes too soon to make the increase more bearable and, in Sutherland's view, the full effects will arouse too much opposition to be enacted (Sutherland 1998).

There are other notable studies, but the reports discussed above identify the strategic issues. The complexity of the issues sometimes led to varying interpretations of the same data. For example, the Department of Energy (DOE) studied Kyoto effects (Office of Policy and International Affairs 1997). The DOE study assumed a goal of achieving 1990 emission levels by 2010 and found that if the market for tradable permits is strictly domestic, permit prices will rise to $150 per ton of carbon emissions during the control period. The price of U.S. coal will triple, and consumption of coal will fall by 50 percent by 2010. Total GDP losses generated by the controls will reach $418 billion. With a world market in permits, however, the price of permits would be only $40 per ton, the department estimated. The relative magnitudes of costs varied significantly across different scenarios about timing and permit prices assumed by the DOE analysts.

In another DOE study prepared by the Interlaboratory Working Group on Energy-Efficient and Low-Carbon Technologies (1997), the analysts found the effects of meeting Kyoto's constraint would hardly be felt. When the scientific journal *Nature* reported this good news, it indicated there would be "no net cost in cutting carbon emissions" (429). The reason: The DOE study argued that if the federal government invested "far beyond current efforts" to encourage switching to energy-efficient technologies, payments for fuel would go down by between $50 and $90 billion per year. These savings would be enough to offset the costs of switching (Reichhardt 1997, 429). Unfortunately, when calculating costs and benefits, the DOE study did not account for the cost of government efforts to bring about the amazing changes.

In the face of multiple studies indicating that implementation of Kyoto will impose substantial economic costs on the U.S. economy, Janet Yellen (1998), Chairperson of the Council of Economic Advisers, offered a more optimistic outlook. But Yellen's more sanguine view was based on the assumptions that the United States would purchase emission credits from a host of developing countries, that global technology transfers would induce "clean economic development" yielding U.S. emission credits, and that carbon sinks developed by improved forestry practices would cheaply offset carbon emissions. With all these forces working favorably, her calculations indicated that the cost of Kyoto would fall from $240 per ton of carbon reduced to just $23. Yellen indicated that her estimates were not based on a single model but were derived by applying different assumptions to existing econometric models. With world trade in emission credits working away, Kyoto would not interfere with U.S. economic growth and prosperity, she indicated.

In spite of differences in emphasis and wide-ranging estimates of overall effects, the larger studies are consistent in arguing that energy-intensive sectors of the economy will face high costs and that coal production will carry the brunt of the load. It is also clear that substitutes for coal, such as natural gas and oil, have much to gain.

## POLITICAL JOCKEYING

The potential cost of the Kyoto Protocol to the United States is far greater than for other industrialized countries, even if trading is allowed. A number of major European countries have already reduced their use of coal. Others, like France, depend largely on nuclear energy, which produces no carbon emissions but leaves the country facing the challenge of reducing auto emissions.

Yet the prospect of having the United States reduce its costs by buying overseas permits is more than some international politicians can bear. British Deputy Prime Minister John Prescott, for one, wants to make certain that the United States feels the pain of implementing the Kyoto accord. Prescott expressed concern that Washington would "buy tradable greenhouse emission permits from Russia." As he put it, "Europe has always been clear that while we accept the trading possibilities in this matter, they should not be used as a reason for avoiding taking action in your own country" (Raven 1998).

United Kingdom negotiators oppose an international market in carbon emission offsets in general and also oppose trades that allow two countries to increase their emissions. John Prescott's idea of trade requires that one party must always reduce emissions if another party increases them.

Yet, as we have seen, some countries' emissions are already approaching their target levels. Under some proposed trading plans, those countries would have little difficulty in selling their carbon emission rights. With Russia's carbon emissions 30 percent below the country's target level of zero reduction, Russia could sell emission credits to another country (such as the United States) and both countries could increase emissions. To many economists, the fact that under some circumstances both countries can increase emissions is one of the beauties of a permit-marketing scheme.

Even as the European Union (EU) tries to limit gains from trade for the United States, it has come up with a way by which its member states hope to minimize their emission reduction costs. The European Union will use a "bubble" concept to achieve overall emission reductions for member states. A bubble is a way of measuring the success of a group of emitters by focusing on their overall collective action—what is emitted from the bubble, not the action taken by any one particular emitter. Under this plan, some countries will be able to emit more and others less because only the collective total matters.

The bubble allows the European Union to minimize the overall cost of emission reductions by allocating emission cutbacks differently to different countries. It is generally cheaper to reduce emissions when concentrations are higher, so it is logical and technically efficient to require countries that produce more $CO_2$ per unit of output to make larger cutbacks. The system obviously provides a framework for trading. Those that face high costs in cutting back their emissions can buy permits or credits from other European countries that face lower control costs.

By encouraging bubble trading within the EU while managing Europe's external trades so that its competitors' costs go up, Europe's new central government takes on the traditional protectionist position of many nation-states, controlling exports and imports. The difference is that the items traded are permits (emission reductions), not commodities.

Not surprisingly, U.S. negotiators did not like the European bubble when it came up during Kyoto negotiations. In its own way, the United States also played the "increase the rivals' cost game." During the negotiations, the United States pushed for treating each

TABLE 1

EU MEMBER STATE EMISSION
REDUCTION GOALS: 1990–2010

| Country | Percent Change from 1990 Levels |
|---|---|
| Luxembourg | –28.0 |
| Denmark | –21.0 |
| Germany | –21.0 |
| Austria | –13.0 |
| United Kingdom | –12.5 |
| Belgium | –7.5 |
| Italy | –6.5 |
| Netherlands | –6.0 |
| France | 0.0 |
| Finland | 0.0 |
| Sweden | +4.0 |
| Ireland | +13.0 |
| Spain | +15.0 |
| Greece | +25.0 |
| Portugal | +27.0 |

SOURCE:   Friends of the Earth (1998).

European country, whatever its size, as the equal of the United States. American negotiators argued that each European state should have specific reduction goals that must be met internally, rather than being allowed to trade within Europe under the bubble. Each small country, such as Portugal and Greece, would have to meet its own Kyoto-specified target. But internal trading within Portugal is a far cry from the internal trading that could go on in the much more vast United States. From the perspective of the United States, this arrangement would have been doubly beneficial: The United States could trade with the less-developed European countries and at the same time impose higher costs on its competitors.

Although jockeying for competitive advantage between Europe and the United States is evident, countries within Europe, too, are strategically positioning themselves. The proposed allocation of emissions under the bubble is shown in Table 1. The bubble policy gives more leeway to southern European, lower income countries, such as Spain, Portugal, and Greece—countries that are rapidly industrializing and emitting high quantities of carbon. Countries such as the United Kingdom, the Netherlands, and France already have relatively low carbon emissions, having transformed their coal-based energy economies to cleaner fuels. Through trading, the latter countries can purchase the emissions credits of the high carbon emitters at relatively low cost.

To gain a better understanding of the EU allocation scheme, I developed a multivariable statistical model that attempted to determine factors explaining it (Yandle 1999). My modeling efforts showed that newer EU members received more allowances, all else being equal. In addition, less populous countries are allowed to emit more tons of $CO_2$ per person, which means relative costs are lower where population is smaller. Countries that currently produce higher levels of carbon emissions per unit of GDP and countries with higher per capita income received fewer allowances.

My study of the scheme suggests that the allocations are designed to keep the bootlegger community intact. The bubble minimizes overall costs, as we have seen, and other concessions (what economists sometimes call side payments) are being made to keep reluctant community members (the newer members) from trading outside the community. The study allows one to infer that populous nations with tighter emissions allowances will probably buy permits from countries with higher carbon streams and larger allowances for emission growth. Wealth will flow generally from northern to southern European countries for trades within the European bubble.

## INTERNATIONAL INDUSTRIAL POLICY

As the post-Kyoto bargaining continues, there are at least two major institutional problems to be settled. The first is the permit markets—how they will be defined and operated and the extent to which this budding market will be unfettered by international rules and regulations. The second problem is the enforcement of agreements within and among countries that ratify the Kyoto

Protocol. In efforts to clamp down on all forms of environmental cheating, ministers from the Group of Seven and Russia met recently to line up cooperation against environmental crime. Britain's John Prescott said that he "wanted to see the equivalent of Interpol to allow police, customs and enforcement agencies to combat . . . global illegal trade" (Morrison 1998, 1).

Singled out for attention was the illegal trade in chlorofluorocarbons (CFCs), which are greenhouse gases as well as probable sources of ozone depletion. Because the Montreal Protocol of 1988 led to a ban on the manufacture of these chemicals in industrial countries, CFCs have become one of the most widely smuggled items across borders. Perhaps an international environmental police force is in the making.

In any case, a world industrial policy is in the making. In the past, governments such as France and Japan, and to a lesser extent the United States, engaged in industrial planning within their countries. The idea was to select the industries and firms that potentially would be the engines of the economy and allow the others to phase out gradually. Such industrial policy aimed at improving a nation's economic well-being. It was never effective over the long run, but it created opportunities for favor-seeking that gave some industries advantages over others.

The Kyoto agreement is setting up a system of industrial policy as well, although its purpose is not economic growth. Officials who manage the system will identify winners and losers in the battle over which nations will bear the greater pain of cutting back on carbon emissions. In this international system, as the Baptists work hard to adopt the treaty, the bootleggers will be converting environmental policy to an industrial policy that favors them.

## CONCLUSION

Day after day, newspapers report the pleas and alarms of the "Baptists" urging world leaders to do something about global warming, but, by and large, the machinations of the "bootleggers" go unnoticed. Yet there is ample evidence that Kyoto is already being used as a crutch to help conventional special interest groups secure political favors. There is also evidence that some nations and at least one community of nations are acting in strategic ways to enhance their positions relative to other nations.

In the final analysis, we should hope that fear of global warming will subside and that efforts to control the world's energy economies will gradually dissipate because the worry that ignited it will subside. Yet even if this happens, the regulatory concrete delivered by Kyoto will endure. History teaches us that once a major concern becomes transformed into institutional rules, interest groups that invested in those rules will work to maintain them.

In its present form, the Kyoto Protocol is an extraordinarily costly treaty for the U.S. economy, and the United States would do well to reject it. If global warming is an illusion, the treaty will be a waste of time and a misuse of our resources. If global warming turns out to be genuine, those economies that maintain market flexibility will be best equipped to adapt to it. Yet Kyoto's bootleggers are doing everything they can to destroy that flexibility. Either way, we are heading down the wrong road.

## ENDNOTES

1. For a quick lay summary of the protocol, see Sparber and O'Rourke (1998). For a rendering of the complete protocol, see UN Framework Convention on Climate Change (1997). A nonbinding resolution (S Res 98) passed the U.S. Senate, 95–0, on July 25, 1997, requesting the executive branch to sign an agreement only if a commitment is made by developing countries to reduce emissions (Freedman 1997).

2. These data, from Antonelli and Schaefer (1997, 18), were drawn from reports of the Intergovernmental Panel on Climate Change.

3. See Committee to Preserve American Security and Sovereignty (1998).

4. The theories here are discussed more completely in Yandle (1989). The public interest and capture theories are not associated with particular researchers. The economic theory was developed by Stigler (1971) and extended by Posner (1974) and Peltzman (1976). The bootlegger-and-Baptist theory first appeared in Yandle (1983).

5. Archer-Daniels-Midland has received $7 billion in the past sixteen years (Bandow 1997).

6. As it turns out, they incorrectly assumed that a 14.4-percent reduction in year-2020 emissions would achieve 1990 levels. Recent data indicate reductions in the range of 40 percent are necessary.

7. The Sutherland (1998) study is noteworthy for drawing an unusual amount of information from a simple economic relationship.

## REFERENCES

Allen, Vicki. 1998. Costa Rica to Save Forest with Carbon Credits. Reuters, 24 April.

Antonelli, Angela, and Brett D. Schaefer. 1997. The Road to Kyoto. *Backgrounder.* Washington, D.C.: Heritage Foundation.

Bandow, Doug. 1997. *Ethanol Keeps ADM Drunk on Tax Dollars.* Washington, D.C.: Cato Institute.

Carrato, Carlo, Marzio Galeotti, and Massimo Gallo. 1996. Environmental Taxation and Unemployment: Some Evidence on the "Double Dividend Hypothesis in Europe." *Journal of Public Economics* 62(1–2): 141–181.

Chen, Zihoi. 1997. Negotiating an Agreement on Global Warming. *Journal of Environmental Economics and Management* 32: 170–178.

Commercial Alcohols Canada. 1998. Fuel Ethanol. At <http://www.comalc.com> (May 5, 1998).

Committee to Preserve American Security and Sovereignty. 1998. *Treaties, National Sovereignty, and Executive Power.* A Report on the Kyoto Protocol at Alexandria, Va., 18 May.

DRI/McGraw-Hill. 1997. *The Impact of Carbon Mitigation Strategies on Energy Markets, the National Economy, Industry and Regional Economies.* Report prepared for UMWA/BCOA, July.

Environmental Defense Fund (EDF). 1997. British Petroleum to Take Action on Climate Change. *EDF Letter* 28(4).

Freedman, Allan. 1997. Senate Sends Signal to Clinton on Global Warming Treaty. *Congressional Quarterly* (July 26): 1785.

Friends of the Earth. 1998. *EU Greenhouse Gas Deal Too Much Hot Air.* Press Release. Washington, D.C., 11 July.

Holtz-Eakin, Douglas, and Thomas M. Selden. 1995. Stoking the Fires? $CO_2$ Emissions and Economic Growth. *Journal of Public Economics* 57: 85–101.

Interlaboratory Working Group on Energy-Efficient and Low-Carbon Technologies. 1997. *Scenarios of U.S. Carbon Reductions.* Washington, D.C.: Office of Energy Efficiency and Renewable Energy, Department of Energy.

Jorgenson, Dale W., and Peter J. Wilcoxen. 1993. Reducing U.S. Carbon Dioxide Emissions: An Assessment of Different Instruments. *Journal of Policy Modeling* 115(5–6): 491–520.

Kosobud, Richard F., Thomas A. Daly, David W. South, and Kevin G. Quinn. 1994. Tradable Cumulative $CO_2$ Permits and Global Warming Control. *Energy Journal* 15(2): 213–232.

Larsen, Bjorn, and Anwar Shah. 1994. Global Tradeable Carbon Permits, Participation Incentives, and Transfers. *Oxford Economic Papers* 46(5): 841–856.

Magada, Dominique. 1998. Focus: Shell Revamps Image. Reuters, 21 April.

Manne, Allan S., and Richard G. Richels. 1991. Global $CO_2$ Emission Reductions: The Impacts of Rising Energy Costs. *Energy Journal* 12(1): 87–107.

Morrison, John. 1998. G8 Countries to Act Against Environmental Crime. Reuters, 5 April.

National Biodiesel Board. 1998. Agricultural Products Are Key to National Energy Security. Press Release. 24 February. At <http://biz.yahoo.com> (March 2, 1998).

National Corn Growers Association. 1998. National Corn Growers Report. At <http://www.ncga.com> (May 5, 1998).

Nordhaus, William D. 1991. The Cost of Slowing Climate Change: A Survey. *Energy Journal* 12(1): 37–65.

Office of Policy and International Affairs. 1997. Analysis of Carbon Stabilization Cases. No. SR-OIAF/97-01 (October). Washington, D.C.: Department of Energy.

Pearce, David, and Edward Barbier. 1991. The Greenhouse Effect: A View from Europe. *Energy Journal* 12(1): 147–161.

Peltzman, Sam. 1976. Toward a More General Theory of Regulation. *Journal of Law & Economics* (August): 211–240.

Pianin, Eric. 1998. Gingrich Halts Move to End Ethanol Subsidy. *Greenville News*, 7 May, 6D.

Posner, Richard A. 1974. Theories of Economic Regulation. *Bell Journal* (Autumn): 335–358.

Raven, Gerrard. 1998. EU Urges U.S. to Implement Kyoto Global Warming Deal. Reuters, 26 April.

Reichhardt, Tony. 1997. No Net Cost in Cutting Carbon Emissions. *Nature* 389 (2 October): 429.

Renewable Fuels Association. 1998a. Ethanol's Contributions to Clean Air Celebrated on Earth Day. Press Release. Washington, D.C., 21 April.

———. 1998b. *Ethanol Report* (May 7). At <http://www.ethanolrfa.org/er050798> (May 7, 1998).

Salisbury, Laney. 1998. Enron Exec Wants Clean Energy Tax Break. Reuters, 26 February.

Sinclair, Peter J. N. 1994. On the Optimum Trend of Fossil Fuel Taxation. *Oxford Economic Papers* 46(5): 869–877.

Sparber, Peter G., and Peter E. O'Rourke. 1998. Understanding the Kyoto Protocol. *Perspectives on Legislation, Regulation, and Litigation* 2(4).

Stark, Craig. 1998. Inventory of Greenhouse Gases. *Iowa Energy Bulletin*. At <http://www.state.ia.us/government> (May 5, 1998).

Stigler, George J. 1971. The Economic Theory of Regulation. *Bell Journal* (Spring): 3–21.

Sutherland, Ronald J. 1998. *Achieving the Kyoto Protocol: An Analysis of Policy Options*. Washington, D.C.: American Petroleum Institute.

Takenaka, Kiyoshi. 1998. Japan, Russia Conclude Landmark Greenhouse Gas Swap. Reuters, 19 April.

United Methodist News Service. 1997. Church Executive Calls for Ratification, December 17. At <http://www.umc.org> (May 4, 1998).

United Nations. 1997. Framework Convention on Climate Change (UNFCCC). The Kyoto Protocol. At <http://www.unfcc.de/fccc/conv/file01.htm> (October 19, 1998).

WEFA, Inc. 1998. *Global Warming: The High Cost of the Kyoto Protocol: National and State Impacts—Executive Summary.* Eddystone, Penn.: WEFA.

Whaley, John, and Randall Wigle. 1991. Cutting $CO_2$ Emissions: The Effects of Alternative Policy Approaches. *Energy Journal* 12(1): 109–124.

Yandle, Bruce. 1983. Bootleggers and Baptists: The Education of a Regulatory Economist. *Regulation* (May/June): 12–16.

———. 1989. *The Political Limits of Environmental Quality Regulation.* Westport, Conn.: Greenwood.

———. 1999. A Global Scramble for Advantage. *Independent Review* 4(1): 19–40.

Yellen, Janet. 1998. Testimony before the House Commerce Committee. 4 March.

# CHAPTER 8

# Biotechnology Regulation and Foreign Policy: Eccentric Environmentalism Instead of Sound Science

## Henry I. Miller

During a speech at Stanford University in April 1996, then-Secretary of State Warren Christopher announced a major new foreign policy initiative that, he said, would make environmental concerns coequal with American economic and national security in U.S. foreign relations. One effect of this initiative has been to enlist the might of the U.S. diplomatic apparatus to proselytize for ideological, idiosyncratic, and often scientifically insupportable environmentalism. A broad spectrum of environmental—*pseudo*-environmental might be more apt—policies is being implemented via the negotiation of treaties and other agreements; collaboration with agencies and programs of the United Nations; bilateral and regional diplomacy; distribution of the largesse of the State Department and the U.S. Agency for International Development; increased involvement by the CIA in "environmental intelligence"; and new "regional environmental hubs" within certain U.S. embassies.

Scientists around the world are using the techniques of the new biotechnology—recombinant DNA, or gene splicing—to improve plants for food and fiber. In 1999, these genetically improved plants were cultivated on approximately 98.6 million acres (39.9 million hectares), up from 69.5 million (27.8 million hectares) in 1998. The five predominant crops grown in 1999 were, in descending order of area: soybean, corn/maize, cotton, oilseed rape, and potato. Enhanced traits include resistance to pests, disease, drought, salinity, frost, and herbicides, as well as enhanced nutritional value, improved processing characteristics, and better taste. Thus, the new biotechnology holds great promise for increasing the overall yields of crops; equally important, it makes possible enhanced productivity in ways that are beneficial to the environment.

Biotechnology research and development, however, have been special and systematic casualties of the initiative. International biotechnology regulation implemented by various agencies and instruments of the United Nations offers an example of how the policies encompassed in Christopher's pronouncement have redounded against the interests of researchers and companies in a number of industrial sectors throughout the world. Half a dozen UN programs or agencies have targeted biotechnology with a sweeping variety of new, unnecessary, burdensome regulations. At a time when hunger remains a serious problem for perhaps a billion people, per capita yields of the major cereal crops have leveled off or decreased, and poor countries are moving from becoming exporters to importers of food. The new biotechnology—the use of precise, state-of-the-art molecular techniques for genetically improving plants, animals, and microorganisms—holds great promise for raising productivity. For that reason, it is cruelly ironic that the State Department's current policies front for and encourage UN policies that actually block advances in agriculture and the development of environment-friendly products, while perpetuating the use (and misuse) of agricultural chemicals.

## ENVIRONMENTAL DIPLOMACY

The Christopher initiative was announced in April 1996, and by the following year it had progressed both rhetorically and programmatically, according to *Environmental Diplomacy* (Department of State 1997). With forewords by Vice President Al Gore and Christopher's successor, Secretary of State Madeleine Albright, its theme is that "[t]oday environmental issues are part of the mainstream of American foreign policy," because "environmental problems are often at the heart of the political and economic challenges we face around the world" (Department of State 1997, 2). In other words, it is not tyrannical forms of government, not state-sponsored genocide or terrorism, not disease, poverty, or economic turmoil, but environmental problems that are at the heart of America's foreign policy challenges.

*Environmental Diplomacy* is similar in philosophy to a Greenpeace manifesto or to Al Gore's (1992) radical *Earth in the Balance,* and that is no coincidence. The document claims that the World Bank must factor "environmental implications into its lending decisions" (Department of State 1997, 4), echoing Gore's position that "[c]lassical economics defines productivity narrowly and encourages us to equate gains in productivity with economic progress" and that "the Holy Grail of progress is so alluring that economists tend to overlook the bad side effects that often accompany improvements" (Gore 1992, 188). Gore's—and now the State Department's—remedy is to redefine the relevant measures of economic activity. The purpose of this redefinition is clear: to enable governments to obscure the costs of environmental protection by calling those costs benefits, and to force businesses to list as societal costs some wealth-creating activity that would normally be considered beneficial to society. Employing this kind of Orwellian doublespeak, a dam or nuclear power plant that brings electricity to an entire region would be considered a societal cost, while a UN grant to Greenpeace could be counted as income.

*Environmental Diplomacy* expresses concerns about "the rapid conversion of land to human uses, increased pollution and the spread of exotic species to non-native habitats" (Department of State 1997, 6). These developments can reduce biodiversity, it observes correctly, which can in turn cause us to lose the benefits of breakthroughs in agriculture such as a strain of "disease-free" wheat. (Biology not being the State Department's—or, for that matter, Mr. Gore's—strong suit, presumably the document meant a disease-*resistant* new variety of wheat.) In any case, U.S. foreign policy toward biotechnology regulation has decreased the amount and robustness of research and development while increasing expense when R&D involves improving plant varieties with the most precise and sophisticated available genetic techniques. At a time when hunger remains a serious problem for many parts of the world and per capita yields of the major cereal crops have leveled off or decreased, biotechnology holds great promise for raising productivity. But in an original but bizarre twist, Gore worries even about biotechnology's possible success:

> The most lasting impact of biotechnology on the food supply may come not from something going wrong, but from all going right. My biggest fear is not that by accident we will set loose some genetically defective Andromeda strain. Given our past record in dealing with agriculture, we're far more likely to accidentally drown ourselves in a sea of excess grain. (Gore 1991, 28)

Unlike many new technologies of our age, biotechnology has almost immediately been available outside the wealthier countries of the northern hemisphere. Because it builds on traditional agriculture and microbiology to improve regionally important crops, biotechnology facilitates that highest goal of developing-world politics, self-sufficiency. It is cruelly ironic, therefore, that the State Department's current policies defend and encourage UN schemes that block the development of environment-friendly products and advances in agriculture. Half a dozen UN programs or agencies have targeted the new biotechnology with a sweeping variety of new, unnecessary, burdensome regulations. The UN's major regulatory and policing initiatives—a code of conduct promulgated by the UN Industrial Development Organization (UNIDO), on behalf of three other UN agencies and a biosafety protocol mandated by the Convention on Biological Diversity (CBD), which is under the control of the UN Environment Program (UNEP)—are discussed in detail below. These regulations have already severely compromised the potential of the new technology. Agricultural biotechnology has been particularly vulnerable, because even though innovation is high, market incentives are small and fragile. Putting this another way, the regulations remove an important tool of crop breeders—namely, the ability to test readily and rapidly large numbers of new varieties in field trials. Each year an individual breeder of corn, soybean, wheat, or potato commonly tests in the field as many as 50,000 distinct new genetic variants (National Research Council,

1989). The vastly increased paperwork and costs of field testing associated with new regulations, which apply only to plant varieties created with the new biotechnology, are potent disincentives to research and development in many countries. The products of this R&D could be particularly environmentally friendly—plants with greater yields and greater resistance to disease and pests, biological alternatives to chemical pesticides, and various biological methods of cleaning up toxic wastes. However, as a result of unscientific and excessive regulation of biotechnology, companies around the world have seen their regulatory expenses skyrocket and their potential markets shrink. Many agricultural biotechnology companies have failed; in contrast to other biotech sectors, there are actually fewer agbiotech companies now than a decade ago. Ultimately, consumers will pay inflated prices for overregulated products and higher taxes to support bloated bureaucracies, and they will have fewer options in the marketplace. Agricultural biotechnology, touted in the 1970s as promising to increase food productivity in the developing world, has increasingly become a boutique technology applied to high-value-added products for affluent consumers in industrialized countries.

Land use is identified in *Environmental Diplomacy* as a critical concern for foreign policy. Critical issues therein include foreign countries' "local and national leaders weigh[ing] the competing goals of protecting a forest against providing additional croplands [and] whether regulations and protective measures to preserve a cropland's long-term viability . . . place too much of an economic burden on their citizens by limiting crop yields in the short-term" (Department of State 1997, 13). These decisions by foreign sovereign governments, we are told, "have social, environmental, and economic implications, which in turn affect our foreign policy" (Department of State 1997, 14). This approach to international land use issues raises two crucial points. First, as described above, the aspirations of the United Nations to become the world's bio-cops—abetted by the United States—have discouraged the application of the new biotechnology to developing higher-yielding plant varieties. Such varieties would decrease the use of agricultural chemicals (which are often dangerously misused in developing countries) and also make higher productivity possible without expanding cultivation to less arable land. If current U.S. foreign policy flaunts scientific consensus and actually works against the nation's stated environmental goals, what are we to make of plans to intensify those efforts?

The second question is, should American foreign policy decisions turn on whether, for example, the French government permits the harvesting of an old forest in Provence, or whether Mexico City decides to build highways instead of a subway system? Americans were overwhelmingly convinced that our national interests were at stake in the Middle East when Iraq invaded Kuwait, but how would they feel about the deployment of troops to enforce limits on carbon dioxide emissions? And how would Americans (to say nothing of citizens of other countries) react to Washington launching cruise missiles at China's Three Gorges Dam because it has negative environmental consequences?

If these examples seem extreme, they are no more so than the philosophy that underlies the U.S. government's new pseudo-environmentalism, namely Vice President Gore's musings in *Earth in the Balance*. Gore's apocalyptic central thesis is that we need to take "bold and unequivocal action . . . [to] make the rescue of the environment the central organizing principle for civilization" (starting at p. 269) (Gore 1992). Throughout the book, Gore uses the metaphor that those who believe in technological progress are as sinister, and polluters are as evil, as the perpetrators of the World War II Holocaust. Our civilization is "dysfunctional," according to Gore, who believes we have created

> a false world of plastic flowers and AstroTurf, air conditioning and fluorescent lights, windows that don't open and background music that never stops, days when we don't know whether it has rained or not, nights when the sky never stops glowing, Walkman and Watchman entertainment cocoons, frozen food for the microwave oven, sleepy hearts jump-started with caffeine, alcohol, drugs, and illusions. (Gore 1992, 232)

Gore analogizes American society to "Nazi Germany [where] dysfunctional thinking was institutionalized in the totalitarian state, its dogma, and its war machine" (Gore 1992, 275). In that foreboding light, extreme measures may seem justified—and, as discussed throughout this volume, extreme measures are being taken aplenty.

The State Department's environmental initiatives will bring to the world, in several new ways, Vice President Gore's inimitable view of environmentalism. Fundamental to his view of government policy, particularly regulation, is the precautionary principle, the essence of which is that in the face of incomplete data, caution—that is, worst-case scenarios—should dictate the choice of governmental policy alternatives. Dr. Elizabeth M. Whelan, the president of the American Council on Science and Health, notes objections to the precautionary principle:

> First, it always assumes worst-case scenarios. Second, it distracts consumers and policy makers alike from the known and proven threats to human health. And third, it assumes no health detriment from the proposed regulations and restrictions. By that I mean that the Precautionary Principle overlooks the possibility that real public health risks can be associated with eliminating minuscule, hypothetical risks. (CEQ 1982, 223)

Christopher Douglass (1988), of the Center for the Study of American Business, has described the stepwise process by which the precautionary principle is incorporated into international public policy for, say, an environmental problem. The ultimate goal (of bureaucrats) is to attain the twin goals of bolstering "scientific support" for the most risk-averse public policy outcome and for reaching a binding international agreement. UN agencies, national governments, and NGOs work in concert, often in a carefully orchestrated way, to develop consensus on an international agreement via five steps (Douglass 1988):

1. Scientific or interest group concern

2. Agenda-setting at unofficial conferences

3. Intergovernmental (usually ministerial level) meetings

4. Creation of a voluntary, or "soft," multilateral agreement

5. Development of a binding, or "hard," agreement

As pointed out by Cohrssen (this volume), the precautionary principle has infiltrated into many multilateral treaties, including the 1987 Montreal Protocol on Substances that Deplete the Ozone Layer; the 1992 Convention on Biological Diversity; the 1992 Climate Change Convention; the 1992 Treaty on European Union; the 1992 Convention for the Protection of the Marine Environment of the North-East Atlantic; and the 1992 Helsinki Convention, which deals with protection of the marine environment of the Baltic. International declarations incorporating the precautionary principle include the 1990 Bergen Declaration, issued by ministerial representatives from European countries (as well as Canada and the United States), and the 1992 Rio Declaration on Environment and Development. An important development has been Vice President Gore and his acolytes throughout the government widely, aggressively embracing and applying this flawed and highly risk-averse notion to domestic and international policy making.

According to *Environmental Diplomacy,* selected U.S. embassies have established "environmental hubs" to advance environmental goals. Some see this as a valuable opportunity to make widely available to foreigners a vast array of ecological, environmental, and other scientific information—computerized data and models of erosion, population growth, climatic patterns, and so on. But given Gore's views of environmentalism and his technophobia, it is a foregone conclusion that the State Department will reflect the vice president's version of such issues as ozone depletion, global warming, sustainable agriculture, and biotechnology regulation. Whatever its virtues, the State Department is not charged to do a great deal of independent thinking on arcane scientific issues. If anything, scientific and technological expertise have been downgraded in importance at the State Department in recent years, with a decrease in the number of scientifically qualified people assigned to the assistant secretary of state for Oceans and International Environmental and Scientific Affairs (Watkins 1997). It is ominous that at the same time that the numbers of scientifically trained personnel were being reduced, "[a]n unannounced reorganization has redistributed those functions within a slimmed-down department bureau that's increasingly focused on global environmental issues," according to former Secretary of Energy Admiral James Watkins (Watkins 1997, 650–651).

Even prior to the announcement of the State Department initiative, Gore had already begun to insinuate these ideas into U.S. foreign policy. The U.S. Agency for International Development (USAID) has provided a kind of slush fund for the schemes of radical environmentalists. USAID foreign aid funds—derived, of course, from American taxpayers—are being used to undermine market economies abroad and to put American businesses at a competitive disadvantage. In Indonesia, for example, USAID gave more than $1.3 million—virtually the entire operating budget—to the Wahana Lingkungan Hidup Indonesia (WALHI), which is affiliated with Friends of the Earth. WALHI has long campaigned against New Orleans-based Freeport McMoRan Copper & Gold, accusing the mining company of polluting an Indonesian river, destroying crops, and inciting military attacks on civilians. But none of these accusations against the company has been substantiated. In addition, through U.S. environmental activists, WALHI successfully lobbied the Overseas Private Investment Corporation (OPIC), a federal agency that promotes business abroad by insuring companies against the risk of nationalization, to cancel Freeport's $100 million policy (McMenamin 1996).

## BIOTECH, THE UNITED NATIONS, AND U.S. FOREIGN POLICY

Secretary of State Christopher took pains in his 1996 speech to underscore the importance of the CBD, and Undersecretary Tim Wirth, during a speech at Stanford University, characterized the CBD as having "top priority among all treaties" and agreements awaiting confirmation. However, this international agreement, which has been signed by President Clinton but not ratified by the U.S. Senate, is a volatile combination of poor-quality science and flawed environmental and foreign policy. When it is fully implemented, it will be bad for the United States and disastrous for the countries of the developing world. The new State Department environmental initiative, as it applies to the CBD, has the United States fronting for the United Nations and promoting it as the world's biosafety police force—even though the U.S. Senate has declined to ratify the treaty. (This is only one of the police forces contemplated for creation and management by the United Nations: With reference to the trading of carbon dioxide emissions permits that could occur under the Kyoto Treaty, UK Deputy Prime Minister John Prescott said that he "wanted to see the equivalent of Interpol to allow police, customs and enforcement agencies to combat . . . global illegal trade" (Morrisson 1998).

The UN's regulatory and policing proposals have compromised the new biotechnology's potential: In the face of overregulation, which has inflated the costs of R&D and consumer products, whence will come the impetus to work on plants that are the staples of subsistence agriculture, such as millet, yams, sorghum, and cassava? There won't be any such impetus, of course, and the result of UN regulatory policies will be disease and famine. Among those threatened most by this regulatory impulse are those Asian countries that have made substantial investments in agricultural biotechnology. The list includes the Philippines, Thailand, India, Singapore, and China, whose programs are among the largest and most vigorous in the world.

As described above, one of the new biotechnology's great advantages is that it has been available almost immediately outside the West. Because it builds on traditional agriculture and microbiology to help improve regionally important crops, biotechnology could be an important element in developing countries' self-sufficiency in food. But a burdensome international bureaucracy enforcing ill-conceived and excessive regulation will stall many of these benefits. Because market incentives are often small and fragile, agricultural biotechnology is particularly vulnerable. Vastly increased paperwork and costs for field testing will be potent disincentives to research and development in many countries. Ironically, many proposed UN biotechnology regulations will actually harm the environment. They will stifle the development of environment-friendly innovations that can help clean up toxic wastes, purify water, and replace agricultural chemicals. Classical plant genetics has already supplanted some chemical pesticides with pest- and disease-resistant varieties of wheat, rice, soybeans, corn, and other staple crops, but further advances of this kind resulting from the use of gene splicing will be slowed by UN policies.

## BIOTECHNOLOGY AND THE UNITED NATIONS: NEW CHALLENGES, NEW FAILURES

Two regulatory documents are of particular concern to the future of agricultural biotechnology: the UN Industrial Development Organization's (UNIDO) 1992 "code of conduct" (1992) for field trials and the 1992 Convention on Biological Diversity (CBD, or informally, the Biodiversity Treaty) (UNEP 1992). The CBD's goals are crafted to seem laudable, but the agreement has become the UN's Trojan horse, surreptitiously delivering biotechnology-averse regulatory policies to the developing world. The UNIDO code of conduct shares all the disadvantages of the CBD but offers none of the latter's ostensible benefits.

### THE UNIDO CODE OF CONDUCT

UNIDO's proposal, a paragon of unscientific, ill-conceived regulation, was published on behalf of three other UN agencies: the UN Environment Program (UNEP), the World Health Organization (WHO), and the Food and Agriculture Organization (FAO). The preamble states that the purpose of this (currently) voluntary code of conduct is to "provide help to governments in developing their own regulatory infrastructure and in establishing standards" for research and use of GMOs. It defines such "genetically manipulated organisms" as those crafted with the most precise and sophisticated molecular techniques and dictates regulatory requirements in the most stringent, unscientific, and self-serving terms. The document asserts that "[t]he UN is an obvious system through which to coordinate a worldwide effort to ensure that all [research and commercial applications of GMOs are] preceded by an appropriate assessment of risks" but it demonstrates a lack of even a rudimentary understanding of risk analysis. The document also defines as a principal goal to "encourage and assist the establishment of appropriate national regulatory frameworks, particularly where no adequate infrastructure presently exists" (UNIDO 1992), but provides no economic strategies by which such frameworks could be created and sustained in developing countries.

The code requires the establishment of new environmental bureaucracies and demands resources from impoverished developing countries if researchers in those countries wish to perform even small-scale field trials of crops of local agronomic value, such as cassava, potatoes, rice, wheat, and ornamental flowers. "Every member country should designate a national authority or authorities to be responsible for handling inquiries and proposals, i.e., all contacts concerning the use and introductions of GMOs. More than one authority may be necessary. . . . Case-by-case evaluation should be the rule."

Finally, we get to the payoff for the international regulators-in-waiting themselves. The code proposes that the United Nations "establish an international biosafety information network and advisory service" (UNIDO 1992). These entities would have a number of functions, among them information-gathering, advising, technical assistance on monitoring the environmental impacts of GMOs, and "on request provid[ing] advice to assist in working toward the setting up of a designated national authority(ies) in each country."

Because UNIDO has produced this code of conduct, it should come as no surprise that "UNIDO should take the lead" in offering these new services. The resources required would include "a scientific steering committee . . . [and] a small technical/administrative secretariat" (UNIDO 1992). And "as a starting point, the service should conduct an international survey to identify existing expertise in the various scientific disciplines required for the safety assessment of biotechnology use."

Nothing at all redeems this ill-conceived document or the "makework" program for bureaucrats and consultants it proposes. Having gotten the scope of risk assessment completely wrong, the drafters hopefully invoke the language—but not the intent—of the scientific consensus about biotech regulation: "Regulatory oversight and risk assessment should focus on the characteristics of the product rather than the molecular or cellular techniques used to produce it." The drafters reduce that pivotal point of scientific consensus to mere rhetoric as they forge ahead with a contradictory, expensive, and regressive regulatory system. Thereby, they erect steep barriers to research and development, particularly for developing countries that aspire to meet some of their economic development and security goals through the new biotechnology.

Resources intended to improve public health and promote environmental protection could be better spent on health promotion and protection than on this UN regulatory humbug: research on schistosomiasis, malaria, and AIDS; immunizing children against cholera, polio, and hepatitis; and developing high-yielding genetically improved cultivars of staple crops like millet, yams, rice, potatoes, and cassava.

## THE CONVENTION ON BIOLOGICAL DIVERSITY

A product of the 1992 UN Conference on Environment and Development (UNCED) held in Rio, the CBD addresses a broad spectrum of issues related to the protection of biological diversity. Its stated intention—the conservation of habitats in developing nations—is commendable:

1.   Identifying and monitoring components of biological diversity, such as specific ecosystems and communities (Article 7)

2.   Establishing a system of protected areas (Article 8)

3.   Adopting measures for *ex situ* conservation (that is, preserving seeds or sperm in repositories under appropriate conditions)

4.   Integrating genetic resource conservation considerations into national decision making and adopting incentives for the conservation of biological resources (Articles 10 and 11)

5.   Developing assessment procedures for ensuring that impacts on biological diversity are considered in project design (Article 14). (UNEP 1992)

But the intentions are heavy on centralized planning and implementation, and light on market-based alternatives.

The treaty was conceived as an opportunity for industrialized and developing countries to reconcile issues of conservation and access to biological resources. However, the treaty is burdened with the prospect of an international biosafety protocol (that is, regulations for biotechnology), expected to be finalized in 1999, which will exacerbate rather than lessen the challenges facing biodiversity.

### The Devil in the Details

It is difficult to determine from the vague and sometimes contradictory language of the treaty whether the CBD actually requires that a biosafety protocol be adopted by ratifying countries. For example, Article 8 calls for measures to "regulate, manage or control the risks associated with the use and release of living modified organisms resulting from biotechnology which are *likely to have adverse environmental impacts* [emphasis added] that could affect the conservation and sustainable use of biological diversity . . ." (UNEP 1992). Article 19 specifies that "the Parties shall *consider the need for* [emphasis added] and modalities of a protocol setting out appropriate procedures, including, in particular, advance informed agreement, in the field of safe transfer, handling and use of any living modified organism resulting from biotechnology *that may have adverse effect on the conservation and sustainable use of biological diversity* [emphasis added]" (UNEP 1992).

At the heart of controversy over the protocol is the meaning of the CBD's phrase, "any living modified organism resulting from biotechnology." Among field trials of living organisms, including microorganisms, insects, fish, farm animals, crop plants, and ornamental flowers, what, exactly, would be subject to regulation? All field trials? Certain organisms or field trials judged to be high risk? Organisms crafted with certain specific genetic techniques? The CBD's scope is potentially broad: "Biotechnology means any technological application that uses biological systems, living organisms or derivatives thereof, to make or modify products or processes for specific use" (UNEP 1992). And the advantage of such a broad definition is that, in theory, it provides latitude for circumscribing categories of organisms to be field-tested that deserve a government safety review—that is, a risk-based approach focused on the product. In other words, case-by-case review could be limited to those categories judged to be of possible significant risk. Such a risk-based approach (Miller, Burns, Vidaver, et al. 1990; Miller, Altman, Barton, et al. 1995) would be more defensible scientifically than the process- or technique-focused approaches of the European Union (1994), the UNIDO code of conduct (1992), or the biotechnology regulations at the EPA and USDA (Miller 1997). However, as discussed below, the scope of what is to be subject to case-by-case review has been narrowed in a way that encompasses only organisms modified with the newer, molecular techniques and is wholly unrelated to the likelihood of risk that might be posed by their testing or use. This violates the fundamental principle of regulation that the degree of oversight should be commensurate with risk.

The rational possibilities afforded by the wording of the CBD are being overlooked. From the beginning, the international bureaucrats charged with crafting the details of the regulations have consistently and purposefully ignored the scientific consensus, which repudiates their regulatory approach. An official document that describes the April 1993 proceedings of the expert panel established to implement these aspects of the CBD clarified the scope of the proposed regulations. According to paragraphs 57 and 58,

> a majority of the Panel members believed the organisms covered by a possible protocol should be restricted to genetically modified organisms, along the lines of the EEC-Directive 90/220 on the Deliberate Release into the Environment of Genetically Modified Organisms which defines GMOs as organisms in which the genetic material has been altered in a way that does not occur naturally by mating and/or natural recombination. Annex 1 A of the Directive further specifies which techniques are covered and which are not. (UNEP 1993)

Annex 1 of the document states explicitly that the scope of regulation "does not include organisms modified by traditional breeding methods," regardless of pathogenicity, likelihood of constituting an environmental nuisance, or other potential risks. Thus, the panel unabashedly endorsed an unscientific, process-based definition of what requires regulation that is wholly irrelevant to risk. It is noteworthy that the panel did so in spite of a minority viewpoint, cited in the panel's report, that argued against limiting the scope to GMOs. The dissenting (and correct) view held that such a scope would be irrational and counterproductive because it "would ignore organisms actually known to present a threat to biodiversity, while focusing on others for which only hypothetical analyses can be offered" (UNEP 1993).

The scientific view did not carry the day. Representatives from the European Union, Holland, and the United Kingdom successfully convinced developing countries that their regulatory and development needs could be met by the same heavy-handed regulatory approach that currently impedes biotechnology research and commercialization in Europe. In characteristically paternalistic, if not imperialist fashion, they offered themselves as consultants to perform the required environmental assessments for their lesser-prepared counterparts in developing countries.

These tactics deserve comment. The national representatives attending the CBD panels have primarily been environmental regulators. It may be that they feel there is reason to believe that the products of the new biotechnology do, indeed, pose incremental hazards; or it may be that they believe that public concerns argue for excessive regulation. It is far more likely, however, that they are acting according to the principle that bureaucrats tend to make decisions that favor their own self-interest even when those decisions are incompatible with the public interest. Environmental regulators see biotechnology as a growth industry, an opportunity to aggrandize their own professional responsibilities, budgets, and influence. (The precautionary principle, discussed above, is thus a useful tool to the ambitious bureaucrat.) Science/technology or trade ministers, with quite different self-interest, would likely have dictated a different outcome of the discussions on biotech regulation.

The overall miasma surrounding the crafting of the CBD's biosafety protocol was aptly summarized by senior Department of Agriculture scientist Val Giddings (now vice president of the Biotechnology Industry Organization), while he was seconded to the U.S. Department of State as special advisor on biotechnology:

> It reveals how factions, driven more by hostility to biotechnology and other goals than concern for biodiversity, brought about the hi-

jacking of a major portion of the energy and resources of the Convention. The impetus has thus been directed away from real and present threats to biodiversity toward an area (biotechnology) that is not a significant threat; furthermore, one that promises to enable major strides toward improved agricultural sustainability in both the industrial and developing worlds. A sadder litany of missed opportunities and misdirected efforts would be hard to find. (Giddings 1996, 1304–1305)

*Negative Impacts on Foreign and Domestic Biotechnology*
The CBD's unscientific regulations will exert negative impacts on research and development that are not limited to the developing world, or even to international transfers and transactions. Consider that in paragraphs 74 and 75 of the April 1993 panel proceedings report, there is the ominous observation that

> a majority of the Panel members interpreted the language of Article 19.3 "safe transfer, handling and use" as if both international transfer of organisms *and domestic handling and use* [emphasis added] of organisms were covered. The majority of the Panel members thought that *domestic regulation should be covered by a possible protocol* [emphasis added]. (Giddings 1996, 1304–1305)

After several meetings and the production of prodigious amounts of paper by participants on discussion panels, the nations that have ratified the CBD appeared to reach agreement on this issue at a conference in Jakarta in November 1995. At first, it appeared that the regulations would encompass both international (that is, transnational) and domestic research and development. Then, according to a November 20, 1995, report in the Bureau of National Affairs (BNA) *Environment Daily,* one of the key decisions made by the 1,000-plus delegates at the Conference of the Parties was "an agreement to draw up a protocol governing the *transboundary* [emphasis added] movement of living modified organisms" (BNA 1995). Thus, signatory nations agreed to formulate an international protocol regulating the transfer of GMOs between states. The agreement appeared not to extend to regulation of purely domestic testing or uses of organisms. The journal *Nature* reported, "The agreement represents a compromise between the Group of 77 (G77) countries, which favored early enactment of a comprehensive protocol on biosafety, and the industrialized nations, which have been seeking the adoption of looser guidelines" (Masood 1995, 326). An open-ended Biosafety Working Group (BSWG), whose function was actually to craft definitions, procedures, and the other details of regulations, was created at that meeting. The issue of exactly which activities will be regulated remains unresolved.

At a meeting held in Cairo, 11–14 December 1995, by UNEP, the BSWG adopted the "final text" of the UNEP Guidelines for Safety in Biotechnology and requested the United Nations to widely distribute those guidelines. Despite appearances to the contrary, this was not the actual biosafety protocol. That protocol would be produced by yet another panel, an "open-ended Ad Hoc Working Group to develop in the field of the safe transfer, handling and use of living modified organisms, a protocol on biosafety." But since it "may take several years to conclude the protocol . . . a number of countries and intergovernmental, private sector and other organizations will need technical guidance of the kind contained in these Guidelines to fulfill their commitments under such an international agreement" (Masood 1995, 326). The required technical guidance was offered in a forty-two page treatise, entitled "Report of the Global Consultation of Government-Designated Experts on International Technical Guidelines for Safety in Biotechnology" (UNEP 1995). Whilst appropriating the concept of "familiarity" from earlier work, such as the 1989 U.S. National Research Council (NRC) report and various OECD publications (see, e.g., OECD 1995), the UNEP group in Cairo tortured and misrepresented the concept, asserting that there is

> generally less familiarity with the behavior of organisms whose genetic make-up is unlikely to develop naturally, such as organisms produced by modern genetic modification techniques, than with the behavior of organisms developed traditionally. This has been the reason why many countries have focused on such organisms and products containing them. . . .
>
> The guidelines provide assistance for identifying organisms whose characteristics may differ from those of the parent organisms from which they are derived in ways that would suggest additional scrutiny

might be appropriate. This may be because they produce substances which are not found in the species concerned. (UNEP 1995)

These are precisely the rationales that the scientific community has repudiated consistently and categorically during the past fifteen years. The UNEP document confuses—intentionally or otherwise—various concepts, including novelty, familiarity, and risk. The introduction of a new gene—even one in a location unlikely to occur in nature—does not necessarily affect an organism's relative risk. For example, a microorganism or plant may have been modified to carry a biochemical or visual marker (such as firefly lucifierase, the protein that makes the insects glow in the dark) introduced by recombinant DNA techniques. If the host organism is known to pose negligible risk and the introduced gene does not make the new construct "unfamiliar" with respect to risk, then the modified organism should be treated no differently than the host organism or organisms with similar traits modified by traditional techniques. It is significant that field tests of living organisms are traditionally unregulated, unless they are known or suspected plant or animal pathogens, or otherwise known to be a hazard.

At the first meeting of the Biosafety Working Group (BSWG-1), held in Aarhus, Denmark, in July 1996, the group tried to begin the drafting of a protocol, but accomplished little. Rather, it was little more than a forum for defining issues and staking out positions. Governments listed issues for future discussion and negotiation and outlined the information required to guide their future work (Bai, Burgiel, Prather, and Wagner 1998). At the next meeting of the working group (BSWG-2), held in Montreal in May 1997, the issues discussed included objectives; "advance informed agreement" (AIA) notification procedures for transfers of living modified organisms (LMOs); competent authorities/focal points; information sharing and a clearinghouse mechanism; capacity building; public participation and awareness; risk assessment and management; unintentional transboundary movement; handling, transportation, packaging, and transit requirements; and monitoring and compliance (Bai et al. 1998). At the third meeting (BSWG-3), held in Montreal in October 1997, delegates produced a draft text to serve as the basis for negotiation. Two sub-working groups were established to address the basic issues to be addressed in the protocol, as well as a "contact group" on "institutional matters" and "final clauses." In full, the issues addressed included objectives, socioeconomic considerations, liability and compensation, illegal traffic, nondiscrimination, and trade with non-Parties (countries that have not ratified the CBD) (Bai et al. 1998). A meeting of the parent group, the Conference of the Parties (COP) to the CBD, took place in May 1998 in Bratislava, Slovakia, and provided for two more meetings to finalize the biosafety protocol (Bai et al. 1998). In August of that year in Montreal, at BSWG-5, in the face of obvious polarization on many issues between developed and developing countries, there appeared to be greater progress on bureaucratic procedures than on issues more basic (and potentially devastating to research and development), such as the scope of which activities should actually be regulated, liability and redress (in case of mishap), consideration of socioeconomic impacts as part of biosafety evaluation, and trade issues.

The February 1999 meeting (BSWG-6), which lacked coherent goals or ground rules, was marked by disorganization and acrimony. A bloc consisting of the United States, Canada, Australia, Argentina, Chile, and Uruguay prevented agreement on a protocol at the meeting, deferring deliberations until "no later than May 2000" (Pollack 1999). But the contentiousness was over the degree to which various trade interests would be disadvantaged. Any mention of the scientific deficiencies of the proposal was conspicuously absent. The chief U.S. negotiator, Rafe Pomerance, said that the talks broke down because "there were two compromises we were not prepared to make. One is to tie up trade . . . [and] the second is to allow this regime, without a lot of deliberation, to undermine the WTO [world trade organization] trading regime" (Pollack 1999). In other words, the United States and its allies were willing to tolerate onerous case-by-case review of research using innocuous genetically improved plants (a catastrophe for academics and small companies), as long as big agribusiness's commercial products were not disadvantaged. There is every reason to believe that the ongoing deliberations on the protocol will continue to be based on politics, expediency, and perceived narrow self-interest, rather than on scientific principles, product risk, or the public interest. What is likely to emerge eventually is a package that is less objectionable to the United States and its allies because it is more favorable to their products. But this package will likely be utterly lacking in scientific and common sense.

In view of these extraordinary efforts, one might wonder what motivates the UN and national officials involved in the CBD's biosafety protocol. Repeatedly, participants have built an unstable edifice: misstatements are heaped upon misapprehensions, all on a foundation of nescience, and implemented at exorbitant cost via thousands of documents. Careful examination of the nations' positions reveals that the underlying agenda is various manifestations of self-interest.

Consider, first, the regulators. As mentioned above, most regulators participating in the drafting of the biosafety protocol are environmental regulators, whose mandates, domains, and budgets traditionally have not been large. It is hardly surprising, then, that these regulators would welcome the opportunity for an international agreement that dictates new regulatory responsibilities that would require that the regulators review proposals and grant approval prior to field testing. A more rational, risk-based approach would leave the vast majority of field trials exempt from case-by-case government review, denying regulators any enhancement of professional responsibilities, budgets, and influence.

Second, and less obvious, many developing countries' interventions at various COP and BSWG meetings reveal their hunger for "capacity-building and financial resources along with compensatory guarantees through liability and socio-economic considerations" (Pollack 1999). These are the code words for more largesse flowing from the Northern to the Southern Hemisphere. Specifically, officials from the developing countries appear to believe that the industrialized countries are going to bankroll the establishment and maintenance of their new regulatory apparatuses and to pay large compensatory damages if, say, Japanese microbiologists develop a yeast that produces extractable vanilla and disenfranchises exporters of vanilla beans in Madagascar and Mauritius.

Third, it seems obvious that the extravagant and gratuitous regulation required by the nascent biosafety protocol will not be implemented in developing countries if industrialized countries do not provide the resources for capacity building and finance. And even if regulatory infrastructures were established, in many countries they would likely be inefficient and corrupt, a particular concern where every field trial would be subject to the vagaries of case-by-case pretesting review. Would this arrangement be a positive incentive for research and development using a new technology?

Biotech regulators in developing countries think mistakenly that they are in a no-lose situation. They know that in the best of worlds, there will be little research or commercial activity in biotech originating in their countries. So, if they do not receive funding to establish new regulatory infrastructures, they simply will not create them; and if they do receive outside support for such capacity building, they are that much ahead. However, the myopic decisions of their regulators have real costs for citizens of the UN member nations, for it is these citizens who continue to pay for both the direct expense of the recurring international seances and the indirect expense of ultimate compliance with the new regulations. In the longer term, the added expense of unnecessary case-by-case review of essentially negligible-risk activities will, as discussed above, serve as a potent disincentive to research and development, especially on low-value-added products like those involved in agriculture in general and subsistence farming in particular. The result will be that many countries will become no more than spectators to the revolution in agricultural biotechnology, and research on plants and microorganisms important to developing countries will never be cost-effective.

The U.S. Senate must ratify the CBD if the United States is to be a party to it and subject to the biosafety protocol. This is unlikely to happen while Republicans control the Senate. Some observers have urged ratification, interpreting the presumed requirement for Senate consent to a biosafety protocol as a fail-safe against U.S. participation in an imprudent agreement. However, were the CBD to be ratified, the president would not be required to seek congressional advice or consent to any of the new language developed by a conference of the ratifying nations. Moreover, even if the Senate were consulted, various blandishments and pressures could be brought to bear on them by the administration and others. This latter scenario is of particular concern with the CBD high on the administration's agenda. As noted above, then-Undersecretary of State for Global Affairs Timothy Wirth said in 1995 that the CBD has the "top priority among all treaties" and agreements awaiting confirmation. By the end of 1997, as Wirth was departing from government service, he observed that, "Despite a growing constituency in support of the United Nations Convention on Biodiversity (CBD), which was signed in 1993, and ever-growing evidence that the earth's biological diversity is diminishing, the Senate has not yet ratified the treaty. Nonetheless, the U.S. has remained active in negotiations under the Convention. *We have played a lead role in negotiations on a biosafety protocol and a global agreement on the protection and management of plant and genetic resources* [emphasis added]" (USIS 1997).

The U.S. government has actively pursued this international agreement, which contravenes broad scientific consensus about biotechnology regulation, which does violence to domestic and international biotechnology research and development, and which the Senate explicitly has chosen not to ratify. This cannot but reflect disdain for science, scorn for the public interest, and contempt for the Senate on the part of the U.S. technology czar, Vice President Al Gore. Gore has placed his acolytes in key positions in various government departments and agencies and, after a lifetime in elected politics, he knows how to wire an issue, how to ensure that key government organizations are focused on furthering his agenda. For example, wishing to add the unique resources of the intelligence community to the influence of the State Department in order to advance the kinds of initiatives described in *Environmental Diplomacy,* Gore maneuvered behind the scenes and in a speech at the World Affairs Council in Los Angeles on July 25, 1996, John Deutch, director of the CIA and the coordinator of all U.S. intelligence activities, signed on, "Just as Secretary Christopher promised 'to put environmental issues in the mainstream of American foreign policy,' I intend to make sure that Environmental Intelligence remains in the mainstream of U.S. intelligence activities. Even in times of declining budgets we will support policymakers" (Deutch 1996). In addition, Secretary of Defense William Cohen gibbers that "environmental considerations shall be integrated into all defense activities," and his principal deputy undersecretary (environmental security) struggles to link sustainable development and the waging of twenty-first-century warfare.

## CONCLUSION

During the Clinton administration, U.S. foreign policy has aggressively embraced and established Vice President Gore's ideological, idiosyncratic, and often scientifically insupportable version of environmentalism. Perhaps pseudo-environmentalism would be more apt. A central component of U.S. policy is to collaborate with UN agencies and programs that favor bureaucrats' self-interest but stifle the development of environment-friendly biotechnology innovations that can help to increase food production, clean up toxic wastes, purify water, and supplant agricultural chemicals. Two egregious examples of unscientific and anti-innovative biotechnology regulation include a UNIDO code of conduct and the biosafety protocol within the Convention on Biological Diversity (CBD), both supported by the United States.

Such poorly crafted and unscientific regulatory proposals have made the products of the new biotechnology unnecessarily expensive to test, produce, and use. The result will be diminished commercial potential and markets for companies in industrialized countries and greater scientific and commercial marginalization of developing countries. Unnecessary government scrutiny in the form of case-by-case reviews will cause delays in biotechnology product testing, increase the potential for corruption, and markedly inhibit the diffusion of this useful new technology to the developing world. Developing countries will be prevented from participating in worldwide technological trends, and the technology gap between industrialized and developing countries will widen. Even more disturbing, the income gap between the have and have-not nations, which more than doubled during the past thirty years, will widen further.

There are bitter ironies in the pressure from regulators at the United Nations, European Union, and United States on developing countries to adopt unscientific, technique-based, and anti-innovative regulatory approaches. Regulators and environmentalists from industrialized countries regard third-world regulation as an opportunity to realize their weltanschauung, validate their own minority view of biotechnology risks, and promote their own importance as policy players on a larger stage. The policies favored by regulators at the United Nations and in industrialized countries will systematically undermine research on precisely the kinds of products that are most needed in developing countries—more plentiful and nutritious foods and biological alternatives to chemical pesticides and fertilizers. At the same time that their poorly conceived policies afford no improvement in environmental or public health protection, the industrialized countries exact unacceptable opportunity costs in the form of deferred enhancements in food production, health care, and entry into international markets.

The U.S. Senate should, therefore, continue to oppose ratification of the CBD and, further, should withhold funding of any UN organization that proposes, implements, or has any connection whatever with unscientific regulation. Were the Senate to ratify the CBD, the United States would thereby commit itself to negotiating biosafety regulations in an intellectual and political miasma. For example, Article 23 of the CBD, in effect, limits eligible NGO participants to only the "greenest"—the most radical—of the environmentalist groups. NGOs can be excluded if one-third of the countries present object to the admission (UNEP 1992). This limit virtually precludes the participation of organizations that represent commercial mining, timber, agribusiness, livestock, fishing, and energy interests. It is ominous that at the 1995 biosafety protocol drafting meeting in Jakarta described above, the more radical NGOs such as Greenpeace and Friends of the Earth—and only such groups—were permitted to participate in the usually closed negotiations.

The debacle of the biosafety protocol contaminates irreversibly the CBD's otherwise commendable biodiversity goals. Stanford University biologist Donald Kennedy has emphasized eloquently that each vanishing species is an irreplaceable resource, the unique endpoint of a long evolutionary process. "One may be the keystone of a complex ecosystem that plays some role in climate stabilization. Another contains gene sequences that may yield new understanding about the control of behavior. Still another may, because of its beauty or its grandeur, have a special hold on the human imagination—as eagles have for some of us, or otters for others" (Kennedy 1994, B9).

There are problems, however, even with the laudable portions of the CBD. For example, the mechanisms that underlie programs intended to preserve biodiversity are variously ambiguous, vague, or impotent. Moreover, the Global Environment Facility (GEF), a $2 billion UN fund organized through the World Bank and which would fund the CBD's biodiversity-related projects, has a variety of problems. A recent twenty-six-country survey of GEF fund recipients, carried out by the CBD secretariat, "revealed concern about the scale of spending on international consultants, whose costs often consume up to half the total project expenditure. It also revealed deep unease over the method used to calculate the size of project grants" (Jayaraman and Masood 1998, 640).

The systematic, significant problems of the United Nations include the desire to expand its mandates and its seeming unawareness of what constitutes legitimate scientific advice. In May 1998, at the Bratislava conference of the parties to the CBD, the newly installed head of UNEP, Klaus Töpfer, announced his intention to have the UNEP play a stronger role in the implementation of five UN conventions that relate to conservation (one of which is the CBD), including taking a lead in providing relevant scientific advice. At the same time, he continued, he wants much of this advice to come from nongovernment environment groups (or NGOs), including the Union for the Conservation of Nature (IUCN) and the World Wide Fund for Nature (WWF) (Masood 1998). From my experience, turning to NGOs for such scientific advice is tantamount to asking the Mafia to help with the relocation of participants in the Federal Witness Protection Program.

If the United Nations is to have a role in international regulation—a big if—several conditions must be met. First, there is the most fundamental requirement that binding international regulation must only occur when circumstances are exceptional—in order to avoid some sort of otherwise likely catastrophe, for example. But, as noted by Jeremy Rabkin, in many UN-inspired conventions "the focus is not on extreme, overriding challenges but on fostering a 'global perspective' which invites an ongoing grab-bag of special concerns, piled onto the international environmental agenda like baggage on an airport carousel" (Rabkin, this volume). Second, policies must make scientific and economic sense.

Thus far, the United Nations has failed spectacularly to meet these conditions.

## REFERENCES

Anon. 1994. *Biotechnology Risk Control.* Luxembourg: Office for Official Publications of the European Communities.

Bai, C., Rajmani L. Burgiel, T. Prather, and L. Wagner. 1998. Earth Negotiations Bulletin 9 (31 August). At <http://www.isisd.ca/linkages/download/asc/enb09108e.txt> (1/7/99).

Bureau of National Affairs (BNA). 1995. *Environment Daily,* 20 November.

Council on Environmental Quality (CEQ). 1982. *1982 Annual Report.*

Deutch, John. 1996. Speech before the World Affairs Council, in Los Angeles, 25 July.

Douglass, Christopher. 1988. *Environmental Crossing Guards: International Environmental Treaties and U.S. Foreign Policy.* Working Paper No. 168. Center for the Study of American Business.

Giddings, L. V. 1996. A Convention Unmasked. *Nature Biotechnology* 14: 1304–1305.

Gore, Albert. 1991. Planning a New Biotechnology Policy. *Harvard Journal of Law and Technology* 5: 19–30.

———. 1992. *Earth in the Balance.* New York: Plume.

Jayaraman, K. S., and Ehsan Masood. 1998. UNECS Fund under Pressure to Open Up. *Nature* 392: 640.

Kennedy, D. 1994. Don't Be Distracted by Alien Cows. *Los Angeles Times,* 24 October, B9.

Masood, Ehsan. 1995. Biosafety Rules Will Regulate International GMO Transfers. *Nature* 378: 326.

———. 1998. UN Agency Chief Seeks Advice from Environmental Groups. *Nature* 393: 99–100.

McMenamin, B. 1996. Environmental Imperialism. *Forbes* (20 May): 124–136.

Miller, Henry I. 1997. *Policy Controversy in Biotechnology: An Insider's View.* Austin, Tex.: R. G. Landes and Academic Press.

Miller, Henry I., D. W. Altman, J. H. Barton, et al. 1995. Biotechnology Oversight in Developing Countries: A Risk-Based Algorithm. *Bio-Technology* 13: 955.

Miller, Henry I., R. H. Burns, A. K. Vidaver, et al. 1990. Risk-Based Oversight of Experiments in the Environment. *Science* 250: 490.

Morrisson, J. 1998. G8 Countries to Act Against Environmental Crime. Reuters (4 May).

National Research Council. 1989. *Field Testing Genetically Modified Organisms: Framework for Decisions.* Washington, D.C.: National Academy Press.

Organization for Economic Cooperation and Development (OECD). 1995. *Safety Considerations for Biotechnology: Scale-Up of Microorganisms as Biofertilizers.* Paris: OECD.

Pollack, A. 1999. U.S. and Allies Block Treaty on Genetically Altered Goods. *The New York Times,* 25 February.

UNIDO Code of Conduct. 1992. *Biotechnology Forum Europe* 9: 218–221.

United Nations. 1992. Environment Program (UNEP). Convention on Biological Diversity.

United Nations. 1993. Environment Program (UNEP). *Expert Panels Established to Follow-Up on the Convention on Biological Diversity.* Report of the Panel IV, 28 April.

United Nations. 1995. Environment Program (UNEP). Global Consultation on Biosafety 4, 19 December.

U.S. Department of State. 1997. *Environmental Diplomacy: The Environment and U.S. Foreign Policy.* Washington, D.C.

U.S. Information Service. 1997. Briefing of Tim Wirth on Global Issues, 23 December, Washington File.

Watkins, James. 1997. Science and Technology in Foreign Affairs. *Science* 277: 650.

CHAPTER 9

# Bucking the Tide of Globalism: Developing Property Rights from the Ground Up

*Terry L. Anderson*

The most salient case for government intervention into private activities arises when the actions of one individual affect another without his or her consent. This happens when people compete for the use of a resource such as air. One individual wants clean air for breathing or viewing and another wants it as a waste receptacle. If the first person has a right to clean air, then the second, by disposing of waste, imposes a cost on the other by violating his or her right; the polluter creates a third-party effect. Alternatively, one party may create a benefit, such as preservation of endangered species habitat, that another may enjoy without paying. In this case, the actions of the free rider may result in underproduction of the good. The greening of U.S. foreign policy has been justified on both grounds. Indeed the title of a recent book, *The Global Commons* (Buck 1998), captures what happens when the actions of one person impinge on the well-being of another. By arguing that the world is one large commons, everything in the world becomes interconnected so that action in one country can affect goings on in every other. Who is to say that a butterfly flapping its wings in Japan may not influence the likelihood of hurricanes in the Caribbean? Hence, the world's oceans and atmosphere become a commons subject to tragedy. This argument opens endless arguments for governmental regulations at the international level under the rubric of third-party effects.

The free rider argument also provides numerous justifications for the greening of foreign policy. If people in New York derive value from the existence of tigers in southeast Asia but will never visit tiger reserves, and if people living with the tigers must forego economic values in order to preserve the habitat, there is no way of charging the people who benefit and compensating those who bear the costs (see 't Sas-Rolfes 1998). And who can refute the argument, assuming global warming is a problem, that people in one corner of the world benefit from the preservation of forests as carbon sinks in another corner, but would free ride on the provision of those benefits? Environmentalists argue that these existence values, as they are known, justify using the regulatory and taxation powers of government to produce environmental goods from something as specific as wildlife habitat to something as nebulous as biodiversity (see Boudreaux and Meiners 1998).

These arguments for the greening of foreign policy assume that governmental intervention is necessary to internalize costs and benefits. In other words, government must regulate the use of the global commons or provide the public goods for which there are free riders.

Turning to political regulation, however, ignores the costs of implementing this action and the potential for getting the desired result. The command-and-control approach assumes that benevolent politicians and bureaucrats will pursue the public interest. But, as this chapter suggests, political costs are positive and perhaps even grow exponentially with the size of the governing unit. Hence, although there may be positive benefits from using higher levels of government to internalize externalities, these benefits must be balanced against the costs. In short, the net gains from regulation should determine whether moving resource decisions from individuals and small groups to national governments or international bodies is optimal.

The ideas that people are imposing costs on others in society or are free riding on the actions of others also fail to capture the essence of the problems as outlined by Coase (1960) in his seminal article, "The Problem of Social Cost." In the Coasean framework, third-party effects are better thought of as competing uses for the same resource for which property rights have not been clearly specified. Bruce Yandle (1998) succinctly summarizes Coase's approach, which considers the paper mill and others who wish to consume or enjoy water quality as a part of a competitive market where people bargain for the use of the rights to scarce property. This analysis has nothing to do with polluters' imposing costs on society, but everything to do with competing demands for use of an asset (120).

Once property rights are clarified, negotiation over the competing uses can begin. Hence, the competing-use paradigm described by Coase focuses our attention on the potential for property rights solutions that vest ownership in individuals and allow competitors to bargain over conflicting uses. If private property rights can be established, a growing body of evidence shows that those rights form the basis for wealth creation that then allows us to worry about and deal with environmental problems. Moreover, property rights give owners the incentive to husband their resources. Both of these points are examined in detail below.

How property rights evolve can be just as important as whether they evolve. Simply saying that there should be property rights ignores the process whereby they are produced. Property rights may evolve from the ground up through customs, culture, and common law, or they may be designated from the top down through legislation and treaties. This chapter examines the potential success of each and argues that when property rights evolve from the bottom up, there is more chance that they will respond to local resource conflicts and conserve on resources used in the definition and enforcement process. Standing in the way of this evolutionary process may be significant enforcement problems when the individual competitors live on opposite sides of political boundaries. In contrast, when property rights are dictated from the top down, especially through international treaties, people will engage in efforts to influence the political process that determines who gets the rights and, in that process, will dissipate some of the gains available from establishing property rights in the first place. Because these costs, known to economists as rent-seeking costs, cannot be avoided, the question is whether they can be minimized. And even then, once rights are handed out from the top down, enforcement costs remain.

## FREE MARKET ENVIRONMENTALISM

The property rights approach to environmental problems is summarized in the paradigm known as free market environmentalism (see Anderson and Leal 1991), which concentrates on the potential for decentralization, as opposed to centralization, to improve resource stewardship and environmental quality by improving the information and incentives available to decision makers. The key to effective markets in general, and free market environmentalism in particular, is the establishment of well-specified and transferable property rights.

To have property rights and markets, the physical attributes of the resources must be specified in a clear and concise manner; in other words, the attributes must be measurable. The rectangular survey system allows us to define ownership rights over land and clarifies some disputes over ownership. This system may also help define ownership of the air space over land, but more questions arise here because of the fluidity of air and the infinite vertical third dimension above ground. If property rights to resources cannot be defined, they cannot be exchanged for other property rights.

Property rights must also be defendable. A rectangular survey may define surface rights to land, but conflicts are inevitable if there is no way to defend the boundaries and prevent other incompatible uses. On the Western frontier of the United States, barbed wire provided an inexpensive way to defend property rights; locks and chains do the same for parked bicycles. But enforcing one's rights to peace and quiet by fencing out sound waves is more difficult, as is keeping other people's hazardous wastes out of a groundwater supply. Whenever the use of property cannot be monitored or enforced, conflicts are inevitable and bargaining to resolve conflicts becomes more difficult if not impossible.

Finally, property rights must be transferable. In contrast to the costs of measuring and monitoring resource uses, which are mainly determined by the physical nature of the property and technology, the ability to exchange is determined largely by the legal environment. Although well-defined and enforced rights allow the owner to enjoy the benefits of using his or her property, legal restrictions on the sale of that property may hinder the potential for gains from trade. Suppose, for example, that a group of fishermen values water for fish habitat more highly than farmers value the same water for irrigation. If the fishermen are prohibited from renting or purchasing the water from the farmers, then gains from trade will not be realized, and potential wealth will not be created. The farmer will, therefore, have less incentive to leave the water in the stream.

In sum, free market environmentalism requires well-specified rights to take actions with respect to specific resources. If such rights cannot be measured, monitored, and marketed, then there is little possibility for negotiations to solve conflicts over resource use. Disposal of airborne waste emissions, for example, is more of a problem than solid waste disposal in the ground because property rights to the atmosphere are not as easily defined and enforced as are ones involving the earth's surface. Private ownership of land works well for timber production, but measuring, monitoring, and marketing the land for endangered species habitat requires entrepreneurial imagination—especially if the species migrates over large areas.

Free market environmentalism does not assume that these property rights automatically exist or that they cost nothing to create. Rather, it recognizes the costs of defining and enforcing property rights and emphasizes the role of entrepreneurs in producing new property rights when natural resources and environmental amenities become valuable. Where environmental entrepreneurs can devise ways of marketing environmental values, market incentives can have dramatic results. Entrepreneurs recognize that externalities provide profit opportunities for those who successfully define and enforce property rights where those rights are lacking. A stream owner who devises a way of charging fishermen can internalize the benefits and gain incentive to maintain or improve the quality of the stream. The subdivider who puts covenants on deeds that preserve open space, improve views, and generally harmonize development with environment amenities establishes property rights to the environmental values and captures the value in higher prices for the housing.

The property rights approach to natural resources recognizes that property rights evolve, depending on the benefits and costs associated with defining and enforcing rights. This calculus depends on such variables as the expected value of the resource in question, the technology for measuring and monitoring property rights, and the legal and moral rules that condition the behavior of the competing parties. At any given time, property rights will reflect the perceived costs and benefits of definition and enforcement. Thus, because property rights are continually evolving, the lack of property rights does not necessarily imply a failure of markets. As the perceived costs and benefits of defining and enforcing property rights change, property rights will evolve.

This evolution does not mean that there is no role for government in defining and enforcing property rights or that property rights will always allow bargaining to resolve conflicts over resource use. The costs of establishing property rights are positive and can potentially be reduced by governmental institutions, such as courts. Furthermore, because transaction costs are positive, market contracts will not take all costs into account. In the case of water pollution originating from sources that cannot be identified at low costs (with current technology), for example, the definition and enforcement of property rights governing water use may be impossible. Or excluding nonpayers from the benefits of growing forests as carbon sinks may be so costly that a market solution cannot evolve.

In these cases, there is a utilitarian argument for considering government intervention, but there is no guarantee that the results from political allocation will be any better than a market with positive transaction costs. If markets produce too little clean water because dischargers cannot bargain with those who value clean water, then by contrast, political solutions may produce too much clean water because those who enjoy the benefits do not pay the cost.

Furthermore, how property rights are produced also can make a considerable difference in their efficacy. If property rights evolve from the ground up, those involved in the evolution have more knowledge of the conflicting resources and a more direct incentive to resolve them in less costly ways. For example, cattlemen arriving on the western frontier of the United States recognized the potential for overgrazing the commons. Without surveys and fences to define and enforce property rights, they formed associations that resolved disputes over customary grazing rights and excluded outsiders who would have caused the tragedy of the commons (see Anderson and Hill 1975). The major problem these local associations faced was successfully excluding entrants onto the commons, mainly because they lacked the governmental sanction to use force. Hence, would-be entrants challenged the authority of the local associations, leading to conflicts that sometimes ended in armed range wars. Nonetheless, these associations hammered out a set of rights that worked for the resources in question and could have been all the more effective if they had been enforced by government.

When property rights evolve from the top down—that is, when they are devised at higher levels of government and imposed on the people using the resource—there is a greater likelihood that the institutions will be less compatible with resource use and that more rent-seeking will take place in determining who gets the rights. Again the U.S. Western frontier provides a vivid example. After declaring illegal the customary rights created by cattlemen's associations, the federal government passed a series of homestead acts aimed at establishing property rights to land on the frontier. Under these acts, homesteaders could obtain title to as much as 640 acres only after making specific investments and living on the land for at least five years. Six hundred forty acres were too few for the average viable farming unit and the required investments were unnecessary for viable farming. In addition, homesteading encouraged a race for property rights on the frontier that led to misery and failure (see Anderson and Hill 1990). The lesson is that when property rights are created from the top down, it is difficult to specify the rights in ways that resolve conflicting resource uses. It is perhaps even more difficult to prevent people from wasting resources in the process of trying to get the property rights that are being handed out.

From these basic tenets of free market environmentalism flow several implications for global environmental issues.

• Government intervention as a solution to environmental problems may have unintended consequences that actually exacerbate environmental problems.

- Establishing property rights is the way to encourage bargaining and efficient use of resources.

- Defining and enforcing property rights is costly, especially in terms of having the necessary coercive power to exclude would-be entrants into the commons.

- Property rights that evolve from the ground up are more likely to be appropriate to the resource constraints but are more difficult to enforce against outsiders who do not recognize the sovereignty of the local group.

- Developing property rights from the top down, on the other hand, is less likely to tailor the rights to local needs, more likely to encourage rent-seeking in the process of establishing the rights, and, when done at the international level, still faces the problem of enforcing the rights against those who choose to violate the agreements or do not recognize the international authority.

## SUBSIDIZING GLOBAL ENVIRONMENTAL DESTRUCTION

Under the title *Mortgaging the Earth,* Bruce Rich (1994) documents how the World Bank and other international financial institutions have subsidized environmental destruction. This story is essentially the exportation of many U.S. environmental policies. Especially in the case of water policy, the United States and other developed countries have dammed rivers with significant environmental consequences and little solid economic justification. Similar policies have been exported through international financial institutions.

One example of how World Bank financing can work against environmental goals is the Northwest Region Development Program. Between 1981 and 1983, the World Bank loaned a little more than $443 million for the paving of Brazilian national highway number 364, a 1,500-kilometer stretch of road. The purpose of the highway was to connect Brazil's populous south-central region with the rain forest wilderness in the northwest and to connect thirty-nine rural settlements with the highway to attract settlers to the region. These agricultural settlers were to produce crops such as cocoa and coffee for export. The effort was extremely effective in attracting tens of thousands of settlers to the region.

Unfortunately, the settlers who were unable to obtain land titles and credit turned to clearing the rain forest and planting subsistence crops of beans, rice, and maze. Crop failure after a year or two on the poor, exposed soils forced many of the colonists to move back to the populated south-central region. Meanwhile, the program increased the rate of forest destruction in a region the size of Oregon from 1.7 percent in 1978 to 16.1 percent in 1991 (see Once It's Here . . . 1997). In addition, settlers and the indigenous population were ravaged by disease. More than 250,000 people were infected with malaria. Some Indian tribes experienced epidemics of measles and influenza with infant mortality rates reaching 50 percent in some tribes.

Brazil is not the only place where a World Bank project has wreaked havoc on the environment and caused social unrest. From 1976 to 1985, the bank loaned about $500 million for another massive resettlement program known as Indonesia Transmigration. The goal was to resettle millions of poor people from the heavily populated inner islands of Indonesia to the sparsely populated outer islands and to provide support for the settlers to grow cacao, coffee, and palm oil. The outer islands contained 10 percent of the world's remaining tropical rain forest and were inhabited mainly by indigenous tribes.

As in Brazil, support for the settlers failed to materialize, and many settlers were forced to clear rain forests to try to survive on subsistence crops. Again, the crops failed due to poor soil conditions. Ironically, if given the $7,000 paid by the World Bank to resettle a family in the remote areas, a household could have lived above the Indonesian poverty level for at least eleven years.

International development efforts illustrate the perils of top-down control. The most recent example is the construction of the Three Rivers Dam in China, arguably the least cost-effective and most environmentally unfriendly international development project ever undertaken. In short, elevating authority to higher and higher levels of government seldom generates fiscal or environmental responsibility. As expenditures are further removed from the citizens paying the costs and as decisions are made by bureaucrats not directly responsible to the electorate, the costs of monitoring governmental agencies rise. As is shown in this chapter, this calls for a careful weighing of the benefits and costs of greater centralization.

## PROPERTY RIGHTS ARE GREENER

A growing body of empirical evidence shows a positive correlation among property rights, economic growth, and environmental quality. Coursey (1992) found that environmental quality has an income elasticity of demand of approximately 2.5, meaning that, above a threshold level, a 10 percent increase in income results in a 25 percent increase in the demand for environmental amenities. Examining specific pollutants such as sulfur dioxide emissions, Grossman and Krueger (1994, 1995) found a "J-curve" relationship between environmental quality and GDP showing that although pollution levels may decline as incomes begin to rise from very low levels, they ultimately decline as annual income levels reach approximately $5,000.

Norton (1998) extends these empirical findings to show the correlation between environmental quality and measures of economic freedom. For a variety of environmental measures and freedom measures, he concludes that

> environmental quality and economic growth rates are greater in regimes where property rights are well defined than in regimes where property rights are poorly defined. Therefore, property rights and growth should be viewed . . . as favorable to environmental quality and conservation of resources. At a minimum, a Pavlovian reaction against the natural concomitants of strong property rights—markets and economic growth—is unwarranted. More to the point, the specification of strong aggregate property rights appears to have an important place in improving human well-being. (Norton 1998, 51)

Economist Robert Deacon (1994) provides a more specific examination of the relationship between property rights and deforestation, concluding that deforestation results mainly from the failure of governments to define and enforce property rights. He argues that insecure property rights contribute to deforestation both directly and indirectly. The direct effect is the obvious tragedy of the commons: If I conserve trees by not cutting, you will still cut. Hence, forests are harvested prematurely and without regard for regeneration. The indirect effect of insecure property rights results from a lack of investment in agricultural productivity and hence a reduction in agricultural yields that requires more forest land to be cleared and planted to crops. Deacon concludes that secure property rights in the pre-Christian Roman Empire and ancient Greece led to forest stewardship, but that the decline of these civilizations weakened the property rights, resulting in deforestation. Using more systematic recent data on forestation and quantifiable measures of political instability and insecure property rights, Deacon finds a direct correlation between good forest management and the rule of law. That is why countries such as Lebanon, Haiti, and El Salvador are experiencing deforestation, while the United States, Canada, and countries of Western Europe are experiencing reforestation. Deacon concludes that it is stable, democratic governments constrained by the rule of law that provide the necessary ingredients for saving the world's forests.

The lesson expressed by Deacon was recently driven home in Nepal. In 1957 the government nationalized all forests in the name of land reform. Deforestation cost the country half its trees, and erosion of steep hillsides caused flooding. To halt the deforestation in the late 1970s, control of forests was put in the hands of corrupt local chieftains, and little changed. Now the government has turned over control of 216,000 hectares of forests to local communities with democratic governments that have a stake in the long-term survival of forests. Nearly 5,000 user groups have rights to harvest fuel wood and animal fodder, and once the forests are mature the groups can selectively harvest trees for a profit. As a result overharvesting has stopped, and nearly 10,000 hectares have been reforested. Although this may not be the purest form of private property, the incentives have changed sufficiently to induce conservation instead of a tragedy of the commons (see Stackhouse 1998).

## THE DEVOLUTION SOLUTION

The well-known environmental slogan "think globally, act lo-cally" admonishes people to seek the appropriate locus for solving environmental problems. This certainly applies to governmental solutions, as David Haddock (1997b) argues.

> The case for centralization has been badly overstated. Gathering all an externality's participants with a single regulatory unit does indeed provide benefits. . . . But many interstate externalities are far from na-tionwide, so the benefit is exhausted before regulation becomes na-tional. Moreover, pointing to the benefits while ignoring concurrent costs is inappropriate, for ideal regulation would maximize net rather than gross benefits. (16)

In short, social cost arguments do not necessarily mean that more centralization is better once we consider the public choice costs of using government. At higher and higher levels of govern-ment, the principal-agent problems become greater and greater. Measuring and monitoring what state political agents deliver to their constituents is more difficult than measuring and monitoring local political agents and so on for national and international po-litical agents. In other words, information and incentive matter.

This point is emphasized by Huffman (1997) and Haddock (1997a) regarding the potential for establishing water manage-ment governance units that balance externalities with costs. Haddock (1997a) states that "much bureaucratic discretion would be better placed in private hands," but "the remainder would predictably be better used at a regional level, because less remote regulators would be better acquainted with constituent preferences, more sensitive to constituent satisfaction, and given the opportunity to observe a wider range of alternative regulatory experiments" (55–56).

There is a growing body of evidence that environmental feder-alism can offer a better way of handling some environmental problems. Two examples come from forests and parks. In side-by-side comparisons of national and state forests, Leal (1995) and Fretwell (1998) have found that states do better on virtually every dimension. Not only do they make money on their operations while the national forests lose, but there is also preliminary evidence of their environmental sustainability. The reason for this difference is largely found in the system of accountability found at the state level. Operated under a trust arrangement, western state forest lands are required to earn revenues for state schools. Hence, recipients and managers alike have a reason to monitor costs and develop revenue opportunities. Such accountability is crucial for both fiscal and environmental responsibility and is more likely if the unit of governance is smaller.

The second example comes from park management. Again, side-by-side comparisons of state and national parks by Leal and Fretwell (1997) reveal that state parks generate more revenues per visitor and reinvest in the long-term economic and environmental health of their assets (see also Anderson and James 1997). Similarly, parks in developing countries are more likely to be economically and environmentally sustainable if local people have a stake in their management and in their revenue-generating capability. In both of these examples, it is devolution, not centralization, that leads to better fiscal and environmental results.

The potential for the common law also should not be ignored as a way of developing property rights from the ground up. A classic example of how this can work is the *Trail Smelter* case discussed in chapter 10. When the effects of pollution from a smelter in Canada got bad enough, citizens from the United States asserted their claim of harm. Ultimately, an international tribunal forced Canada to recognize the rights of the U.S. citizens to clean air and forced the smelter to pay damages. This case demonstrates that property rights solutions including liability rules are possible, even if costly.

In cases where air and water pollution are relatively localized, communities with a direct stake in the problems have a history of forcing cleanup. Pittsburgh was one of the first cities to impose regulations on air pollution, long before the national government addressed the problem. The reason Pittsburgh acted when it did was because the costs of air pollution were rising and because higher incomes increased the citizens' demand for cleanup. As a result, Pittsburgh's air quality has shown substantial improvement from World War II onward, and it certainly does not exhibit a race to the regulatory bottom in an effort to attract industry and create jobs (see Goklany 2000).

## SUCCESSES FROM THE TOP DOWN

To avoid some of the costs of developing property rights through court-adjudicated disputes, governments may be able to lower costs by establishing property rights more directly. One of the best examples comes from southern African countries where property rights are encouraging wild animal, especially elephant, husbandry. The CAMPFIRE program in Zimbabwe gives local groups ownership of elephants in their regions and allows them to profit from hunting and safari operations. The results measured in terms of reduced poaching and increased elephant numbers are well documented (see Bonner 1993; Kreuter and Simmons 1995). In fact, elephant numbers in some regions have grown so rapidly that culling is necessary to prevent overgrazing, which can be catastrophic with such large beasts.

But this example also illustrates how global regulation can thwart a property rights solution. Despite the demonstrated benefits of privatization, international environmental groups have supported the CITES ban on ivory trade even though trading would allow even more returns from good management. Trading is finally being allowed on a very limited and regulated basis only because the southern African countries that are managing their elephants well threatened to pull out of the CITES agreement altogether. The greening of foreign policy is hardly likely to make constructive solutions such as CAMPFIRE more likely.

Another example comes from international fishery regulations. With a few exceptional cases of whaling treaties, international agreements have not been very successful at stopping overfishing of the ocean commons. The few success stories in fisheries management revolve around privatization, not centralization. Community-run fisheries stop short of complete privatization, but they get the incentives right by limiting entry into the fishery and giving community members a stake in asset management (see Leal 1996). Again and again the evidence shows that devolution of fisheries management for local species is the best way to prevent the tragedy of the commons. Along the Pacific Northwest Coast, families and clans of pre-Columbian Indians controlled access to smaller salmon streams and to netting and trapping locations on larger salmon streams. With a stake in the long-term viability of the fisheries, they practiced sustainable management. It was not until non-Indians arrived, ignoring traditional fishing rights and progressively moving nets downstream until they were at the mouths of streams where entire stocks could be depleted, that the tragedy of the commons occurred (see Higgs 1982).

In many small-scale examples from Maine to Brazil to Nova Scotia to Turkey, community management of fisheries has excluded outsiders and prevented overfishing. On a larger scale, the Norwegian Lofoten fishery has been self-regulated since the end of the nineteenth century. The system operates with fifteen control districts, each with separate, well-defined territories and each with its own regulatory and enforcement body. As a result of this ownership system, the Lofoten fishery is one of the largest and most lucrative in the world. Donald Leal (1996) concludes that "community-run fisheries challenge the notion that fishers will always be locked into the tragedy of the commons unless there is state control. . . . Given the failure of government to regulate fishing successfully, a self-regulated fishery is an idea whose time has come" (22).

Expanding territorial limits to 200 miles and establishing individual transferable quotas (ITQs) is another way that governments can encourage property rights and better management of fisheries. Several countries, most notably Australia and New Zealand, have implemented ITQs where other forms of regulation have failed. Australia is using the ITQ system for its southern bluefin tuna fishery, which was declining dramatically. Just six months after ITQs were established, the fleet capacity in the fishery was reduced by 60 percent as those who intended to stay in the fishery bought quotas from those who could earn more elsewhere. There was also a dramatic increase in the size of the catch as more efficient operators bought out less efficient operators, giving the fewer number of remaining fishers a greater stake in the fishery. As an indication of the increased value of the fishery, ITQs began selling for just under $1,000 per ton on October 1, 1984, but were selling for $2,000 per ton almost six months later. New Zealand and Iceland have experienced similar improvements (Anderson and Leal 1991, 131–132).

## CONCLUSION

Global environmentalism in general and the greening of foreign policy in particular are based on the assumption that externalities are pervasive and that international political control is the necessary solution. There are, to be sure, significant conflicts over resource uses that transcend political boundaries, and centralization has the potential for solving these conflicts. However, this solution presumes that international political institutions can develop regulations that are appropriate and enforceable, a presumption that is questionable. Measuring and monitoring the activities of political agents grows with the size of government, which necessitates balancing the benefits of solving resource conflicts at higher levels of government with the costs of doing so.

If the costs of international political solutions outweigh the benefits, we need not despair. There is, in fact, an alternative solution—decentralization and privatization. The former calls for devolving the locus of authority for resolving disputes over resource use to lower levels of government where agents can be held more accountable, and the latter calls for encouraging the definition and enforcement of private property rights so that individuals and small groups can bargain with one another to resolve conflicts.

Of course there is no way to define and enforce private property rights to the atmospheric commons, but there is also no way to implement and enforce international regulations on carbon emissions. For that reason we have no choice but to "think globally and act locally." By trying to act globally through the greening of foreign policy, the likely result will be impediments to devolution and privatization because global regulation calls for larger units of governance and creates less secure property rights. The CAMPFIRE program for elephant conservation in southern Africa is a case in point. Once top-down regulations under CITES were in place, it was more difficult for innovative property rights solutions and markets to evolve from the ground up.

If the greening of foreign policy is to have a positive impact, it should foster institutions that encourage political and economic freedom, the traditional goals of U.S. foreign policy. Given the high correlation between measures of freedom and environmental quality, this is the surest way to bring good natural resource stewardship and environmental quality to the developing world. With freedom comes economic growth, and with economic growth comes the wherewithal to afford environmental amenities. Perhaps the most important parts to this recipe are private property rights and the rule of law. Hence a greener foreign policy should be one that encourages these fundamental institutions both at home and abroad.

## REFERENCES

Anderson, Terry L., and Peter J. Hill. 1975. The Evolution of Property Rights: A Study of the American West. *The Journal of Law and Economics* 28(1), April, 163–179.

———. 1990. The Race for Property Rights. *The Journal of Law and Economics* 33, 177–197.

Anderson, Terry L., and Alexander James, eds. 1997. *The Politics and Economics of Park Management*. Unpublished manuscript. Bozeman, Mont.: Political Economy Research Center.

Anderson, Terry L., and Donald R. Leal. 1991. *Free Market Environmentalism*. San Francisco: Pacific Research Institute.

Bonner, Raymond. 1993. *At the Hand of Man: Peril and Hope for Africa's Wildlife*. New York: Alfred A. Knopf.

Boudreaux, Donald J., and Roger E. Meiners. 1998. Existence Value and Other of Life's Ills. In *Who Owns the Environment?*, edited by Peter J. Hill and Roger E. Meiners. Lanham, Md.: Rowman & Littlefield.

Buck, Susan J. 1998. *The Global Commons: An Introduction*. Washington, D.C.: Island Press.

Coase, Ronald H. 1960. The Problem of Social Cost. *Journal of Law and Economics* 3(1), 1–44.

Coursey, Don. 1992. *The Demand for Environmental Quality*. St. Louis, Mo.: Washington University, Department of Economics.

Deacon, Robert. 1994. Deforestation and the Rule of Law in a Cross-Section of Countries. *Land Economics* (November): 414–430.

Fretwell, Holly. 1998. *Public Lands: The Price We Pay*. Bozeman, Mont.: Political Economy Research Center.

Goklany, Indur M. 2000. Empirical Evidence Regarding the Role of Nationalism in Improving U.S. Air Quality. In *The Common Law and the Environment:*

*Rethinking the Statutory Basis for Modern Environmental Law*, edited by Roger E. Meiners and Andrew P. Morriss. Lanham, Md.: Rowman & Littlefield.

Grossman, Gene M., and Alan B. Krueger. 1994. Environmental Impacts of North American Free Trade Agreement. In *The U.S.–Mexico Free Trade Agreement*, edited by P. Garber. Cambridge: MIT Press.

———. 1995. Economic Growth and the Environment. *Quarterly Journal of Economics* 112: 353–378.

Haddock, David D. 1997a. Must Water Regulation Be Centralized? In *Water Markets—The Next Generation*, edited by Terry L. Anderson and Peter J. Hill. Lanham, Md.: Rowman & Littlefield.

———. 1997b. Sizing Up Sovereigns: Federal Systems, Their Origin, Their Decline, Their Prospects. In *Environmental Federalism*, edited by Terry L. Anderson and Peter J. Hill. Lanham, Md.: Rowman & Littlefield.

Higgs, Robert. 1982. Legally Induced Technical Regress in the Washington Salmon Fishery. *Research in Economic History* 7, 55–86.

Huffman, James L. 1997. International Constraints on Transboundary Water Marketing. In *Water Markets—The Next Generation*, edited by Terry L. Anderson and Peter J. Hill. Lanham, Md.: Rowman & Littlefield.

Kreuter, Urs P., and Randy T. Simmons. 1995. Who Owns the Elephants? The Political Economy of Saving the African Elephant. In *Wildlife in the Marketplace*, edited by Terry L. Anderson and Peter J. Hill. Lanham, Md.: Rowman & Littlefield.

Leal, Donald R. 1995. Turning a Profit on Forests. PERC Policy Series No. 4. Bozeman, Mont.: Political Economy Research Center.

———. 1996. Community-Run Fisheries: Avoiding the Tragedy of the Commons. PERC Policy Series No. 7. Bozeman, Mont.: Political Economy Research Center.

Leal, Donald R., and Holly Fretwell. 1997. Back to the Future for Our Parks. PERC Policy Series No. 10. Bozeman, Mont.: Political Economy Research Center.

Norton, Seth W. 1998. Property Rights, the Environment, and Economic Well-Being. In *Who Owns the Environment?*, edited by Peter J. Hill and Roger E. Meiners. Lanham, Md.: Rowman & Littlefield.

Once It's Here . . . . 1997. *The Economist*, 1 March, 19–20.

Rich, Bruce. 1994. *Mortgaging the Earth: The World Bank, Environmental Impoverishment, and the Crisis of Development*. Boston: Beacon Press.

Stackhouse, John. 1998. Forests Returning to the Himalayas: First Nepal's Forestry Program Failed, Then the People Took Over and Saved the Trees. *Globe Mail*, 22 October.

't Sas-Rolfes, Michael. 1998. Who Will Save the Wild Tiger? PERC Policy Series No. 12. Bozeman, Mont.: Political Economy Research Center.

Yandle, Bruce. 1998. Coase, Pigou, and Environmental Rights. In *Who Owns the Environment?*, edited by Peter J. Hill and Roger E. Meiners. Lanham, Md.: Rowman & Littlefield.

# CHAPTER 10

# International Environmental Agreements: Developing Another Path

*Julian Morris*

## INTRODUCTION

International agreements differ from ordinary legislation in two ways.[1] First, international agreements typically are not directly binding on signatory states (to become binding they must usually be subsequently introduced into the legislation of each state).[2] Second, they are not directly enforceable: there is no international regulatory agency with enforcement powers. These differences mean that if international agreements are to be implemented and enforced, the benefits to each signatory party must be significantly greater than the implementation costs (Kosobud and Daly 1984; Barrett 1994, 1997a). Most commentators have left unstated the fact that these benefits and costs are essentially political, so they are not necessarily directly related to any actual environmental or economic effects. In fact it may be the case that an international environmental agreement (IEA) with negative economic and environmental consequences for the majority of people in all signatory states is pushed through because certain politicians, civil servants, businesses, scientists, intergovernmental bodies, and NGOs benefit from it (Bate 1996).

There are three main types of agreement:

1.   Agreements that relate to genuine environmental problems and that address those problems in an appropriate way.

2.   Agreements that relate to genuine environmental problems and are ostensibly intended to resolve those problems, but are based on a misunderstanding of the political economy of the problem.

3.   Agreements that are based on a mischaracterization (or lopsided characterization) of the scientific issues surrounding a purported environmental problem.

Because of the complex nature of many agreements (in particular, the fact that agreements are often predicated on contentious scientific assumptions and implemented through a political process that is far from ideal), it is often not possible to pigeonhole any particular agreement into one of these categories. The typology nevertheless remains useful as a means of identifying features of agreements that either should or do (and perhaps should not) exist. In the latter case, I consider certain hypothetical situations; for example, what might be the most appropriate form of agreement if it is assumed that governments around the world are determined to restrict emissions of carbon dioxide or CFCs (regardless of whether such restrictions are scientifically justified)? The three types are considered in turn.

## INTERNATIONAL AGREEMENTS RESULTING IN PROTECTION OF THE ENVIRONMENT

There are essentially three kinds of international agreements that are capable of resulting in genuine environmental benefits: first, agreements relating to interjurisdictional application of private law; second, agreements relating to spillover effects from national environmental regulations; and third, agreements relating to the use of resources not subject to the exclusive jurisdiction of any nation. These subtypes are not necessarily distinct and in the discussion that follows, it is clear that there is much overlap among them. For example, an agreement that relates to the interjurisdictional application of contract law may reduce the spillover effects of a national regulation pertaining to a resource that is partially outside the current jurisdiction of any nation.

### AGREEMENTS RELATING TO INTERJURISDICTIONAL APPLICATION OF PRIVATE LAW

Agreements relating to interjurisdictional application of private law are beneficial if they enable parties to obtain redress that they would otherwise be denied because of the transnational nature of the problem. Using the language of the civil law, the relevant areas of private law would include contract law and property law.[3]

#### Contract Law

No contract is perfect, in the sense that breach, misrepresentation, mistake, and other problems (including impacts on third parties) are possible. Such problems are less likely when:

(a)   The contract forms part of a series of commercial transactions between the two parties. In that case, the contract is likely to become self-enforcing; the parties have incentives to avoid potential problems because failure to do so would have adverse consequences for their future relationship.[4] For example, if one party were to breach a term of the contract, the credibility of its commitment to perform future contracts would be reduced.[5]

(b)   The parties are concerned about their reputations with other potential or actual contracting parties. Again, and for similar reasons, the contract is likely to be self-enforcing.

(c)   The contract is readily enforceable in the courts.[6] In that case, the threat of enforcement increases the incentives of both parties to avoid potential problems.

Where both parties are domiciled in a single jurisdiction and where the courts in that jurisdiction are willing to enforce such contracts, (c) is a highly effective measure for ensuring contractual performance.

However, where the two parties are not both domiciled in the same jurisdiction, the decisions of the court in one jurisdiction will not automatically be binding on a party that is domiciled in another jurisdiction, because the court cannot enforce its decision extrajurisdictionally. One way to overcome this problem is for the respective nations to enter into an agreement on mutual enforcement of contracts. Such an agreement should increase the probability that contracts relating to the sale of goods between the two countries would be honored and hence would lead to an increase in the number of such contracts.[7] The net result is that the amount of trade that takes place across international borders will increase. Because international trade increases the efficiency of resource use (in the absence of market distortions, production will occur in the most appropriate place, taking into consideration the cost of all factors), such an agreement would tend to benefit the environment. In addition, efficient allocation of resources should foster more rapid growth, which itself is associated with long-term environmental benefits (Grossman and Krueger 1995; Xepapadeas and Amri 1998).[8] Furthermore, contractual agreements between parties in different nations can have direct environmental benefits. For example, pharmaceutical companies and other research organizations have entered into deals in which the owners of tropical rain forests are remunerated for the provision of newly discovered biotic matter that has pharmaceutical potential (Deacon and Murphy 1993). This remuneration provides direct incentives for the owners of the forest to conserve the resources in it.

Of course, it may be the case that national courts choose autonomously to enforce such contracts, in which case no formal international agreement is necessary. One reason courts might favor such autonomous enforcement is that the benefits, in terms of encouraging trade and investment, are tangible to those making and enforcing the decisions. In addition, were international contracts to be repudiated by the judiciary, politicians would be wary of the political implications of discouraging trade. So, to the extent that there is political oversight of the court system, there will be pressure to enforce contracts.[9]

A further consideration is that in many cases law will have evolved somewhat independently of the action of the legislature, so it is possible that attempting to formalize the enforcement of contracts through an international agreement might lead to inappropriate restrictions on contract structure.[10] For example, certain NGOs might lobby for mandatory restrictions on certain kinds of exclusion clauses or, perhaps more worryingly, restrictions on the kinds of goods that can be exchanged (e.g., parts of animals such as turtles, rhinos, and elephants). Notwithstanding this caveat, it is evident that where no reciprocal arrangement for enforcement of contracts has emerged spontaneously, it may be desirable to create one.

*Property Law*

Consider a river that crosses national boundaries. If a person in the upstream country extracts water from the river or discharges effluent into it, river users in the downstream country may be adversely affected. Given the difficulties of extraterritorial application of tort law, Scott (1994, 172) argues that "special reciprocal legislation under an interjurisdictional agreement or treaty" is needed to enable downstream users to obtain redress. Ideally this redress might take the form of an injunction combined with damages for harm already caused, thereby allowing a Coasean bargain to take place between the two parties, if desired.

By defining the rights associated with use of water, such an agreement would—if combined with appropriate enforcement of transnational contracts, licenses, covenants, and easements—enable trading of those rights, with attendant efficiency improvements and environmental benefits (Anderson 1994; Scott 1994). The argument applies equally to other resources, such as oil, coal, gas, and gold.

Relatively few transboundary environmental harms have been the subject of legal dispute. Probably the most famous of these is the *Trail Smelter* (United States v Canada, 3 RIIA 1905 [1949]) arbitration, which has been described as "the only adjudicative decision of an international tribunal that speaks directly to the substantive law of transboundary pollution (Merrill 1997, 947). The facts of the case are that from the early 1920s onward, fumes emitted by a smelter operated by Cominco in Trail, British Columbia, had been causing harm to cattle ranchers in the United States. Instead of attempting to sue Cominco directly, a course that according to experts on international law would not have had

a great chance of success (Scott 1994, 172), the ranchers applied
to their own government, which, jointly with the government of
Canada then appointed the International Joint Commission (IJC)
as a special tribunal. The IJC awarded damages, but the harm
continued, and the United States, on behalf of the ranchers, rejected the award. The two countries then set up a special arbitration of three judges, one from the United States, one from Canada,
and one from Belgium. The arbitration granted an injunction and
awarded more substantial damages to the United States, to be paid
to the ranchers. In reaching its decision, the arbitration panel considered in particular the case of *Georgia v Tennessee Copper Co.*
(206 U.S. 230 [1907]). In that case, a copper smelter in eastern
Tennessee, located very close to the Georgia state line, had been
emitting sulfurous fumes, which caused headaches and other
physical symptoms in residents living in Georgia. In response to
complaints from those residents, Georgia filed an original action
in the U.S. Supreme Court on their behalf, seeking an injunction
against the continued operation of the smelter. The leading judgment was given by Oliver Wendell Holmes, who found in favor of
Georgia, arguing that the sovereignty of states entitles them to
choose not to permit entrance of pollution emanating from within
the borders of another state.[11] The arbitrators in *Trail Smelter* followed this decision, arguing that "under the principles of international law, as well as the law of the United States, no State has the
right to use or permit the use of its territory in such a manner as
to cause injury by fumes in or to the territory of another or the
properties or persons therein, when the case is of serious consequence and the injury is established by clear and convincing evidence" (*Trail Smelter* 1949, at 1965).

While *Georgia v Tennessee Copper Co.* and the *Trail Smelter*
arbitration suggest a potential mechanism for resolving transboundary pollution incidents, there are problems. In particular,
the transaction costs associated with protecting property rights in
this way may be prohibitive (Scott 1994, 172).[12] Even where the
transaction costs are not prohibitive of a solution in general, the
fact that the government acts as an intermediary for the plaintiff
(and also in some cases, as in *Trail Smelter,* the defendant) imposes

a barrier to any potential Coasean bargain that might otherwise have been reached between plaintiff and defendant in respect of the sale of the injunction. It seems that a far superior solution would be to agree on an interjurisdictional system of law that could be applied on either side of the boundary and that would be enforced by both nations. Such a legal system would enable parties to negotiate and settle disputes privately, in the shadow of the decided law, thereby incurring far fewer costs.

## AGREEMENTS RELATING TO SPILLOVER EFFECTS FROM NATIONAL ENVIRONMENTAL REGULATIONS

National environmental regulations may result in economic and/or environmental spillovers. An example of the former would be a regulation in one state requiring certain products to conform with certain criteria (e.g., minimum content of recycled material, ban on certain types of packaging material, maximum energy consumption during use) that favors firms that produce in that state (Barrett 1991). An example of the latter would be a regulation limiting ambient emissions within one state that encourages firms to design and locate plants in such a way as to ensure that much of the emissions flow into neighboring states.

Regulation or direct control over natural resources, such as fish and oil, can also have spillover effects. For example, pelagic fish often straddle national boundaries, so national regulations that permit high levels of harvesting are likely to reduce the stock available for harvest by people in neighboring states. Indeed, the incentives for officials of national governments, who are subject to lobbying by vested interests, will likely favor excessive harvesting because of the fear that failure to harvest at high levels will simply allow other states to take a higher share.[13] In such circumstances, an IEA might result in a reduction of total harvest levels leading to an increase in stocks and, hence, long-term flows. A danger of such agreements is that, because they will be subject to political lobbying by vested interests,[14] the comparative outcome may not be far superior to the noncooperative outcome. This has been the case with the European Common Fisheries Policy, which

permits catch levels for some fish that are probably higher than
the bioeconomic optimum (De Alessi 1998).

## AGREEMENTS RELATING TO THE USE OF RESOURCES NOT SUBJECT TO THE EXCLUSIVE JURISDICTION OF ANY NATION

Many resources are not subject to the exclusive jurisdiction of any
nation. Examples are found in the high seas or in Antarctica, as
well as in certain parts of the atmosphere, including the ozone
layer and outer space. In the absence of some agreement on the
use of these resources, the resources would be subject to a regime
of open access. Depending on the nature of the resource, three approaches seem applicable here. First, if the value of the resource is
low relative to the costs of implementing any property regime, it
may be desirable simply to leave the resource as open access.
Second, those resources that are readily excludable (low cost of
exclusion, monitoring, and enforcement relative to benefits) might
best be deemed the exclusive property of their appropriators and
subject to the protection of the member state of which the appro-
priator is a national. Third, resources that cannot readily be made
the exclusive property of specific individuals but nevertheless are
relatively cheaply monitored might better be managed as shared
property, subject to rules governing use that are set by an agency
on behalf of the owners.

### The North Pacific Fur Seal Treaty

A step toward privatization of one oceanic resource was taken in
1911, with the signing of the North Pacific Fur Seal Treaty. This
IEA was signed by only the United States, Canada, Russia, and
Japan, who all asserted their right to be the exclusive owners of
the North Pacific Fur Seals.[15] Quotas were set for each country
and breach of the treaty terms by one of the parties was punishable by dissolution of the treaty. Entrance by nonparties was discouraged by the credible threat of trade sanctions. The treaty was
highly successful in reversing the decline in numbers of these
pelagic seals (Barrett 1997b).

   The North Pacific Fur Seal Treaty was effective in large part because of the small number of parties. Barrett (1994, 1997b) has

shown that as the number of parties to such a convention increases, the probability of the cooperative outcome exceeding the noncooperative outcome declines. Ironically, this result would actually seem to support the argument that nations should devolve ownership of resources to individuals and corporations. The reasons for this argument are as follows:

- The incentives faced by a resource user to conserve that resource depend on the benefits of conservation in terms of increased future yields and on the costs of conservation, including such things as investments in habitat improvements as well as in monitoring and enforcing exclusive rights.

- When individuals own a resource, they must weigh the costs and benefits of conservation themselves. In general, individuals are concerned about obtaining the greatest value possible from a resource.

- When a state owns a resource, the state officials may attempt a rational calculation of the costs and benefits of conservation. Often, however, the state will be subject to lobbying by individual resource users, each of whom will attempt to grab as much of the resource as possible. Individual users behave differently when the state is the owner because they remain uncertain about who will be granted use rights in the future.[16]

- In general, private ownership will tend to result in better resource management than state ownership will.

- If the resource is not within the exclusive jurisdiction of an individual state and two or more states jointly claim ownership, the pressures on state officials to set inappropriate rules for resource use are greater because of the heterogeneity of interests and because of other international political decisions that may be logrolled together.[17] As noted previously, as the number of parties increases and the total benefits from cooperation decline, such international management regimes approach the noncooperative solution.

- If such resources are owned privately, the individual owners face stronger incentives to cooperate because they each have similar goals to increase the value of the resource that they own. They also cannot trade off increases. For example, an increase in this year's herring quota for Denmark could not be traded with an agreement to increase tobacco subsidies to Greece.

• For resources that are currently being used by many different people, the best method for privatization would be to create a joint-stock corporation that would own the resource, with each user given a share in that corporation.[18] These corporations would most likely domicile in nations that have credible powers to defend their property rights, thereby overcoming the problem of commitment that so bedevils multiparty intergovernmental agreements on resource ownership.[19]

### Individual Transferable Fish Quota Trading

Fish are one of the common pool resources that have been partially privatized in some jurisdictions through the creation of individual transferable quotas (ITQs). In New Zealand and Iceland, ITQ systems have been relatively successful in creating incentives to conserve stocks (De Alessi 1998; Gissurarson 1999). However, stocks of fish and other marine life on the high seas (especially tuna and whales) are not subject to such systems; nor are many stocks of fish that straddle the territorial waters of several nations (for example, those in the European Union). As a first step toward sustainable management, it would seem desirable to set up ITQ systems for these stocks. For such a system to function, it would be necessary to have an international agreement establishing interjurisdictional authority. Most likely this would entail signatory countries agreeing to hold nationals accountable for breaches of their quota.[20] An international agreement on tradable fish quotas should be self-enforcing, because the benefits for each country under the cooperative solution (enforcement of quota and quota trades) should be significantly greater than the benefits under a noncooperative solution (no enforcement).

### UN Convention on the Law of the Sea

At this time, one of the forces obstructing the creation of such self-enforcing rights is the UN Convention on the Law of the Sea, an IEA with signatories from 125 countries, many of which have no citizens who currently harvest resources from the high seas.[21] This convention reinforces the seventeenth-century doctrine of mare liberum—freedom of the seas—which includes both freedom of passage and freedom to fish. Although most fish are found within the territorial waters of one nation or another, many straddle both national and international waters, and it is not possible under the convention to assert private ownership of those fish.

The Law of the Sea encourages the creation of international agreements in order to resolve problems associated with pelagic species that are caught within territorial waters. One such agreement is the North Atlantic Fishery Organisation (NAFO), which was created to resolve conflicts among the United States, Canada, Iceland, Greenland, Norway, the United Kingdom, Spain, and Portugal over fishing in the North Atlantic. However, NAFO recently and rather spectacularly failed to resolve the very kind of dispute that it was set up to prevent, namely a conflict between Spain and Canada over the rights to fish Greenland Halibut (De Alessi 1995).

*Objects in Outer Space*

Another resource that is not subject to the exclusive jurisdiction of any nation is outer space. Objects in outer space are governed by various international treaties, including the Treaty on Principles Governing the Activities of States in the Exploration and Use of Outer Space, Including the Moon and Other Celestial Bodies 1967 and the Convention on International Liability for Damage Caused by Space Objects. Article II of the latter convention imposes absolute liability on the parties responsible for launching objects into space for any damage caused to persons or property on earth or to aircraft in flight (Shaw 1997, 384). This convention, then, has similar merits and drawbacks to the rules that governed transboundary air pollution at the time of the *Trail Smelter* arbitration: The sovereignty of nations is upheld, but the only parties that have standing under the convention are nation states.

## AGREEMENTS RELATED TO GENUINE PROBLEMS

The discussion has thus far focused primarily on the role of government as an intermediary for settlement of private disputes. There are many cases, however, in which the acts of government go beyond dispute resolution. In particular, states often assert ownership over resources and attempt either to control use of those resources or to permit certain individuals to use those resources in specified ways. Examples include systems of public lands, national parks, oil reserves, and forestry concessions. In addition, states often impose restrictions on the types of possession and use that are permissible. Examples of restrictions on types of possession include bans on possession of several property;[22] examples of restrictions on types of use include zoning laws and other types of land use planning.

These statutory interventions in the use of resources often have unintended consequences. State officials are not usually the residual claimants of the resources they manage, so they have less incentive to discover the most appropriate uses of those resources than do private owners (Alchian 1965). Where government asserts direct control over resources, the outcome ranges from poor, for example in the western United States where the Bureau of Land Management (BLM) mismanages land (Nelson 1995), to disastrous, for example in the former Soviet Union where the state systematically destroyed the Aral Sea and other areas (Bernstam 1991). Government restrictions on the types of permissible possession are often combined with other measures, such as monopsonistic purchasing boards and regulations limiting herd densities. As a result, the possessors of the land are discouraged from making investments in improvements (Deninger and Binswanger 1995; Morris 1995). Where government restricts the types of use that are permissible, two effects are observed: first, rent is dissipated through the process of seeking permission for changes of use; and second, permits may be seen as tantamount to statutory authority, allowing pollution to occur beyond what would normally be legally permissible. The problems that arise from these state interventions have sometimes become the subject of IEAs, as the following examples illustrate.

## CITES

The Convention on International Trade in Endangered Species (CITES) primarily arose as a result of concerns about dwindling numbers of charismatic fauna, such as rhino, elephant, tiger, and turtles. But the convention itself failed to deal with the root cause of the problem. CITES imposes restrictions on trade in certain species. The ostensible ground for such restrictions is that demand for parts of those species outside the territory of the nations in which those species live is encouraging people to poach those species, leading to dwindling stocks. However, this characterization of the problem entirely misses what for most species is the most important factor in determining numbers, namely the opportunity cost of their continued existence to those people who live nearby (Norton-Griffiths 1996). Indeed, by reducing the value of various species to the locals, CITES may in fact discourage conservation ('t Sas-Rolfes, Bate, and Morris 1994; 't Sas-Rolfes, 1995).

## CONVENTION ON BIOLOGICAL DIVERSITY

The Convention on Biological Diversity (CBD) is predicated on the assumption that through mismanagement we are killing off species that are crucial to human survival. The problem of biodiversity loss seems to have been exaggerated (Simon and Wildavsky 1984). Of course, it may be occurring; we cannot know for sure, because we do not know how many species there are (estimates vary between 10 and 100 million). But the evidence, such as it exists, does not support the contentions of people who claim that species loss is occurring at an alarming rate. Per contra, the largest study yet undertaken, by the International Union for the Conservation of Nature, concluded that, globally, "the number of recorded extinctions for both plants and animals is very small" (Whitmore and Sayer 1992, cited by Simon 1996, 445–446). Nevertheless, even moderate species loss may have some adverse consequences for humanity. It is arguable, however, that the loss of some species is worthwhile given the benefits that may be entailed in converting land to other uses. It is also arguable that species can be conserved equally well and far less expensively *ex situ* (outside natural habitat; e.g., in zoos). In spite of these observations, there are many places where habitat is being destroyed at a faster rate than is economically efficient primarily because of government intervention.

In those cases, it would be rational to encourage better manage-ment by removing the perverse incentives created by state inter-vention (Deacon 1994; Southgate 1998). Unlike CITES, the CBD places less emphasis on the role of international trade and more on in situ and, to some extent, *ex situ* management.

Nevertheless, to date little attention has been given to the prob-lems entailed in state control over resources, and it is implicitly as-sumed that simply increasing the funding of state-run national parks will solve the problem. (The primary means of implement-ing the convention is the Global Environment Facility, which is principally a mechanism for transferring monies to the govern-ments of poor states to help them fund conservation efforts.) Although it is true that increasing the level of funds available to park operators will in many cases lead to improvements in the management of those parks, lack of autonomy will remain a prob-lem. In particular, the incentives of those who operate the parks and of those who fund them will tend to favor excessive expendi-ture on administration while simultaneously underfunding protec-tion. In addition, there may be a reluctance to take sufficient ac-count of the local people whose actions crucially affect the management of parks in developing countries.

Parks that are operated privately tend to be better managed (Sugg and Kreuter 1994; 't Sas-Rolfes 1995). In most African countries, wildlife is the property of the state, so local people have little in-centive to conserve it. In Kenya, for example, elephant numbers fell from more than 100,000 in the 1960s to 20,000 in the 1980s. In Zimbabwe, by contrast, the policy has been to encourage private management by entitling individuals and communities to own the wildlife that traverses their property.[23] As a result, elephant num-bers in Zimbabwe rose from fewer than 40,000 in the 1960s to more than 50,000 by 1993 (Sugg and Kreuter 1994).

Possibly worse than the main convention is the Biosafety Protocol to the CBD, which was due to be finalized in 1999.[24] If implemented, this protocol is likely to slow down, if not halt, the introduction of genetically modified plants into the agriculture of developing countries (Miller, this volume), thereby denying the people in those countries the benefits, in terms of more abundant, cheaper, and better food, that such plants are likely to represent. The environmental consequences are also likely to be significant. One of the benefits of modern genetic engineering technologies is that they enable the creation of plant types that require less fertilizer and pesticide and have higher yields. The use of such plants would enable more food to be grown on less land, causing less pollution. An indirect consequence of this is that there would be less pressure to convert land that is currently habitat for wild species. So, by reducing the speed of uptake of genetically modified plants, the Biosafety Protocol to the CBD may have the very opposite effect to that intended by the CBD as a whole; it will increase the rate of conversion of land from wilderness to domestic use and might thereby increase the likelihood of species extinction.

## CONVENTION ON DESERTIFICATION

Government intervention, especially attempts at direct control, but also inappropriate restrictions on ownership and use, has resulted in what might be called land degradation (Sneath 1998). Under apartheid, for example, most South Africans were prevented from owning several properties (Mbaku 1991), so they overused the soil, causing severe degradation. Around the world, government irrigation projects have led to salinization of land and reduced nutrient deposition (Mahmood 1987; OED 1989).

However, this problem has been mischaracterized by international agencies, especially the United Nations Environment Programme (UNEP), as one that results not from too much government intervention but from too little. The Convention on Desertification explicitly claims that land degradation is the result of poverty and that it can thus be alleviated by reducing poverty, that is, by transferring resources from the governments of developed countries to the governments of developing countries. According to this theory, poverty is supposed to encourage excessive use of resources. The assumption is that poor people, having higher discount rates than wealthy people, will care less about the long-term impacts of their actions. There is some logic to this argument, but the evidence suggests that the effect is not as strong as is supposed and that land tenure is a far more important cause of the problem (Tiffen, Mortimore, and Gichuki 1993; Deacon 1994; Morris 1995; Leach and Mearns 1996; Southgate 1998).

Even if poverty were a significant determinant of land degradation, it does not necessarily follow that financial transfers to governments of developing countries should alleviate the problem, as experience over the past forty years attests. Indeed, areas that have received relatively little aid or intervention have typically fared better than those that have soaked up vast sums. In the Machakos district of Kenya, for example, land degradation has been reversed and famines, once common, no longer occur because more people now own real property and everyone is freer to engage in market transactions (Tiffen, Mortimore, and Gichuki 1993). Contrast that with Sudan and Ethiopia, where billions of dollars of aid probably made famines worse by enabling the ruling elite to continue their oppressive activities (Morris 1995).

## BASEL CONVENTION

The Basel Convention on the Control of Transboundary Movements of Hazardous Waste and Their Disposal was motivated by a concern that toxic waste from developed countries was being dumped illegally in developing countries, causing harm to the people in those countries. However, a careful assessment of the evidence compiled by Greenpeace shows that there are only five recorded episodes of illegal export of hazardous waste from developed to developing countries, and four of these were cases of fraud (Montgomery 1995). Although it is feasible (even likely) that there are other cases that have gone unreported, the belief that this is just the "tip of the iceberg" is rather implausible.

A question arises as to whether an agreement relating to international trade in hazardous waste is in principle an appropriate means of reducing the likelihood that hazardous waste will be dumped in a way that endangers people living in developing countries. The answer to this question must be no. First, it is unlikely that even an outright ban on international trade in hazardous waste would in fact eliminate the trade. Consider other bans on high-value commodities, such as heroin and rhino horn. Such bans have conspicuously failed to eliminate the trade in those commodities; the bans have merely driven trade underground, making it more difficult to monitor the activities of those involved and making it more difficult to ensure the quality of the product delivered to consumers ('t Sas-Rolfes, Bate, and Morris 1994). Second, such a ban does not address the root cause of the problem, if indeed there is a problem, which is either that the laws in the nation where the harmful dumping is occurring are not sufficient to protect the citizens of that country and their property or that the laws are not being enforced.[25] Moreover, given the small volume of hazardous waste that is currently brought into developing countries from developed countries, the waste disposal and recycling sites that exist in developing nations must be receiving most of their waste from domestic or other developing country sources, in which case it is absurd and counterproductive to focus on waste emanating from developed nations (Montgomery 1995).

## INTERNATIONAL CONVENTION FOR THE REGULATION OF WHALING

The International Convention for the Regulation of Whaling established the International Whaling Commission (IWC) "to provide for the proper conservation of whale stocks and thus make possible the orderly development of the whaling industry." It is clear that the IWC was initially conceptualized as a means of ensuring sustainable harvests of whales. However, unlike the Pelagic Seal Treaty and subsequent convention, membership of the IWC was not restricted only to those nations with citizens who hunt whales. As a result, the IWC was captured by interests that are in principle opposed to whaling. In 1986 the IWC imposed an international moratorium on whaling with some exceptions for scientific and aboriginal whaling. Despite the protestations of the scientific advisory committee to the IWC, which has argued vehemently for a reintroduction of hunting of certain superabundant species (such as the CITES listed minke whale), the moratorium persists. However, Norway has chosen simply to ignore the moratorium and set its own quota for whale hunting in spite of threats by the U.S. government to invoke the Pelly Amendment (see below).

It is perhaps interesting to consider what might have happened had membership of the IWC been restricted to parties who are actively involved in whaling. The experience of the North Pacific Fur Seal Treaty suggests that such a restriction might have prevented capture and enabled the parties to set and enforce sustainable catches. Nevertheless, it also seems plausible that partial capture could have resulted from, say, environmentalists in the United States influencing decisions by U.S. delegates. Under such circumstances, a system of private ownership of whales, which is now at least technically feasible, might be superior (De Alessi 1997). Aside from providing incentives for sustainable harvesting, private ownership offers the possibility for resolution of conflicts between environmentalists or animal rights activists and whalers; if an environmentalist does not want a whale to die, he or she can buy it from its current owner. Furthermore, owners of whales could be held liable for the consumption of other oceanic resources such as fish, thereby making explicit the opportunity costs of conserving these leviathans.

## CONVENTION ON THE LAW OF THE SEA

In addition to permitting freedom to fish, which, as discussed previously, causes problems for the privatization of fish stocks, the Law of the Sea Convention vests the seabed and all resources on it in the International Seabed Authority (ISA). The ISA has responsibility for managing the resources as "the common heritage" of humankind, and benefits accruing from the seabed are to be shared equitably (Shaw 1997, 444–446). The consequence is that the incentive to invest in technologies for discovering and using the vast reserves that we know to be on the seabed is significantly diminished. A far superior solution would have been to allow private parties to homestead the seabed, with claims being recognized by the domicile state of the legal person making the claim (Denman 1984, 50–52).

## AGREEMENTS BASED ON FLAWED
## SCIENTIFIC ANALYSIS

Many IEAs are based on flawed or biased interpretation and representation of scientific evidence. In large part this misinformation is the consequence of manipulation by the persons charged with producing executive summaries of that evidence and of the perverse incentives faced by people producing the underlying research (Lindzen 1992; Morris 1995; Bate 1996; Lieberman 1998).

### ACID RAIN

In the 1970s and early 1980s, environmentalists expressed concern at the acidification of lakes and tree die-off in northern Europe and North America. As a result, extensive research was carried out to discover the causes of these problems. The research initially focused on the relationship between sulfur dioxide emissions and the pH of rainwater. These studies confirmed that emissions of sulfur dioxide did result in weak sulfuric acid falling as rain. Some scientists assumed, based largely on laboratory experiments, that this acid rain was the cause of the acidification of lakes and tree die-off. Armed with these results, environmentalists encouraged politicians to push through legislation limiting emissions of sulfur dioxide.

However, more detailed and comprehensive studies recently published show that acid rain was not and is not causing any significant damage either to trees or to lakes (NAPAP 1990; Howells 1995). Indeed, the very claim that trees were dying off in large numbers has been disputed. Moreover, an alternative and better explanation for the rising levels of acidity in lakes was offered, namely that increasing concentrations of decomposing acidic pine needles resulted in the rising acidity. During the early part of the twentieth century, deforestation led to declining levels of acidity in many northern European lakes, allowing fish and other aquatic life to thrive. However, the subsequent reforestation reversed this process; the lakes became acidic once more and the fish died (NAPAP 1990; Howells 1995).

Adding concentrated sulfuric acid to water will make the water acid, and spraying the same solution onto plants grown in hydroponic conditions may cause those plants to die. But these laboratory conditions are very different from the conditions that prevail in the forests and lakes of northern Europe and North America, where weak sulfuric acid is metabolized by the flora as fertilizer and only very slowly leaches through soil, thereby having relatively little impact on the pH of lakes. (Acid rain may have increased the effect of other stresses on trees and may have caused an increase in the acidity of some lakes, but these effects have been difficult to differentiate from other possible causes.) Nevertheless, the laboratory experiments were used to justify pointless—indeed possibly counterproductive—regulations, including the Large Combustion Plant Directive in Europe. This directive was the result of political bargaining at both the member state and the European Communities (EC) level. The directive had the effect of favoring the extant big emitters of sulfur dioxide in Europe, as well as the nuclear industry, while coal production continued to be subsidized (Boehmer-Christiansen 1993). Elsewhere it has been shown that such regulations tend to favor incumbent firms over entrants (Buchanan and Tullock 1975; Maloney and McCormick 1982; Pashigan 1984). What often seems to happen in these circumstances is that firms form a coalition with environmental groups, supporting them in both word and deed. Bruce Yandle (1983, 1989, 1998) has made the analogy between this situation and the tacit coalition that exists between Baptist ministers, who are opposed to the sale of alcohol on Sundays, and bootleggers, who make monopolistic profits from the sale of illicit alcohol.

## Montreal Protocol

The 1987 Montreal Protocol to the 1985 Vienna Convention called for the gradual phaseout of putative ozone-depleting chemicals such as CFCs and halons. By 1990, however, the parties to the protocol had decided to impose a total ban on CFCs and halons by 2000, and in 1992 they decided to phase out CFCs by 1995. The explanation for this rapid ratcheting up of targets is perhaps the classic example of a Baptist–bootlegger coalition (see Yandle, this volume) in the international environmental sphere.

Concern amongst some in the scientific community over the possible impact of CFC emissions on the ozone layer began in 1974. As understanding of the interactions between CFCs and ozone improved, the early theories of ozone depletion were overturned and new mechanisms were postulated. In addition, satellite data indicating an annual springtime decline in ozone levels over the Antarctic began to appear in the mid-1980s (accurate records go back only to 1979). Environmentalists seized on these data and sprang into action, calling for bans on CFCs and other putative ozone-depleting chemicals. The big producers of CFCs were initially resistant to this threat to their business. However, perhaps realizing that they would benefit from a regulatory-induced reduction in output, they soon changed their tune. By the mid-1980s, the patents on several of Du Pont's CFCs had run out and competition was driving profit margins down. Seeing a potential for artificial market restriction, the big CFC producers began lobbying for an international treaty to limit production and, within the United States, restrictions on who would have the right to produce CFCs. In 1988, production rights were formally limited to those companies that were already producing in 1986 (McInnis 1992, 149). The output restrictions agreed upon at Montreal were music to the ears of an industry with pretensions to oligopoly pricing. In 1988, the U.S. EPA estimated that the benefits to U.S. CFC manufacturers of the output restrictions under the Montreal Protocol would be between $1.2 billion and $1.8 billion (Barrett 1991).

Another factor ultimately weighed in favor of U.S. producers of CFCs. In 1978, the EPA had banned the use of CFCs in pressurized containers for any purpose other than those deemed essential by the FDA (such as for asthma inhalers) (McInnis 1992, 137). This ban spurred the producers to begin developing substitutes, and although development at Du Pont was suspended in 1980 because of the high costs that were predicted for the alternatives, it began again in the mid-1980s following renewed claims that the ozone layer was being destroyed. In response to these claims, the UN organized the Vienna Convention for Protection of the Ozone

Layer, which was signed by more than twenty nations and empowered UNEP to conduct future meetings (Lieberman 1998). This convention led directly to the signing of the Montreal Protocol in 1987, after which the major producers of CFCs and CFC substitutes continued to lobby in favor of tighter restrictions in order to protect their investment in research into substitutes. Environmental organizations also continued to lobby for tighter restrictions in order to protect their membership by keeping their names in the media. Finally, UNEP and the World Meteorological Organization (WMO), which had begun to rely on research into ozone depletion for funding, both supported further restrictions.

The result is that we now have nearly a blanket ban on the production and use of CFCs and halons in developed countries, although production in China, India, and Russia is increasing. The impact of these chemicals on the stratospheric ozone layer remains uncertain while the impact of this thinning on humans and on the environment is negligible (Lieberman 1998).

### CFC Trading

As a mechanism for reducing the production of CFCs and halons, the Montreal Protocol has been somewhat effective, but at what cost? Economic theory suggests that a more efficient mechanism for reducing production would have been to create a regime of tradable production permits. The regime would have enabled high-cost abaters, such as users of air conditioning, to have continued using their relatively expensive equipment. At the same time, it would have enabled producers to continue using their own expensive plants rather than shutting them down and encouraged producers in developing countries to build new plants.

## THE FRAMEWORK CONVENTION ON CLIMATE CHANGE

The United Nations Framework Convention on Climate Change (UNFCCC) was motivated by a concern that continued emissions of greenhouse gases (GHGs) at current or higher levels would result in catastrophic global climate change. This concern was not justified by a reasonable analysis of the evidence presented by the 1990 report of the Intergovernmental Panel on Climate Change (IPCC), although it was certainly encouraged by implication in the Policymakers' Summary of the report. The so-called consensus that catastrophic global climate change is imminent was manufactured through a careful manipulation of the wording of the Policymakers' Summary. Moreover, the models whose output formed the basis of the claims made in that summary inaccurately reflected what was known about the impact of water vapor. This inaccuracy led to significant upward bias in predictions of temperature in a raised–carbon dioxide ($CO_2$) world (Lindzen 1992). Our knowledge of the impact of increasing concentrations of carbon dioxide and other GHGs has improved little over the past six years (ESEF 1996, 1997). It is simply too soon to provide a prognosis, dire or otherwise, on this matter. Nevertheless, the balance of evidence (if surveys of climatologists are tantamount to such evidentiary balancing—which is doubtful) suggests that the impact of humankind on the world's climate will not be catastrophic (Morris 1997; Salmon, this volume).

Bate (1996) argues that the movement to control carbon dioxide emissions owes more to satisfying interest groups than to a dispassionate desire to protect humanity. Environmentalists, scientists, government officials, UN officials, and even certain businesses seem to have formed a grand, if mostly tacit, coalition to control the climate. Indeed, this seems the only plausible explanation for the UNFCCC and its offspring, such as the Kyoto Protocol.

Given the relatively small effect that the proposed emission limits are likely to have on the concentration of GHGs in the atmosphere, it seems reasonable to suggest that we might be better off not imposing any limits on carbon dioxide emissions. Moore (1998) has stressed the fact that the climate is constantly changing and that humankind has historically shown a remarkable ability to adapt to such changes. As we become wealthier and more technologically advanced, our ability to adapt to changes in climate increases. Restricting emissions of carbon dioxide far below the level that would pertain in an unfettered free market will divert resources away from useful technological developments, including those that enable us to adapt to a changing climate, and will reduce the overall wealth of society. In other words, if we restrict carbon dioxide emissions, we restrict our ability to adapt (Morris 1997; Smith 1997). It seems that the most logical policy with regard to climate change is to free up energy markets, not to regulate them.

Although restricting emissions of GHGs almost certainly does not make sense at this point in time, it seems that many governments around the world are likely to impose such restrictions. In light of this fact, it is perhaps worth considering how this might be done at least cost and whether a global agreement to restrict emissions is realistically enforceable.

*Carbon Trading*

The cost of measures to mitigate emissions of greenhouse gases varies widely. Some measures—for example, eliminating subsidies to coal mining and the deregulation of markets for lower-carbon substitutes, such as natural gas—would provide economic benefits to society. Others, such as mandating zero-emission vehicles or zero-emission power plants, would be hugely expensive.

Aside from eliminating subsidies, the most efficient way to achieve a specified reduction in GHG emissions is probably through permit trading. This trading would be done by setting an overall target level of permissible emissions, allocating those permits among the various emitters either through grandfathering or by auction, and then allowing people to trade their emissions permits. A particularly interesting feature of emission trading for GHGs is that it should allow for carbon swaps. For example, a firm increases emissions of carbon dioxide while simultaneously planting a sufficient number of trees to absorb the same amount of carbon dioxide,[26] adding a sufficient amount of iron to the oceans to achieve the same end through fertilizing plankton, or engaging in some other equivalent procedure. Allowing carbon trading will encourage innovative mechanisms for reducing carbon dioxide concentrations.

Fundamental to the success of a carbon trading regime is the enforceability of the property rights entailed in the tradable permits. Experience with other trading regimes shows that the likelihood of success is increased if (1) the rights are clearly specified, (2) the likelihood of arbitrary revocation is very small, and (3) there is minimal bureaucratic intervention in the trading regime (McCann

1996). For some pollutants, bureaucratic intervention is almost inevitable given the geographical and biophysical nonuniformity of their effects. However, carbon dioxide is about as close to being a perfectly uniform ambient pollutant as is imaginable. There is little reason for the emission of a ton of carbon dioxide in Australia not being treated as identical, in terms of its impact, to the emission of a ton of carbon dioxide in India, Japan, or Venezuela. Hence, carbon trading could in principle be an entirely private activity. Once emission permits are defined, they can be traded among businesses around the globe.

A necessary requirement for such a carbon trading system would be agreement on enforcement. Ideally, the owners of emission permits might have standing to sue noncompliant emitters, which would effectively privatize enforcement, making the system procedurally independent of the executive branch. The owners of permits could be relied upon to carry out such enforcement because noncompliant firms would otherwise be at a competitive advantage. Under such a regime, the owners of emission permits might set up co-mutual monitoring agencies in order to reduce the duplicative and high expenditures of each firm monitoring on its own.

For a trading system to function, it would be necessary to have an agreement on the interjurisdictional enforcement of transactions. If a firm in the Netherlands sells an emission quota to a firm in South Korea and the latter firm exceeds its permitted emissions level, the firm in the Netherlands should be entitled to obtain redress for breach of contract. This would require that South Korean courts recognize trades in carbon emission permits as legitimate, which, given the peculiar status of the permits, is likely to require an international agreement recognizing carbon emission permits as legitimate items of transferable property.

### Enforcement of an International Agreement to Limit GHG Emissions

Whether GHGs are to be restricted through the use of tradable carbon permits or any other scheme, there must be some mechanism for enforcement of the international agreement. Otherwise, governments could simply fail to implement the restrictions. In light of the significant benefits that would accrue to a noncompliant state in terms of temporarily enhanced economic growth and attendant increase in support for the incumbent political party, it seems implausible to rely upon self-enforcement. Either trade sanctions or military sanctions would be necessary.

The problem with trade sanctions is that they harm both the people in the country targeted and the people in the country imposing them, without necessarily forcing the government of the targeted country to change its policy. The masochistic impact of trade sanctions makes them less credible. A threat to invoke the Pelly Amendment[27] against Norway in 1986 for breach of IWC quotas was followed by an announcement from the Norwegian government that it was suspending commercial whaling after the 1987 season. As a result, the threatened sanctions were not imposed. A similar threat in 1990 was ignored, and no sanctions were imposed (Charnowitz 1994). Failure to impose trade sanctions under the Pelly Amendment because of fear of adverse domestic effects has reduced its credibility as a threat. Sanctions will only be credible if there are sufficient concentrated political interests whose support is able to offset any potential political damage (DeSombre 1995).

The problem with military sanctions is that they have to be credible in order to work, and it is not clear that people will be willing to go to war over the putative threat of global warming.

A further problem is that under the current proposals, emission limits are to be set on a country-by-country basis, so it may be difficult to establish a tradable permit regime. Industries in those countries where emission limits are relatively lax may oppose trading on the grounds that it will reduce their competitive advantage.[28] In addition, environmental NGOs have traditionally been critical of the use of tradable permits, which makes a coalition between these NGOs and the beneficiary industries likely.

## CONCLUSION

The typology of international environmental agreements developed in this chapter suggests that there are significant problems with the way in which such agreements are developed. In particular, it seems that international organizations, such as the United Nations and its various affiliates and subsidiaries, are open to capture by vested interests. Where economic and ideological interests are aligned, the outcome may well be a conspiracy that is against the public interest. A question arises as to whether such organizations generally do more harm than good. The evidence presented in this chapter suggests that in the environmental sphere, this is the case.[29]

For nontransboundary issues like desertification and local pollution, such as that resulting from waste disposal, it is far from clear that any international agreement is justified. Certainly the agreements that have been created to deal with these issues are not likely to make any improvements to the situation and may well have the opposite effect.

For issues that have potential transboundary effects, such as loss of biodiversity, IEAs may well be desirable, but they should be structured as contracts between sovereign states, avoiding wherever possible the use or creation of international agencies.[30] Alternatives to IEAs, such as agreements relating to enforcement of private property rights and contracts, are an even better way of dealing with such transboundary environmental problems.

Many IEAs are not only poorly devised with regard to their institutional structure, but are also based on highly contentious science. The funding of basic science has been so heavily dominated by the state that it creates perverse incentives for scientists to encourage us to believe in hobgoblins so we will not flinch when the state hands over more cash for those scientists to research their pet theories. Karl Popper said that overfunding of science may be as detrimental to the evolution of knowledge as underfunding because "big science may destroy great science" (Popper 1981). That certainly seems to have happened in the area of research into environmental problems. To decrease the likelihood of this occurring, it seems that a shift toward more diverse, market-based funding of science is necessary (Kealey 1996; Morris 1998).

From this discussion, it seems that five conditions are likely to increase the probability that an agreement relating to protection of the environment will be successful in achieving its end. First, if possible, the agreement should flow logically from a body of evolved private law and should protect private rights. Second, where the agreement concerns a resource that has become the subject of national or local regulation and where those regulations have transjurisdictional effects, it might be desirable to create inter- or multijurisdictional rules governing the ownership and use of that resource (for example, the creation of multijurisdictional tradable quota systems for certain pelagic species). Third, signatory status to such agreements should be restricted to those nations that have direct economic interests in the resources under threat, and if a nation ceases to have a direct economic interest then it should automatically cease to be a party. Fourth, the use of international agencies should be avoided if at all possible, but where this is not possible, a new nonpartisan agency is likely to be preferable to existing agencies such as the United Nations. Fifth, decision makers should be encouraged to hold a healthy skepticism of claims that there is a scientific consensus about forthcoming environmental apocalypses.

## ENDNOTES

1. International agreements are usually considered to be agreements between states rather than agreements between individuals. Following convention I shall adopt this terminology; however, I shall also discuss agreements between individuals and between individuals and states, where those agreements are transnational in nature.

2. An exception is European Union (EU) legislation, which in some cases has direct effect: *Van Gend en Loos v Nederlanse Administratie der Belastingen* [1963] ECR1; *Grad v Finanzamt Traunstein* [1970] ECR 825; *Van Duyn v Home Office* [1974] ECR 1337.

3. These categories are simpler for the purposes of this chapter than those of the English or American legal system, which would entail a rather complex intertwined discussion of tort, property, equity, contract, and riparian law.

4. The degree to which the contract is self-enforcing will depend on the nature of the prospective transactions. Generally speaking, the larger the costs of future reciprocal breaches, the higher the incentive to abide by the agreed terms.

5. This should logically imply a risk premium for future transactions. That is to say, the party in breach will have to offer some extra consideration on future contracts or will run the risk of reciprocal breach.

6. Decisions made by a court must be backed by the threat of force, for example by the police, in order to be credible. In addition (or alternatively), there may be other dispute resolution mechanisms (e.g., private arbitration) and enforcement procedures (e.g., private security firms) available; for a discussion, see Benson (1991).

7. The number of contracts will increase because potential contracting parties will be more willing to enter into agreements if the chance of those agreements being honored is higher (Goetz and Scott 1980).

8. However, this might not apply to some putative global problems; see Shafik (1994) and the papers in Barbier (1997).

9. Although there is a nominal separation of powers in most countries, judicial appointments are a more or less political decision. Even where appointments are made by a body that is independent of the elected representatives, there are social pressures on the members of the appointing authority.

10. By inappropriate, I mean likely to produce results that are not socially desirable. For example, a restriction on trade in elephant ivory, put in place ostensibly to protect elephants as a species, is likely to reduce the consideration that the owners of elephants are able to receive for the animals they have looked after (although traders in elephant ivory may receive more consideration to compensate for the risk of capture that they face). As a result, people in areas where elephants are common will have less incentive to invest in the conservation of those elephants. Because elephants compete with humans for habitat, the net result will be a decline in elephant numbers (Sugg and Kreuter 1994; see also Schwab 1988).

11. It is worth noting the outcome of an earlier case that was brought before the Tennessee Supreme Court against another nearby copper smelter. At the turn of the century, three copper smelters in eastern Tennessee were operating open pile furnaces, emitting sulfurous fumes, causing headaches and other physical symptoms among residents living in the vicinity. Local residents sued the owners of one of the copper smelters and the case went to the Tennessee Supreme Court. Although the court found that there was a nuisance, the judges ruled that the smelters provided public benefits and so denied injunctive relief. *Madison v Ducktown Sulphur, Copper & Iron Co.* (83 SW 658 [Tenn. 1904]) (cited by Merrill 1997, 943).

12. Three reasons for this seem noteworthy: first, it is costly to organize a petition, and, in any case, the petition may not be successful in motivating the government to take action; second, even if the government does take action, that action may not be successful; third, even if the government is ultimately successful, it may take a considerable amount of time to achieve that success (the *Trail Smelter* arbitration was finally resolved sixteen years after the ranchers initially petitioned the government).

13. This is a variant of the tragedy of the commons argument (Alchian 1965; Demsetz 1967; Hardin 1968).

14. Such interests are likely to include both economic interests, such as fisheries producer groups, and environmental interests, such as World Wide Fund, International Fund for Animal Welfare, and Greenpeace.

15. These four countries remain the exclusive parties to the treaty's successor, the Convention on Conservation of the North Pacific Fur Seal 1957, as amended in 1976.

16. This is obviously a simplification of the situation, which is complicated by such factors as collusion among resource users and by the iterative nature of the process of allocation of use rights, both of which would tend to reduce the malignant consequences of state ownership.

17. For an explanation of the process of logrolling, see Buchanan and Tullock (1962).

18. Nevertheless, very broad ownership (for example, where no individual owns more than 0.1 percent of the total resource) might not be much better than state management, because each individual will have too little incentive to monitor the behavior of the managers. In the absence of government intervention, we would not expect this to present a problem because entrepreneurs will see the profit to be made in buying large shares. Barriers to concentration of ownership, such as a statutory restriction on the total share that can be owned by a single individual or company, would represent a loss of efficiency and would have negative consequences for the environment.

19. It might be objected that governments could form such a management authority more easily; after all, isn't the role of government precisely to obviate the need to form smaller bodies organized for collective action? To this I would respond that (1) the intergovernmental authority would suffer from the enforcement problems already outlined, (2) the intergovernmental body would be motivated by concerns other than maximizing the bioeconomic return on oceanic resources, and (3) the transaction costs associated with forming and running the management companies would almost certainly be smaller than the transaction costs associated with the intergovernmental authority, when dissipation of rent through lobbying and inappropriate harvesting rules is factored in.

20. Under such a system, it would probably make sense for quota holders to have standing to sue other quota holders who exceed their quota. This would provide incentives for fishers to monitor each other's behavior and would effectively privatize enforcement. It would also probably make sense, on cost grounds, for companies to delegate monitoring and enforcement of such actions to agencies (as is the case in New

Zealand, where some individual stocks of fish are regulated by management companies).

21. The convention was signed in 1982 and came into force in 1994.

22. Several property is private property owned by individuals or corporations. Common property (shared private property) was permitted—indeed enforced—but the inability to sever land for individual use distorted the incentives of users.

23. Under the Wildlife and National Parks Act of 1975, wildlife on private land was deemed to be the property of the owner of that land. In the amendment to that act of 1982, property rights were extended to people living in communal areas. In response to this change in the law, several conservation groups, including the Africa Resources Trust and WWF, set up CAMPFIRE, a program that enables local people to benefit from the sale of tourism and hunting rights.

24. The protocol is a consequence of Articles 8 and 19 of the CBD (see Miller, this volume).

25. Montgomery (1995) notes that fraud is not limited to attempts to export hazardous waste illegally. If fraud is a problem, then the solution (insofar as there is a solution) is better enforcement of contracts.

26. For the tree planting to represent a long-term reduction in concentrations of GHGs, the trees and the products derived from them must not subsequently be permitted to decay or burn. This could be achieved by ensuring that the wood is used in a long-lasting building.

27. "The Pelly Amendment is a 1971 amendment to the [U.S.] Fisherman's Protective Act of 1967. (Public Law 92-219, adding section 8 to the Fisherman's Protective Act of 1967, codified at 22 U.S.C. 1978.) It gives the president discretion to restrict imports of fish products or wildlife products from countries that engage in practices that diminish the effectiveness of international fishery conservation programs or international programs for endangered species, respectively" (OTA 1992). Any trade sanctions imposed under the Pelly Amendment would probably violate GATT and WTO trading rules (Charnowitz 1994).

28. We have already seen this to some extent: The UK delegates at Kyoto were not keen on allowing the United States to trade permits with Russia (Yandle 1998). The United Kingdom will likely meet its targets at low cost relative to the United States because of reforms to the UK energy market, which was previously very carbon-intensive.

29. In other areas, the answer seems also to be in the affirmative (Bandow and Vasquez 1994).

30. The only example of an IEA that seems to have provided net benefits, the North Pacific Fur Seal Treaty, was structured as a multilateral contract among four sovereign nations many years before the United Nations came into existence.

# REFERENCES

Alchian, Armen. 1965. Some Economics of Property Rights. *Il Politico* 30(4), 816–829.

Anderson, Terry. 1994. Introduction: From Political Water to Private Water. In *Continental Water Marketing,* edited by Terry Anderson. San Francisco: Pacific Research Institute for Public Policy.

Bandow, Doug, and Ian Vasquez, eds. 1994. *Perpetuating Poverty.* Washington D.C.: Cato Institute.

Barbier, Edward, ed. 1997. Environmental Kuznets Curve Special Issue. *Environment and Development Economics* 2, 369–515.

Barrett, Scott. 1991. Environmental Regulation for Competitive Advantage. *Business Strategy Review* (Spring), 1–15.

———. 1994. Self-Enforcing International Environmental Agreements. *Oxford Economic Papers* 46, 878–894.

———. 1997a. Heterogenous International Environmental Agreements. In *International Environmental Negotiations: Strategic Policy Issues,* edited by Antonio Carraro. Cheltenham, Eng.: Edward Elgar.

———. 1997b. Do International Environmental Agreements Really Work? *Weathervane* (December). At: <http://www.weathervane.rff.org/pointcpoint/pcp4/barrett.html>.

Bate, Roger. 1996. Science Under Siege: The De-Coupling of Science from Climate Policy. *Energy and Environment* 7(4), 323–331.

Benson, Bruce. 1991. *The Enterprise of Law.* San Francisco: Pacific Research Institute for Public Policy.

Bernstam, Mikhail. 1991. *The Wealth of Nations and the Environment.* London: Institute of Economic Affairs.

Boehmer-Christiansen, Sonja. 1993. *The Politics of Acid Rain.* London: Belhaven Press.

Buchanan, James, and Gordon Tullock. 1962. *The Calculus of Consent.* Ann Arbor: University of Michigan Press.

Buchanan, James, and Gordon Tullock. 1975. Polluters' Profits and Political Response. *American Economic Review* 65, 139–147.

Charnowitz, Steve. 1994. Environmental Trade Sanctions and the GATT: An Analysis of the Pelly Amendment on Foreign Environmental Practices. *American University Journal of International Law and Policy* 9(3): 751–808.

Deacon, Robert. 1994. Deforestation and the Rule of Law in a Cross-Section of Countries. *Land Economics* 70(4), 414–430.

Deacon, Robert, and Paul Murphy. 1993. Swapping Debts for Nature. In *NAFTA and the Environment,* edited by Terry Anderson. San Francisco: Pacific Research Institute for Public Policy.

De Alessi, Michael. 1995. The North Atlantic Fishing Feud. *Journal of Commerce,* 13 April, p. 6A.

———. 1997. Emerging Technologies for the Conservation of Marine Resources. Environment Working Paper. London: Institute of Economic Affairs Environment Unit.

————. 1998. *Fishing for Solutions*. IEA Studies on the Environment No. 11. London: Institute of Economic Affairs Environment Unit.

Demsetz, Harold. 1967. Toward a Theory of Property Rights. *American Economic Review* 57, 347–359.

Deninger, Klaus, and Hans Binswanger. 1995. Rent Seeking and the Development of Large-Scale Agriculture in Kenya, South Africa, and Zimbabwe. *Economic Development and Cultural Change* 43, no. 3 (April): 493–522.

Denman, Donald. 1984. *Markets Under the Sea?* Hobart Paperback 17. London: Institute of Economic Affairs.

DeSombre, Elizabeth. 1995. Baptists and Bootleggers for the Environment: The Origins of United States Unilateral Sanctions. *Journal of Environment and Development* 4(1), 53–75.

European Science and Environment Forum (ESEF). 1996. *The Global Warming Debate: The Report of the European Science and Environment Forum*. Cambridge, Eng.: European Science and Environment Forum.

————. 1997. *Global Warming: The Continuing Debate*. Cambridge, Eng.: European Science and Environment Forum.

Gissurarson, Hannes. 1999. *Overfishing: The Icelandic Solution*. IEA Studies on the Environment No. 15. London: Institute of Economic Affairs Environment Unit.

Goetz, Charles, and Robert Scott. 1980. Enforcing Promises: An Examination of the Basis of Contract. *Yale Law Journal* 89, 1261–1322.

Grossman, G., and A. Krueger. 1995. Economic Growth and the Environment. *Quarterly Journal of Economics* 110, 353–357.

Hardin, Garrett. 1968. The Tragedy of the Commons. *Science* 62, 1243–1248.

Howells, G. 1995. *Acid Rain and Acid Waters*, 2nd ed. Cheltenham, Eng.: E. Honvood.

Kealey, Terence. 1996. *The Economic Laws of Scientific Research*. London: Macmillan.

Kosobud, Richard, and Thomas Daly. 1984. Global Conflict or Co-operation Over the $CO_2$ Climate Impact? *Kyklos* 37, 638–659.

Leach, Melissa, and Robin Mearns. 1996. *The Lie of the Land.: Challenging Received Wisdom on the African Environment*. African Issues series. Westport, Conn.: Heinemann.

Lieberman, Ben. 1998. *Doomsday Déjà Vu: Ozone Depletion's Lessons for Global Warming*. Cambridge, Eng.: European Science and Environment Forum.

Lindzen, Richard. 1992. Global Warming: The Origin and Nature of the Alleged Scientific Consensus. Paper presented at the OPEC Seminar on the Environment, at Vienna, 13–15 April.

Mahmood, K. 1987. *Reservoir Sedimentation: Impact, Extent, and Mitigation*. World Bank Technical Paper No. 71. Washington, D.C.: The World Bank.

Maloney, M., and R. McCormick. 1982. A Positive Theory of Environmental Quality Regulation. *Journal of Law and Economics* 25, 99–123.

Mbaku, John. 1991. Property Rights and Rent Seeking in South Africa. *Cato Journal* 11(1), 135–150.

McCann, Richard. 1996. Environmental Commodities Markets: "Messy" Versus "Ideal" Worlds. *Contemporary Economic Policy* 14(3), 85–97.

McInnis, Daniel. 1992. Ozone Layers and Oligopoly Profits. In *Environmental Politics—Public Costs, Private Rewards*, edited by Michael Greve and Fred Smith. New York: Praeger.

Merrill, Thomas. 1997. Golden Rules for Transboundary Pollution. *Duke Law Journal* 46, 931–1019.

Montgomery, Mark. 1995. Reassessing the Waste Trade Crisis: What Do We Really Know? *Journal of Environment and Development* 4(1), 1–28.

Moore, Thomas Gale. 1998. *Climate of Fear*. Washington D.C.: Cato Institute.

Morris, Julian. 1995. *The Political Economy of Land Degradation*. IEA Studies on the Environment No. 5. London: Institute of Economic Affairs.

———. 1997. Introduction: Climate Change: Prevention or Adaptation? In *Climate Change: Challenging the Conventional Wisdom*, edited by Julian Morris. IEA Studies on the Environment No. 10. London: Institute of Economic Affairs.

———. 1998. Popper, Hayek and Environmental Regulation. Paper presented to the Adam Smith Society/British Council, at Milan, June 24.

National Acid Precipitation Assessment Programme (NAPAP). 1990. Acid Deposition: State of Science and Technology.

Nelson, Robert. 1995. *Public Lands and Private Rights*. Lanham, Md.: Rowman and Littlefield.

Norton-Griffiths, Michael. 1996. Property Rights and the Marginal Wildebeest: An Economic Analysis of Wildlife Conservation Options in Kenya. *Biodiversity and Conservation* 5, 1557–1577.

Operations Evaluation Department (OED). 1989. *Renewable Resource Management in Agriculture*. World Bank Operations Evaluations Study. Washington, D.C.: The World Bank.

Pashigan, B. Peter. 1984. The Effect of Environmental Regulation on Optimal Plant Size and Factor Shares. *Journal of Law and Economics* 27, 1–29.

Popper, Karl. 1981. The Rationality of Scientific Revolutions. Reprinted in *Scientific Revolutions*, edited by Ian Hacking. Oxford, Eng.: Oxford University Press.

Schwab, Stewart. 1988. A Coasean Experiment on Contract Presumptions. *Journal of Legal Studies* 17, no. 2: 237–268.

Scott, Anthony. 1994. International Water Marketing: Nations, Agencies or Individuals? In *Continental Water Marketing*, edited by Terry Anderson. San Francisco: Pacific Research Institute for Public Policy.

Shafik, N. 1994. Economic Development and Environmental Quality: An Econometric Analysis. *Oxford Economic Papers* 46, 757–773.

Shaw, Malcolm. 1997. *International Law,* 4th ed. Cambridge: Cambridge University Press.

Simon, Julian. 1996. *The Ultimate Resource 2*. Princeton, N.J.: Princeton University Press.

Simon, Julian, and Aaron Wildavsky. 1984. On Species Loss, the Absence of Data and Risks to Humanity. In *The Resourceful Earth*, edited by Julian Simon and Herman Khan. Oxford, Eng.: Basil Blackwell.

Smith, Fred L. Jr. 1997. Conclusion: The Role of Opportunity Costs in the Global Warming Debate. In *The Costs of Kyoto,* edited by Jonathan Adler. Washington, D.C.: Competitive Enterprise Institute.

Sneath, David. 1998. State Policy and Pasture Degradation in Inner Asia. *Science* 281, 1147–1148.

Southgate, Douglas. 1998. *Tropical Forest Conservation—An Economic Assessment of the Alternatives in Latin America.* New York: Oxford University Press.

Sugg, Ike, and Urs Kreuter. 1994. *Elephants and Ivory: Lessons from the Trade Ban.* IEA Studies on the Environment No. 2. London: Institute of Economic Affairs Environment Unit.

Tiffen, Mary, Michael Mortimore, and Francis Gichuki. 1993. *More People, Less Erosion—Environmental Recovery in Kenya.* Chichester, Eng.: Wiley.

't Sas-Rolfes, Michael. 1995. *Rhinos: Conservation, Economics and Trade-Offs.* IEA Studies on the Environment No. 4. London: Institute of Economic Affairs Environment Unit.

't Sas-Rolfes, Michael, Roger Bate, and Julian Morris. 1994. The Economics of Trade in Rhino Horn. Unpublished paper prepared for the Worldwide Fund for Nature and Save the Rhino International.

U.S. Office of Technology Assessment (OTA). 1992. *Trade and the Environment: Conflicts and Opportunities.* Report no. OTA-BP-ITE-94. Washington, D.C.: Government Printing Office.

Whitmore, T. C., and J. A. Sayer, eds. 1992. *Tropical Deforestation and Species Extinction.* New York: Chapman and Hall; cited by Simon 1996, 445–446.

Xepapadeas, Anastasios, and Esma Amri. 1998. Some Empirical Indications of the Relationship Between Environmental Quality and Economic Development. *Environmental and Resource Economics* 11, 93–106.

Yandle, Bruce. 1983. Bootleggers and Baptists: The Education of a Regulatory Economist. *Regulation* (May/June), 12–16.

———. 1989. *The Political Limits of Environmental Regulation: Tracking the Unicorn.* Westport, Conn.: Quorum.

———. 1998. Kyoto: Bootleggers and Baptists in a Global Contest. *The Independent Review.*

# Contributors

TERRY L. ANDERSON is a senior fellow at the Hoover Institution and executive director of the Political Economy Research Center in Bozeman, Montana.

JOHN J. COHRSSEN is executive director of the Public Health Policy Advisory Board.

FERNAND KEULENEER is a partner of Keuleneer-Storme-Vanneste-Van Varenbergh-Verhelst, a Brussels-based law firm, and is practicing in the areas of corporate and financial law. He is also on the board of the Centre for the New Europe, a Brussels-based think tank. He can be reached at: f.Keuleneer@glo.be

HENRY I. MILLER is a senior research fellow at the Hoover Institution.

JULIAN MORRIS is assistant director of the Environmental Unit at the Institute of Economic Affairs in London.

JEREMY RABKIN is an associate professor of government at Cornell University.

JEFFREY SALMON is executive director of the George C. Marshall Institute and a senior fellow with the Environmental Literacy Council.

BRETT D. SCHAEFER is the Jay Kingham Fellow in International Regulatory Affairs in the Center for International Trade and Economics of the Kathryn and Shelby Cullom Davis Institute for International Studies at the Heritage Foundation.

JAMES M. SHEEHAN is an adjunct scholar of the Competitive Enterprise Institute in Washington, D.C.

BRUCE YANDLE is Alumni Distinguished Professor of Economics at Clemson University and a senior associate with the Political Economy Research Center.

# Conference Agenda

## THE GREENING OF U.S. FOREIGN POLICY

*A symposium sponsored by*
Hoover Institution
Stanford University

Stauffer Auditorium
Hoover Institution
October 13–14, 1998

### Agenda

**Tuesday, October 13**

| | |
|---|---|
| 8:30 a.m. - 10:30 a.m. | *Environmentalism vs. Sovereignty*<br>**John Cohrssen**<br>**Fernand Keuleneer,** Center for the New Europe<br>**Jeremy Rabkin,** Cornell University |
| 10:30 a.m. - 11:00 a.m. | Break |
| 11:00 a.m. - 12:00 noon | Panel Discussion |
| 12:00 noon - 1:30 p.m. | Lunch |
| 1:30 p.m. - 3:00 p.m. | *Kyoto Is the Mother of All*<br>**Jeffrey Salmon,** George C. Marshall Institute<br>**Bruce Yandle,** Clemson University |
| 3:00 p.m. - 3:30 p.m. | Break |
| 3:30 p.m. - 5:00 p.m. | Panel Discussion |

**Wednesday, October 14**

| | |
|---|---|
| 8:30 a.m. - 9:45 a.m. | *And It Doesn't Stop with Kyoto*<br>**Henry Miller,** Hoover Institution<br>**Brett Schaefer,** Heritage Foundation |
| 9:45 a.m. - 10:30 a.m. | *Developing Another Path*<br>**Terry L. Anderson,** Hoover Institution and PERC<br>**Julian Morris,** Institute of Economic Affairs |
| 10:30 a.m. - 12:00 noon | Panel Discussion |
| 12:00 noon | Lunch |

# THE GREENING OF U.S. FOREIGN POLICY

## Conference Organizers

Terry L. Anderson—Martin and Illie Anderson Senior Fellow, Hoover Institution, Stanford University; Executive Director, Political Economy Research Center, Bozeman, Montana; Professor, Department of Agricultural Economics and Economics, Montana State University

Henry Miller—Senior Research Fellow, Hoover Institution, Stanford University

## Presenters

Terry Anderson—Martin and Illie Anderson Senior Fellow, Hoover Institution; Executive Director, Political Economy Research Center, Bozeman, Montana; Professor, Department of Agricultural Economics and Economics, Montana State University

John Cohrssen, Esq.—former Majority Counsel to the House Commerce Committee

Fernand Keuleneer—President, Center for the New Europe

Henry Miller—Senior Research Fellow, Hoover Institution

Julian Morris—Assistant Director, Environment Unit, Institute of Economic Affairs

Jeremy Rabkin—Associate Professor, Cornell University

Jeffrey Salmon—Executive Director, George C. Marshall Institute

Brett Schaefer—Jay Kingham Fellow, Heritage Foundation

Bruce Yandle—Alumni Professor of Economics, Clemson University

## Discussants and Panel Moderators

Tom Bray—Editorial Page Editor, *The Detroit News*

Bonner Cohen—Editor, *EPA Watch*

Addison Davis—National Security Affairs Fellow, Hoover Institution; Lieutenant Colonel, U.S. Army

Judith Goldstein—Professor of Political Science, Stanford University

Donald Kennedy—Bing Professor of Environmental Biological Science, Stanford University; President Emeritus, Stanford University

Thomas Gale Moore—Senior Fellow, Hoover Institution

James Sheehan—Competitive Enterprise Institute

Michael Walker—Executive Director, The Fraser Institute

# Index

Acid rain, 6, 285–86
Adler, Jonathan, 45
Administrative Procedures Act, 20
Agenda 21, 48–49, 123–24, 147–50
 passim, 155
Albright, Madeleine, 45, 47, 118–20,
 134, 183, 222
American Farm Bureau, 205
Anderson, Terry, xii, 255, 261, 264
Antonelli, Angela, 71–73
Archer, Bill, 202
Auto reference, 34
Avery, Denis, 161

Bailey, Ronald, 161
Baliunas, Sallie 158, 159
Balling, Robert C., Jr., 158
Basel Convention, 7, 10, 11, 16, 153,
 154, 282
Bate, Roger, 267, 279, 283, 285, 289
Bergen Declaration, 129, 133, 228
Biodiversity, vii, 24, 49, 70, 148, 223,
 236–37, 243, 279
Biosafety Protocol, 8, 71, 131,
 234–47, 280–81
Biosafety working groups, 238–41

Biotechnology, vii, 221–47; national
 sovereignty and, xii, 225; regulation
 of, 222, 224, 231–47; research and
 development and, 223–25, 230,
 242; land use and, 225–26; United
 Nations Industrial Development
 Organization and, 231–33; 244;
 Convention on Biological Diversity
 and, 234–37, 240–46 passim;
 contentious science and, 235, 239,
 244–47 passim; risk-based
 approach and, 235–36, 241;
 impacts of regulation on, 237–47
Bonner, Raymond, 262
Bootleggers and Baptist theory, xii,
 200–206, 286–87
Boudreaux, Donald J., 250
Bretton Woods Agreement Act, 74, 144
Browne, John, 204
Brubaker, Elizabeth, 161
Brundtland, Gro Harlem, 143
Brundtland Commission, 121, 129
Bubble trading, 212–214
Bureau of Oceans and International
 Environmental and Scientific
 Affairs, 46, 228

Burt, Richard, 182
Bush Administration, 15, 53, 117, 173
Business Council on Sustainable Development, 159

Cameron, James, 130
CAMPFIRE program, 262, 264
Carlucci, Frank Charles, 184–85
Carson, Rachel, 44
Certified Tradeable Offsets, 205
CFC regulation, ix, 11, 18, 67–70, 151–53 passim, 159, 215, 268, 286–90. *See also* Montreal Protocol
*Changing Course: A Global Perspective on Development and the Environment*, 159
Cheney, Dick, 61, 182
Christopher, Warren, 47, 118, 120, 134, 221, 229
Climate change, 128, 148, 169. *See also* Global warming
Clinton administration, xi; sanctions and, 27; environmental national security and, 42; Department of State policy, 46–48; trade regulation and, 53–62 passim; International Monetary Fund and, 76; international environmentalism and, 77–79; sustainable development and, 124–29; precautionary principle and, 133; Climate Change Action Plan and, 158; Kyoto Protocol and, 173–86; global warming and, 202; Convention on Biological Diversity and, 229; environmental foreign policy and, 244
Coase, Ronald H., 250–51, 271–73
Cohen, William, 183, 244
Cohrssen, John J., xi, 227
Commission on Global Governance, 144–45, 149, 156
Committee to Preserve American Sovereignty and Security, 133, 182–83

Conference on Social Development, 149
Contract Law, 269–71
Convention for the Protection of Marine Environment, 133, 228
Convention on Biodiversity, xii, 8–11 passim, 16, 25, 65, 70–71, 96–97, 279–81; trade restrictions and, 65; precautionary principle and, 133, 228; biotechnology and, 224, 231, 233–37, 240, 241–46, 280; Senate ratification and, 229, 242–43, 244, 117–18, 148; as product of United Nations Conference on Environment and Development, 233; science and, 235, 239, 244–47 passim; developing countries and, 236, 241–42
Convention on Climate Change, 7, 20, 65, 133, 228
Convention on Desertification, 281–82
Convention on International Trade of Endangered Species, 65, 154, 262, 264, 278–79, 280, 283
Convention on Liability for Damage Caused by Space Objects, 277
Council on Environmental Quality, 45, 116, 131, 132
Council on Foreign Relations, 144
Coursey, Don, 258

Dagget, Stephen, 61–62
Deacon, Robert, 258–59
De Alessi, Michael, 274, 276, 284
Defense Environmental Alert, 176–78
Defense Environmental Restoration Account, 61
Department of Defense, U.S., xii, 46, 60–63, 79, 120–21, 174–86
Department of Energy, U.S., 210
Department of State, U.S., xii, 45–48, 77–79, 118–20, 134, 174, 178, 221–23, 225, 228–29
Deutch, John, 243–44
Developing countries: Convention on Biological Diversity and, 11, 233; international relations and, 26;

international environmental agreements and, 117; sustainable development and, 147; global environmentalism and, 160–61;
greenhouse gas reductions and,
173, 196, 201; biotechnology and,
224, 229, 236–44
Devolution, 260, 262, 275–76
Douglas, Christopher, 132–33, 227

Earth Charter, 36–37
Earth Council, 124, 127
*Earth in the Balance*, 41–42, 47,
167–68, 169, 223–24, 226
Earth Summit. *See* United Nations
Conference on Environment and
Development
Ecosystem management, 148
Ecosystems, 64, 160, 233
Ehrlich, Paul, 44, 167
Eizenstat, Stewart, 178–79, 180–91
Emerson, Ralph Waldo, 43
Emissions trading, 186, 190
Endangered species. *See* Convention
on International Trade of
Endangered Species
*Environmental Daily*, 237
Environmental Destruction, 256–57
*Environmental Diplomacy*, 47, 48,
77, 222–23, 225, 228, 243
Environmental Education and
Communication Project, 49
Environmentalism: globalization of,
ix–x, 31, 41–42, 115–18, 143,
159–61, 167–69, 249, 255–56,
264; U.S. foreign policy and,
ix–xiii passim, 38, 41–42, 45–50,
118–21, 133, 166–74, 227, 250,
256–58, 264–65; national sovereignty and, 2, 12, 22–23; international, 2–8, 63–66; new global
consensus and, 31–33, 38–39; effect of legalization of, 37–38; history of, xi, 42–45, 201
Environmental Protection Agency,
U.S., 17, 18, 45, 72, 116, 117,
120, 130, 287

Esty, Daniel C., 145
European Commons Fisheries Policy,
273
European Union, 23, 25, 28, 33,
212–14, 228
Existence values, 250
Expected value, 254
Export Expansion and Reciprocal
Trade Agreements Act of 1997, 57
Export Import Bank, 58–60

Fast-track trade negotiating, 45, 53,
56–58, 79
Federal Advisory Committee Act, 20
Federal Communications
Commission, 9
Federalism, 12–16, 260
Figueres, Jose Maria, 205
Food and Agriculture Organization,
94–95, 116, 231
Forest Reserve Act of 1902, 43
Freedom of Information Act, 20
Free market environmentalism, xii,
252, 256
Free rider, 249–50
Fretwell, Holly Lippke, 260–61
Frost, Robert, 4
Fundamental rights, 34–35

G77, 237
General Agreement on Tariffs and
Trade, 26–27, 52–57 passim,
102–3, 155–57, 198
General Circulation Models, 171
Genetically Manipulated Organism,
231–32, 235–36, 237
*Georgia v. Tennessee Copper Co.*,
272
Giddings, L. Val, 236–37
Gingrich, Newt, 202
Glickman, Dan, 202
Global Climate Coalition, 203–4
Global Climate Convention, 148
*Global Commons, The*, 249
Global Environmental Facility, 64,
76, 119, 246
Globalism, 162–63

Global warming, 158, 126, 201, 250;
    Kyoto Protocol and, 71, 170–91,
    195–96; precautionary principle
    and, 133; greenhouse warming and,
    160; as tool of environmental
    movement, 169–70 ; scientific de-
    bate and, 170–73; Department of
    Defense, U.S. and, 173–86; alterna-
    tive energy sources and, 202–3, 205
Golklany, Idur M., 123
Goodman, Sherri, 175, 179–85
Gore, Al, 41–42, 47, 118, 167–68,
    169, 171, 222–24, 226–29, 243,
    244
Greenhouse gases: global warming
    and, 19, 126, 288–92
Grossman, Gene M., 258, 270
Grotius, 3–4

Haddock, David, 260
Hamilton, Alexander, 20
Hansen, James, 171
Hanson, Jaydee R., 200
Harmon, James, 59
Hazardous waste, ix, 7, 282–83
Helsinki Convention, 22, 228
Henkin, Louis, 21
Hicks, Kathleen H., 60–62
Hill, P.J., 255
Holmes, Oliver Wendell, 272
Huffman, James L., 260
Hughes, Charles Evans, 15
Human rights, 15, 32–35, 78. See
    also International law
Hume, David, 5

Individual transferable quotas,
    263–64, 276
International aid, 281–82
International Conference on
    Population and Development,
    148–49
International Convention for the
    Regulation of Whaling, 104–5,
    110–11, 283–84, 292
International Court of Justice, 33
International courts, 189

International Criminal Court, 66,
    73–74
International environmental agree-
    ments: costs of, 2, 11, 19, 25–26,
    28; effects on U.S. domestic policy
    and, 2, 12–29; and national sover-
    eignty, 2, 12, 22–23, 73–74, 115,
    117, 267; history of, 6–7, 63,
    115–16, 150–52; expanding
    agenda of, 7–8, 17, 24, 36–37,
    115; implications of 8–12; non-
    governmental organizations and,
    9–10, 117–18, 157; constitutional
    impacts of, 12–29; international
    relations and, 21–22, 26; effects
    on U.S. foreign policy and, 21–22,
    66–70, 72–74, 77–79, 229–31;
    sustainable development and,
    146–52; types of, 268–84, 292–94.
    See also Developing countries;
    International environmental
    treaties; Trade; and names of indi-
    vidual agreements
International environmentalism. See
    International environmental agree-
    ments; Environmentalism
International environmental regula-
    tion. See International environ-
    mental agreements
International environmental treaties,
    42, 66, 293–94; national sover-
    eignty and, x, 73–74; treaty power
    and, 14–15, 17–23; effects on U.S.
    foreign policy, 21–22, 42, 66–70,
    72–74, 221–22; precedent for 63;
    in which U.S. is a participant,
    90–113; scientific debate and,
    170–71; alternative energy sources
    and, 202–3, 205. See also
    International environmental agree-
    ments and names of individual
    treaties
International institutions. See names
    of individual institutions
International Joint Commission, 272
International Law, 146; environmen-
    talism and, xi, 6, 32, 63; history

of, 2–7; national sovereignty and, 2–7, 37–38; human rights and, 15, 33–35; evolutionary acceptance of, 24, 36, 132–33, 156, 227; and fundamental rights, 34–35, 37; global commons and, 150; Montreal Protocol and, 150; types of, 251; fishing and, 262–64
International Maritime Organization, 10–11
International Monetary Fund, 65, 74–75, 76, 90–91, 155
International Seabed Authority, 152, 284
International Union for the Conservation of Nature, 279
Interstate Commerce Commission, 9

Jefferson, Thomas, 4
Jorgenson and Wilcoxen study, 206–7

Kennedy, Donald, 245–46
Kent, James, 5
Kerry, John, 182
Keuleneer, Fernand, xi
Keynesian schemes, 144
Kleckner, Dean, 205
Kreuter, Urs P., 262
Krueger, Alan B., 258, 270
Kyoto Protocol, ix, xii, 7–11 passim, 16–19 passim, 26, 67, 71–72, 173–74, 195–97, 211–15, 289; national security and, 7–9 passim, 72, 170, 174–75, 178–86, 188–91; costs of, 72, 173–74, 186, 206–21; congressional reaction and, 173, 180–82, 184–86, 190; the Department of Defense, U.S. and, 178; exemptions to, 178–82, 189; national sovereignty and, 184, 186–88; emissions trading and, 186, 197–98, 211–14; economic implications of, 197–06

Lash, Jonathan, 127
Law of the Sea, 19, 151–52, 160, 276–77, 284

Leal, Donald R., 260–61, 263, 264
Liberalism, 3

Manne and Richels Study, 206–7
Market: economy, 161; mechanisms, 186; incentives, 224–25, 230; alternatives, 233
Marketable emissions permits, 197, 211–214
Marshall, Chief Justice John, 23
Marshall Plan, 127
Mathews, Jessica Tuchman, 12, 144–46, 150–52, 156
McCulloch v. Maryland, 23
Meiners, Roger E., 250
Miller, George, 76–77
Miller, Henry I., xii, 71, 235, 280
Missouri v. Holland, 14
Montreal Protocol, 7–11 passim, 65, 67–70, 92–93, 133, 150–54 passim, 159, 228, 286–88
Moody–Stewart, Mark, 203
Morris, Julian, xii, 278–85 passim, 289, 293
Mortgaging the Earth, 256
Multilateral environmental agreements, 54, 66–74, 77. See also International environmental agreements
Murkowski, Frank, 59–60

National Acid Precipitation Assessment Programme, 285
National Council on Sustainable Development, 124
National Performance Review, 47
National Research Council, 224–25
National security, 42, 45–46, 47, 72, 78, 170, 174–86, 188–91, 221
National Security Council, 78, 182–83
National Security Strategy, 78
National sovereignty, x–xii, 115–18 passim, 145–46, 152, 169; history of, 3–7; and Trail Smelter ruling, 6; affected by international law, 12, 22–23; affected by international environmental agreements,

73–74, 79, 115, 225; Kyoto
   Protocol and, 184, 186–88
Natural Resources Defense Council,
   118
New Deal, 13–14, 17
Nichols, Mary, 202
Nixon, Richard, 60, 116
Nongovernmental organizations,
   9–10, 32, 35, 59, 74, 115–19 pas-
   sim, 157, 245–46 passim, 267,
   271, 292
North American Free Trade
   Agreement, 23, 53–54, 106–7,
   154–55
North Atlantic Fishery Organization,
   277
North Atlantic Treaty Organization,
   176
Northern Pacific Fur Seal Treaty, 274
Norton, Seth W., 258

Omnibus Trade and Competitiveness
   Act, 57
Organization for Economic
   Cooperation and Development,
   100–101, 116, 127–29, 134, 153,
   297
O'Riordan, Tim, 130
Our Common Future, 121–22,
   143–44, 155
Overseas Private Investment Corp,
   58–59

Panama operation, 179, 184, 189
Patton, Paul, 204
Peña, Federico, 203
Pomerance, Rafe, 240
Popper, Karl, 293
Precautionary principle, xi, 129–34,
   158, 227–28; sustainable develop-
   ment and, 129; application of,
   130; definition of, 130; no regrets
   policy and, 131; international
   agreements and, 132–33, 158;
   Montreal Protocol and, 133, 228;
   implications of 134–35
Prescott, John, 211, 230

Presidential Council on Sustainable
   Development, 124–27, 159
Pritchard, Sonia Zaide, 6
Private conservation, 43–44
Private interests. See Special interests
Problem of Social Cast, The, 250-51
Property rights, x, 79, 121, 161–63,
   199, 250–65 passim, 272, 290

Rabkin, Jeremy, x, 247
Reagan administration, 132
Regulation, 9, 199–200, 250,
   262–64; See also International en-
   vironmental agreements
Regulatory capture, 283–84
Rent-seeking, 157, 251, 255, 278
Restatement of Foreign Relations
   Law, 15, 21
Rich, Bruce, 256
Richardson, Bill, 78
Rio Declaration on Environment and
   Development, 147, 150
Rio Summit. See United Nations
   Conference on Environment and
   Development
Roosevelt, Theodore, 43, 115

Salmon, Jeffery, xi–xii
Schaefer, Brett, xi, 73
Schneider, Stephen, 170
Schoenbrod, David, 118
Scott, Anthony, 271–72
Shalikashvili, General John M.,
   62–63
Sheehan, James, M., xi, 126
Simmons, Randy T., 262
Singer, Fred, 158
Smith, Adam, 5, 50
Smith, Fred, 126
Smoot–Hawley Tariff Act, 51
Social cost, 250, 260
Southerland, Ronald, 209
Southern Governors Association, 204
Special interests, 10–21, 157, 199–205
Sprague, Merritt W., 123
Stanford, Anna, 203
Strong, Maurice, 36, 124, 127, 147

Sustainable development, xi, 121–29, 134–35, 155; in international environmental agreements, 32, 121, 146–52, 153–56; United States Agency for International Development initiatives and, 49, 120; in United Nations Commission on Sustainable Development, 116, 148; defined, 121–24 passim; political utility of, 121, 134; costs of, 122; Clinton administration and, 124–29; precautionary principle and, 129; Congress, 129; global environmentalism and, 143–44, 145–52, 159, 161–63; doctrine of collective security and, 146; Earth Summit and, 146–49

Taylor, Jerry, 123–24
Third-party effect, 249, 250
Thoreau, Henry David, 43
Three Rivers Dam, China, 226, 257
Trade, international, 3, 5, 26–28, 42, 282; sanctions and, 27–28, 50–51, 55, 292; environmentalism and, 50–60; international treaties and, 50–56, 65, 152–57; trade liberalization and, 51; sustainable development and, 154. See also Convention on International Trade of Endangered Species; Fast-track trade negotiating; and General Agreement on Tariffs and Trade
Trade Act of 1974, 52, 56
Tragedy of the commons, 259
Trail Smelter ruling, 6, 261, 271–72, 277
Treaty on Principles Governing the Activities of States in the Exploration and Use of Outer Space, 277

Underwood, Cecil, 204
United Nations Charter, 2–3, 166

United Nations Commission on Global Governance, 10
United Nations Commission on Sustainable Development, 116, 148
United Nations Conference on Environment and Development, xii, 49, 64–65, 71, 117, 122–24, 133, 146–49, 158, 173, 228
United Nations Conference on the Human Environment, 63–64, 116
United Nations Development Program, 64, 116
United Nations Educational, Scientific, and Cultural Organization, 64, 94–95
United Nations Environment Program, 1, 64, 70, 116, 224, 231, 234–38 passim, 245–46, 281, 288
United Nations Framework Convention on Climate Change, 18, 24, 71–72, 102–3, 148, 173, 175, 288–89
United Nations global consensus, 31–33
United Nations Industrial Development Organization, 94–95, 234, 231–33
United Nations Intergovernmental Panel on Climate Change, 171–72
United Nations International Law Commission, 6
United Nations Stockholm Conference, 116, 121
United States Agency for International Development, 48–50, 119, 120, 221, 229
United States Conference on Human Environment, 64
United States Marine Mammal Protection Act, 50–51 , 55
United States Strategic Plan for International Affairs, 47
Universal Declaration of Human Rights, 33, 36, 78

Vattel, Emmerichde, 4–5

Vest, Gary, 174
Vienna Convention for the Protection
    of the Ozone Layer, 18, 150–51,
    286–87
Vogel, David, 28

War Powers Act, 187
Watkins, James, 228
Whelan, Elizabeth M., 132, 227
White, Tom, 201–2
Wilson, Arlene, 51–55 passim
Wilson, Elizabeth, 130
Wirth, Tim, 47, 229, 243
World Bank, 66, 74–76, 91, 155,
    246, 256–57

World Commission on Environment
    and Development, 121–22, 155
World Health Organization, 63,
    94–95, 201–2, 231
World Heritage Program, 64
World Meteorological Organization,
    96–97, 116, 288
World Trade Organization, 27, 42,
    53–56 passim, 63, 155–56, 240

Yandle, Bruce, xii, 214, 251, 286
Yellen, Janet, 210–11